CHILDREN'S ERRORS IN MATHEMATICS

3RD EDITION

ALICE HANSEN

SAGE | LearningMatters

Los Angeles | London | New Delhi
Singapore | Washington DC

Learning Matters
An imprint of SAGE Publications Ltd
1 Oliver's Yard
55 City Road
London EC1Y 1SP

SAGE Publications Inc.
2455 Teller Road
Thousand Oaks, California 91320

SAGE Publications India Pvt Ltd
B 1/I 1 Mohan Cooperative Industrial Area
Mathura Road
New Delhi 110 044

SAGE Publications Asia-Pacific Pte Ltd
3 Church Street
#10-04 Samsung Hub
Singapore 049483

Editor: Amy Thornton
Development editor: Jennifer Clark
Production controller: Chris Marke
Project management: Deer Park Productions
Marketing manager: Catherine Slinn
Cover design: Wendy Scott
Typeset by: C&M Digitals (P) Ltd, Chennai, India
Printed by Henry Ling Limited at The Dorset Press,
Dorchester DT1 1HD

First published in 2005 by Learning Matters Ltd
Reprinted in 2005
Reprinted in 2007
Reprinted in 2008 (twice)
Reprinted in 2009
Reprinted in 2010
Second edition published in 2011
Third edition published 2014

Library of Congress Control Number: 2014932988

British Library Cataloguing in Publication data

A catalogue record for this book is available from the
British Library

ISBN: 978-1-4462-7443-9 (pbk)
ISBN: 978-1-4462-7442-2

CHILDREN'S ERRORS IN MATHEMATICS

Contents

About the editor and authors

Editor
Alice Hansen

Alice Hansen is an educational consultant who has taught in a wide variety of primary schools in England and abroad. She worked for over a decade in Initial Teacher Education (ITE) as a senior lecturer in primary mathematics education at the University of Cumbria before becoming the Programme Leader for the full-time primary Postgraduate Certificate in Education with Qualified Teacher Status. Since becoming a consultant, she has worked with a significant number of ITE providers across England, supporting the development of their mathematics education courses. Alice is also the director of Children Count Ltd, through which she remains active in researching children's mathematics learning and wider educational issues to support ITE provision nationally.

Authors
Doreen Drews

Doreen Drews taught extensively within the Foundation Stage, Key Stage 1 and Key Stage 2. She was a mathematics advisory teacher for four years before joining St Martin's College (now University of Cumbria). She has a particular interest in Early Years mathematics, and how resources can be used to support children's mathematical understanding effectively.

John Dudgeon

John Dudgeon is the primary mathematics subject leader at the University of Cumbria. He has taught at a wide range of primary schools. John is particularly interested in mathematical development in children in the Early Years Foundation Stage and in the effective use of mathematical resources.

Fiona Lawton

Fiona Lawton has taught in a range of primary and secondary schools. She is a Senior Lecturer in Mathematics Education at the University of Cumbria with responsibility for leading the secondary undergraduate route into teaching. Her current research interest is the use of mobile technologies to enhance learning and teaching in mathematics.

Liz Surtees

Liz Surtees is the Examinations and Assessment Officer at The School of Medicine, University of St Andrews. She is currently researching the impact of different forms of e-learning. She has taught mathematics across the primary and secondary school age ranges, in further education and higher education contexts. She is particularly interested in statistics and problem solving and is co-author (with Sue Fox) of *Mathematics Across the Curriculum: Problem-Solving, Reasoning and Numeracy in Primary Schools* and 'Breaking down the boundaries' ([2010] *Teach Primary*! 4(6): 88–91).

Preface

This third edition of *Children's Errors in Mathematics* has undergone a number of changes to bring it in line with the 2014 National Curriculum for England and the original content has been shifted between chapters. Original content was provided by:

Doreen Drews (Errors and misconceptions: The teacher's role)

John Dudgeon (Measures)

Alice Hansen (How do children learn mathematics? Shape and space)

Fiona Lawton (Number)

Liz Surtees (Handling data)

Acknowledgements

The work for identifying the fractions misconceptions listed here has been partially made possible thanks to the iTalk2Learn project that is co-funded by the European Union under the Information and Communication Technologies (ICT) theme of the 7th Framework Programme for R&D (FP7) GA No 610467. The contents of this chapter do not represent the opinion of the EU, which is not responsible for any use that might be made of them.

Thanks to Amelie Earnshaw and Ella Saltariche for re-constructing some of the misconceptions in the third edition.

Introduction

This third edition has joined the successful *Transforming Primary QTS* series, which was established to reflect current best practice and a more creative and integrated approach to the primary school curriculum. While mathematics is a subject that will keep a strong and discrete identity in the new national curriculum, there is a clear movement within schools to approach mathematics teaching and learning in a way that engages and inspires children.

This book encourages you as a trainee teacher to take a critical and creative look at how you can make best use of children's errors and misconceptions in mathematics to support their learning.

The importance of mathematics should not be underestimated. Not only is it a core national curriculum subject in its own right, it also provides children with the skills of reasoning, problem solving and communication that can be used as tools to learn all subjects.

About the book

This book has been written as a resource for you to develop your knowledge and understanding about children's mathematical conceptual development and how errors and misconceptions are a natural part of learning mathematics.

In Chapter 1, you will read about why and how misconceptions arise. It is important to read this chapter because through understanding this, your planning, teaching and assessment will improve. Chapter 2 develops the ideas introduced in Chapter 1 and discusses the role of the teacher who is following this misconceptions-aware teaching approach. The remaining chapters present a number of common errors that children will exhibit during their Early Years Foundation Stage and primary years. It is essential to understand that this is not an exhaustive list and you should remain vigilant in your working with children to identify others in order to help them progress. In order to make the most of this book, it is essential that you note the following.

1   These errors can be demonstrated by any child, regardless of their attainment level and their age.

2   These errors, while presented in one context in this book, can be often seen in a multitude of mathematical contexts. Cross-references are included as appropriate.

3   All the objectives of the national curriculum have at least one related misconception listed, but this book only scratches the surface of the misconceptions that exist. So, as you come across others it would be useful to note them down and discuss them with your tutor/mentor.

4   Mathematical errors can be observed within mathematics lessons, or just as frequently in sessions or lessons that have a less mathematical focus. For example, a science lesson that explores plant growth or a DT lesson requiring accuracy of measurement both require children to be able to use a ruler accurately and record using the appropriate units of measurement.

5   The discussion of each misconception involves some common reasons why the error may have been made. However, the discussion may not be exhaustive and you should look for alternatives during your own work with children.

The Appendix offers busy students on placement and teachers the opportunity to dip in and out of the errors as they plan in relation to the national curriculum.

Learning Matters have published a number of other mathematics-related titles. This book is complementary to these because it focuses specifically on one aspect of teaching and learning mathematics which will aid you to teach mathematics effectively.

Using this book

You can use this book in a number of ways, which are outlined below.

1   **Planning:** When you are planning a lesson or unit of work, Chapters 3 onwards can be used as a reference guide to help you to consider some of the possible misconceptions and errors the children you are working with may exhibit. If your planning takes into consideration some of the possible misconceptions the children may show, you will be better prepared in your teaching.

2   **Teaching:** As well as feeling more confident in your teaching because of your thorough planning, at times you may present some of the examples in this book to the children you are teaching. This can offer an opportunity for rich mathematical discussion about a potentially difficult aspect in a context that is 'safe' for the children. Additionally, Chapters 1 and 2 may challenge your perception of what errors and misconceptions are, and ultimately this may help you to shape how you teach children.

3   **Children's assessment:** By being able to identify misconceptions and discuss these with children, you will be able to use these opportunities as they present themselves as an excellent Assessment for Learning opportunity.

4   **Your own coursework:** This book will support coursework you are required to complete for your teaching qualification. In addition to assignments directly related to errors and misconceptions, you will also find other supporting material such as theories on how children learn mathematics and ways of teaching mathematics effectively.

5   **Subject knowledge:** Although this book addresses many of the common errors and misconceptions that you may see in primary schools, you may find that you also develop your own subject knowledge by thinking through them as you plan, teach and assess.

1 How do children learn mathematics?

Understanding how children learn mathematics is a critical element of your beginning to understand the errors and misconceptions they make and how you can embrace these in your teaching to support every child's mathematical cognitive development. This chapter aims to:

- develop your understanding of children's mathematical cognitive development (the micro-level);

- develop your understanding of cognitive development within mathematics curricula (the macro-level);

- show that all children (and adults, too) make errors in their mathematics work as they construct their own mis-conceptions of mathematics;

- identify that adults mediate learning for children.

Distinguishing between macro-level and micro-level cognitive development

As a teacher you will be working within two levels of cognitive development as you plan, teach and assess. At the macro level, you will be ensuring that you meet the statutory requirements of the mathematics curriculum. At the micro level, you will be proactively responding to each individual's needs and considering effective personalised learning for every child in your class. This is challenging to do, even for experienced teachers. It is challenging because the spiral curriculum we use presents mathematical concepts hierarchically and it presents conceptual development as a smooth progression throughout a child's primary years. We can expect most children through their primary years to make steady progress, but you will probably know from your own learning experiences and your teaching experience that learning is very much context-dependent, and this has an impact on individual children's progress.

Let's pause to pursue this. Towards the end of their primary education, a child is expected to be able to *compare and classify geometric shapes based on their properties* (DfE, 2013, page 140). Pause here and write down the properties of a square.

You have no doubt stated that is has four interior angles of equal size (all 90°) and four sides of equal length. It is likely that you thought about the order of rotation and number of lines of symmetry (and linked these to the square being a regular polygon with four sides). You may have also visualised the square having equal-length diagonals that are perpendicular.

Now do this with a less familiar shape, such as a kite. You may wish to use these prompts to help you. Using an **inclusive definition** of a kite, what are the:

- number of right angles?

- number of pairs of equal and opposite angles?

- number of pairs of equal and opposite sides?

- number of equal-length sides?

- number of pairs of parallel sides?

- number of lines of symmetry?

- number of perpendicular diagonals?

- number of equal-length diagonals?

- number of bisecting diagonals?

- what is the order of rotation?

How did you get on? Check your answers with those on page 10. I suspect when you were carrying out the task, you had a prototypical picture of a kite in your mind (see Figure 1.1). That might be why you (probably) stated that the kite had just one line of symmetry. However, if we are considering the properties of a kite using **inclusive** definitions, remember a square is also a type of kite (see Figure 1.2). Therefore, if you were using an inclusive definition of 'kite', you should have stated that a kite has 'at least one line of symmetry', or that it has 'an order of rotation of at least 1'.

Is this task confusing you? It was intended to! Afterall, the notion of inclusivity is something that children – and adults – find difficult. (See, for example, Hansen, 2008a; Hansen and Pratt, 2005; Jones, 2000.) The point of this task is to demonstrate that when we track children's progress over time, it appears smooth and (often) reflects the expectations of the prescribed curriculum. However, when we take a closer look at a moment in that learning journey, we no longer see a smooth development. Instead we observe oscillation which is all rather messy. This is represented in Figure 1.3.

One final example, described by Simpson (2009, page 15), may help to describe this phenomenon:

Figure 1.1 A prototypical kite

Figure 1.2 More examples of kites

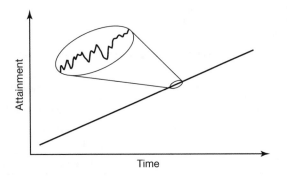

Figure 1.3 Macro- and micro-level cognitive change

Shaun had successfully measured a number of pencils and had been able to record their lengths in order; he knew that 21.4cm was longer than 21.25cm. However, in another lesson later in the same week, he was ordering a list of numbers and stated that 13.65 was bigger than 13.7.

What does this tell you about Shaun's mathematical understanding of number (decimals), measurement (length) and use and application of mathematics? What does it tell you about his attainment at the macro-level and at the micro-level?

Macro- and micro-level cognitive change: planning and assessment

Macro- and micro-level cognitive change is seen reflected in a number of the aspects of a primary teacher's role. Two of these are planning and assessment. Although these two aspects are strongly interrelated, Table 1.1 provides a summary of these discretely in order to exemplify them.

The outcomes associated with macro- and micro-level cognitive change can be seen in many aspects of our teaching. Exploring the literature around these levels helps us to continue to develop our understanding. Therefore, the next section will consider in more detail the two levels. First, it will look at macro-level cognitive change, identifying how the literature represents the hierarchical nature of mathematical

Table 1.1   Comparison of macro- and micro- level planning and assessment

	Macro-level	Micro-level
Planning	Follows long-term curriculum learning objectives	Follows short-term unit/weekly/ lesson learning objectives
	Provides an overview of a yearly/ termly/half-termly intended learning journey	Identifies learning outcomes based on actual data gathered about very recent outcomes
	Focuses on a larger group of children (typically the whole class, a year group or in some instances a key stage)	Focuses on a smaller group of children or individuals
	Focuses mainly on content and context/themes	Considers how the content is learned, e.g. learning styles, resources, grouping, etc.
	Changes may or may not be made to planning	Change is inevitable
	Any changes will be minimal	Changes may be significant
	Any changes will impact on the longer term	Changes will occur in lessons and between lessons
Assessment	Summative in nature	Formative and diagnostic in nature
	Happens at key points in the year/key stage	Happens continuously
	Assesses children's attainment over a longer term using curriculum levels or part thereof (e.g. 1c, 1b, 1a)	Assesses children's attainment according to short-term learning objectives
	Often uses a limited range of assessment strategies (typically pencil-and-paper tests or 'tasks' carried out independently)	Often uses a wide variety of Assessment for Learning strategies
	Assesses the yearly/termly/ half-termly intended learning outcomes	Identifies 'next steps' learning outcomes based on recent assessment data gathered
	Used systematically to inform further long-term planning and to support transition between years	Used spontaneously or systematically to inform pedagogical decisions within a lesson or for the next lesson(s)
	Often used to inform communication to parents at the end of a year	Can be used to inform communication with children, teaching assistants, parents or other adults supporting the child's learning
	Used to inform tracking of individual pupils' progress	Focus on the number of children changes depending on the learning/teaching undertaken
	Can be used to prompt lesson study in a particular area of a teacher's performance	Can be used in lesson study to support professional development through peer support
	Focuses on a narrow curriculum	Focuses on a wider range of knowledge, skills or understanding
	Any assessments will impact on the longer term	Any assessments will occur in lessons and between lessons

learning. Next, the notion of micro-level conceptual change is discussed. This goes on to explore some of the literature related to micro-level conceptual change and offers an explanation for why children make errors and develop 'misconceptions' in mathematics.

Macro-level cognitive change: exploring the notion of hierarchy

The long- and medium-term planning teachers undertake is led by statutory and other curricula, which are in part informed by macro-level theories of learning (e.g. Dubinsky *et al.*, 2005; Tall, 2007; Weber, 2005). These are usually hierarchical in nature, involving earlier concepts becoming the foundations for later concepts to be built upon. This can be explained as a process where a new concept becomes developed sufficiently for it to become an object that can be used in a more advanced concept. For example, addition may be seen as an object that can be used in multiplication. Once we know how to calculate $3 + 3 + 3 + 3$, this knowledge can be used to calculate 3×4.

To explain this, we can use the image of a spiral – as Jerome Bruner did – to model how concepts are expanded upon as they are developed. As you read the literature review below, consider what model you have developed in your mind to explain this process and the different terms that are used to explain this.

Many mathematics educators and theorists have written about these ideas. For example, Anna Sfard explored mathematical development taking guidance from mathematics history. She explained that the history of mathematics can be characterised as an *ongoing process of reification in which the processes are reinterpreted as objects* (Sfard, 1991). We can see this through the historical development of mathematics. For example, the evolution of a base-ten number system enabled written calculations to be developed. This is reflected in the curriculum where children are expected to have a good understanding of place value and mental calculation before they are taught formal written calculation methods (DfE, 2013).

Hans Freudenthal is a well-known figure in mathematics education. He was the founder of the Freudenthal Institute in Holland, where the Realistic Mathematics Education (RME) curriculum is developed. Some aspects of this curriculum, such as the empty number line, have been integrated into the mathematics curriculum for England (DfE, 2013). Freudenthal (1973) proposed that children should develop their mathematical understanding through reinventing mathematics. He suggested that children be given the opportunity to experience a similar process to the way a particular topic of mathematics was invented. He was clear that children should not repeat history as it occurred (Freudenthal, 1981), but rather as if our ancestors had known what we now know. He maintained that conceptual development is psychological, rather than historical, in its progression. Gravemeijer and Doorman (1999), also from the Freudenthal Institute, explain that the core activity within reinvention is 'mathematising' – a way of *organising from a mathematical perspective*. Reification is identifiable here because *the operational matter on one level becomes a subject matter on the next level*.

Dubinsky's A-P-O-S theory (Dubinsky *et al.*, 2005) identifies a common cyclic development called encapsulation. This cycle involves four levels whereby the last relates to a combined object-schema that in turn becomes the first level of a new cycle (**A**ctions that are perceived as external, are interiorised into internal **P**rocesses, encapsulated as mental **O**bjects developing within a coherent mathematical **S**chema) (adapted from Poynter and Tall, 2005). Gray and Tall (2007, page 25) explain how the process of compression involves *taking complicated phenomena, focusing on essential aspects of interest to conceive of them as whole to make them available as an entity to think about*.

While this all seems fairly straightforward at the macro-level, what is unclear in all these approaches is the specific point at which a child has reified, reinvented, encapsulated or compressed a concept. For example, you will read in Chapter 3 that Gelman and Gallistel revealed how complex it is for young children to learn to count. Can we say that a child is able to count because they can recite the number labels to ten in order? Or when they can count to 100, or in tens or hundreds, or when they know that counting is an infinite activity? Is it when they can 'count on' in order to add … using integers … fractional numbers …?

At the macro-level, it is possible to identify a qualitative difference between the attainment of children who are five years of age and ten years of age. However, if we focus on an individual child, their attainment is less straightforward. The clear, smooth progression at the macro-level appears to give way to apparent fluctuation at the micro-level, demonstrating a 'gap' between macro- and micro-level theories of conceptual change (diSessa and Cobb, 2004).

What is micro-level conceptual change?

In the literature review on macro-level conceptual change above it was possible to see that although different theorists use different terminology, there exists a broadly agreed model about the learning of mathematical concepts. This is also observable within the literature about micro-level conceptual change. For example, there is common reference to children cognitively making systematic associations that they develop from their experiences within the rich world around them. This may be thought of as a web, where connections are made between the particular instances (Tennyson, 1996) of a concept that children experience. As these instances become increasingly associated, prototypes (early concepts) are formed.

Similarly, diSessa and Sherin (1998) refer to a co-ordination class. They define it as *systematically connected ways of getting information from the world* (page 1171). This is developed through a process they refer to as *conceptual bootstrapping*. Both of these views of children's early conceptual change rely on children noticing what is happening around them and (usually subconsciously) making connections with other experiences or understanding of the ideas being developed.

Noss and Hoyles (1996, page 105) put forward a case for learning which involves the construction of a web of connections between resources. Resources may be formal or informal, internal (cognitive) and external (physical or virtual). The web is developed through connections being made between these resources. By drawing on the webbing of a particular setting, children will shape the way that they express their mathematical ideas (Noss and Hoyles, 1996, page 122). Noss and Hoyles call this process/object *situated abstraction*. Learners abstract within rather than away from (the literal meaning of 'abstract') a situation, webbing their own knowledge and understanding by acting within the situation.

Wilensky (1991, page 201) also suggests that children establish connections to bring about cognitive change. He sees that this *process of development moves from the abstract to the concrete.* Wilensky labels the process of concretising as *concretion*: the process of new knowledge *coming into relationship with itself and with prior knowledge, and thus becoming concrete.* Wilensky postulates that adults express difficult (higher-order) concepts as abstract because they have little or no understanding of the concept themselves, therefore it is abstract to them. Likewise, the easy (lower-order) concepts are very concrete for them – they understand these concepts because they are grounded. From this, adults then assume that these easier concepts are concrete and as children develop, they move on to more abstract concepts (or, as he calls them, *objects*). Wilensky maintains that all objects are abstract when an individual's relationship with that object is poor. It is only when we use the object in various and multiple ways – when we develop a relationship – that we are able to begin to make sense of it, or it becomes concrete.

Two core aspects emerge from the cognitive change literature. These are the associations (webbing) that enable concretion, and the children's experiences. Chapter 2 deals with children's experiences by discussing in more detail the role of the teacher. How a child develops relationships between resources during concretion or webbing is a process that happens cognitively. Therefore, we can only observe external products of that process, such as verbalised situated abstractions.

Misconceptions and the classroom context

From the literature review on micro-level cognitive change, it is possible to see how misconceptions are inevitable. As situated abstractions develop, or as concretion occurs, children are going to draw on their own understanding of the world around them and unavoidably misconceive some ideas. For example, have you witnessed a young child point to a horse and say 'cow'? They have noticed: (a) an animal in a field; (b) eating grass; (c) swishing its tail; and (d) coloured white and black. These attributes satisfy, for the child, the definition of a cow. They have misconceived the being as a cow. Later they will be able to distinguish between a cow and horse. How can this development be mediated?

The classroom setting is a complex *learning ecology* (Cobb *et al.*, 2003) that *encompasses the historical, cultural, social, and political contexts of both mathematics and mathematics education* (English, 2007, page 122). In the above example, it is likely that an adult or older sibling will correct the young child to explain that the animal is a horse and not a cow.

Cognitive load theory

While misconceptions do occur naturally, it is important to remember that learning can be a laborious (unconscious or conscious) process. Cognitive load theory explains how schemata become automated and become part of our long-term memory. At first, when new information is presented to us, we process it within our working memory, but our working memory is extremely limited in capacity and duration (Miller, 1956; Peterson and Peterson, 1959). Once schemata have transferred from working memory to long-term memory and the information is used, it is no longer limited (Ericsson and Kintsch, 1995). Information can then be returned to the working memory later to be used efficiently (Tabbers, 2002). In recent research, Peters (2010) used eye-tracking technology to observe how mathematicians and non-mathematicians work through mathematical problems. He showed how non-experts require explicit processing while they read and interpret mathematics. They tended to read fully all the questions, and after working out the most relevant information, they would check to see if it was actually relevant. Mathematicians, on the other hand, were able to process information effectively by selecting the relevant information very quickly.

Alloway (2006, page 134) undertook a comprehensive literature review that considered how working memory works in the classroom. She identified how *a child with a poor working memory capacity will struggle and often fail in such activities, disrupting and delaying learning* and notes that children with low working memory scores also have poor computational skills. Therefore, Alloway suggests reducing working memory demands in the classroom. This involves:

- ensuring the children know what they are doing (i.e. they can remember the next step);

- reducing processing demands (e.g. simplifying vocabulary);

- breaking down tasks into simpler steps (displaying *aides-mémoire*; encouraging use of memory aids);

- developing effective strategies for coping with situations where a child experiences a failure in working memory. (Adapted from Alloway, 2006, page 138)

Thinking about the process of learning as one which can be mediated in school by the teacher may be helpful. It is likely that you will have already come across

Vygotsky's (1978) zone of proximal development (ZPD). It is defined as *the distance between the actual development level as determined by independent problem-solving and the level of potential to development as determined through problem-solving through adult guidance or in collaboration with more capable peers* (Vygotsky, 1978, page 86). The notion of the ZPD was developed by Wood *et al.* (1979), who considered how teachers and peers could build (scaffold) and withdraw (fade) support as necessary to help a child bridge the ZPD.

Cognitive load theory may explain the difference between a 'novice' and an 'expert' (in this case, a child and teacher). Sweller (1988, page 7) explains that the amount of information and how the information is organised are quite different between working memory and long-term memory. He points out that novices *fall back on weak problem-solving strategies ... which leads to a high cognitive load* because they do not have the schemata to support their work.

Vygotsky played a major role in relation to individual and social processes of cognitive change (John-Steiner and Mahn, 2003). Vygotsky understood the power and versatility of speech: *For not only does speech function as a tool that mediates social action, it also {mediates} the individual mental activities of remembering, thinking and reasoning* (Wells, 1999, page 136).

Misconceptions can become rigid and resistant to revision later on (Furani, 2003). Therefore, it is the role of teachers to be aware of potential misconceptions and the possible reasons why they have developed (overgeneralisation is common). Doreen Drews discusses the role of the teacher in Chapter 2.

Summary

This chapter has identified two levels of cognitive change. The first is the framework that teachers are required by law to work within: that of macro-level change that can be observed in curricula. Over a child's school career it is likely that a fairly smooth progression through the attainment levels will be mapped out through summative assessments. However, when we focus a microscope on any one moment in that child's progression, the cognitive change is no longer smooth. Instead it is messy, with oscillation. You may have experienced this yourself by feeling confused in the kite-defining activity or other mathematics tasks you have undertaken or even taught. Micro-level cognitive change has been explored by many theorists. This chapter has explored the notion of developing situated abstractions and the process of concretion as ways of thinking about how cognitive change occurs.

The chapter has also highlighted how difficult cognitive development can be, by briefly referring to cognitive load theory. The role of the adult in mediating learning concluded this chapter and paves the way for a more detailed discussion of the role of the adult in relation to children's errors and misconceptions in the next chapter.

Inclusive definitions of a kite

On page 2 you were asked to consider the inclusive definition of a kite. It is possible to identify the following attributes of a kite.

Number of right angles?	At least 0
Number of pairs of equal and opposite angles?	At least 1 pair
Number of pairs of equal and opposite sides?	At least 0
Number of equal length sides?	At least 0
Number of pairs of parallel sides?	At least 0
Number of lines of symmetry?	At least 1
Number of perpendicular diagonals?	At least 2
Number of equal length diagonals?	At least 0
Number of bisecting diagonals?	At least 1
What is the order of rotation?	At least 0

2 Errors and misconceptions: the teacher's role

This chapter explores recent research into teaching approaches to 'deal' with the common mathematical errors and misconceptions made by primary-aged children. It focuses on whether employing teaching approaches which seek to minimise or avoid children making errors and forming misconceptions is likely to be successful. Alternative teaching approaches are considered, based on discussion, dialogue and challenge to children's existing mathematical constructions. Choices and changes in mathematics teaching practices carry with them implications not only for considerations of teaching approaches but also for how teachers view their role within Early Years Foundation Stage settings (nursery and reception classes) and Key Stage 1 (Years 1 and 2), lower Key Stage 2 (Years 3 and 4) and upper Key Stage 2 (Years 5 and 6) classrooms.

Distinguishing between mathematical errors and misconceptions

A teacher's response to dealing with a child's mathematical error demands skill in diagnostic terms: different responses will be appropriate depending upon the nature (and frequency) of the error observed.

An error could be made for many reasons. It could be the result of carelessness, misinterpretation of symbols or text, lack of relevant experience or knowledge related to that mathematical topic/learning objective/concept, a lack of awareness or inability to check the answer given, or the result of a misconception. Ryan and Williams (2007, page 16) considered different levels of knowledge and view mathematical errors to be principally formed within surface levels of knowledge: as such, a child's response to a task is procedural and can be corrected by the teacher providing correct alternatives.

In addition to this, Cockburn (1999) discusses the nature of the mathematical tasks selected by the teacher as having potential for children making errors: she suggests that consideration must be given to the complexity of the task (is it sufficiently challenging or too challenging?), the way the task is presented and the ability of the child to *translate* the task, i.e. does the pupil know what is required in mathematical terms? This latter point is fundamental, for example, to a child's ability to solve word problems.

Sometimes errors can be exacerbated by teachers making assumptions about their children's experiences: this has particular resonance for teachers of young children. Some young children may, or may not, have had experiences of handling money, using or observing the use of a balance to measure an item's mass, or 'reading' time on analogue timepieces.

Incorrect uses of resources can lead to children making errors: a number line can only be an effective tool for assisting 'counting on' and 'counting back' if children are shown, and understand, how to count on/back from the first number without including that number in the count. This issue is discussed further on pages 21–2.

The term 'misconception' is discussed in detail in Chapter 1. It is commonly used when a learner's conception is considered to be in conflict with the accepted meanings and understandings in mathematics (Barmby *et al.*, 2009). A misconception could be the misapplication of a rule, an over- or under-generalisation, or an alternative conception of the situation. For example, *a number with three digits is bigger than a number with two digits* works in some situations (e.g. 328 is bigger than 35) but not necessarily in others where decimals are involved (e.g. 3.28 is not bigger than 3.5).

Misconceptions are far more problematic than errors as they are set within deeper levels of knowledge (Ryan and Williams, 2007, page 16). They demand diagnosis and dialogue to ascertain the misconception, which can be time-consuming. Nevertheless, Barmby *et al.* (2009, page 4) argue that misconceptions should be regarded as *evolving understandings in mathematics ... essential and productive for the development of more sophisticated conceptions and understanding.*

It is important to note that misconceptions are not limited to children who need additional support: more able children also make incorrect generalisations.

Should we teach to hide or avoid mathematical errors and misconceptions?

There is no doubt that some mathematical errors could be avoided by teacher awareness, skilful choice of task and clarity of explanation. However, Swan (2001) suggests that, despite what they are taught, children seem to make the same mathematical errors, and construct their own alternative meanings for mathematics, all over the world. This challenges notions about teaching to avoid children developing such mistakes and misconceptions.

The Primary National Strategy (PNS) advocated diagnosis and intervention schemes that provide *focused teaching activities which tackle fundamental errors and misconceptions that are preventing progress* (DfES, 2005a, page 6). Wave 3 materials emphasised individualised diagnosis of the errors and misconceptions shown by children with significant difficulties, specific or non-specific, with mathematical learning. As Dowker (2009) points out, the focus here is one of using teacher assessment to *correct* identified errors and misconceptions. In order to use Assessment for Learning (AfL) effectively, emphasis also needs to be placed on children recognising themselves that errors and misconceptions are part of the learning process.

Opinions on whether this is possible or even desirable alter from the differing perspectives of primary children and their teachers. Koshy (2000) reports that when primary children were asked how they felt about making mathematical mistakes, they expressed strong feelings of anger, frustration and disappointment. In contrast, Cockburn (1999) and Koshy (2000) both reflect a growing view in the research evidence that mathematical errors can provide a useful insight for teachers into a child's thinking and understanding, an effective mechanism for assessment for learning and, with sensitive handling, can enable children to learn from mathematical mistakes.

Current thinking and research are recommending a shift in how both teachers and children regard mathematical errors and misconceptions, moving from a 'let's plan to avoid' strategy to one which seeks to give greater status and value to diagnosis, explanation and negotiation of meaning. Lee (2006) argues that such strategies lead to more creative approaches to AfL, help pupils see themselves as successful learners, and encourage both teachers and pupils to attempt more challenging work. Rather than simply correcting an error or misconception, it would appear far more productive for teachers to investigate the reason a child provides a given answer. Indeed, Barmby *et al.* (2009, page 5) maintain that *identifying and building on incomplete or incorrect conceptions are important ways of developing coherent mathematical knowledge.*

It is self-evident that that such a shift will necessitate teachers adopting *a constructive attitude to their children's mistakes* (Koshy, 2000, page 173), and children recognising that analysis and discussion of mistakes or misconceptions can be helpful to their mathematical development.

Spooner (2002) suggests that placing children in situations where they feel in control of identifying mathematical errors/misconceptions leads to greater openness on the part of the children to explore and discuss their own misconceptions. Working with specifically designed pre-National Test materials for Key Stage 2, he discusses children exploring answers produced by an 'unknown pupil'. In order to do so they had to engage with the mathematical question set, discuss the errors with peers and explore why the error/misconception may have been made. The children appeared willing to engage in such discussions as it wasn't 'their' work under investigation. The process allowed children to be placed in the role of the teacher, encouraged open dialogue and consolidated their understanding of the concepts which underpinned the given examples.

This approach has an underlying belief that children's mathematical understanding is more likely to be developed if children are given opportunities to:

- explain their thinking;
- compare their thinking with that of peers and teachers.

To be effective in terms of long-term gains these opportunities need to be embedded within a school and classroom 'culture' which accepts and promotes that children can learn effectively from their peers and need encouragement to 'be brave' to express their mathematical ideas. Support for this can be found in a report by Ofsted into the Primary National Strategies and their impact upon the rest of the primary curriculum.

> *The most effective teachers ... cultivate an ethos where children do not mind making mistakes because errors are seen as part of the learning. In these cases, children are pre-pared to take risks with their answers.*

(Ofsted, 2003, page 18)

A significant feature of such approaches would be a recognition by children that learning often involves having to 'shift' one's thinking.

Swan (2001) encourages a more radical shift in teachers' thinking, suggesting that far from trying to teach to avoid children developing misconceptions, the latter should be viewed as helpful and, possibly, 'necessary' stages in children's mathematical development. This suggests that a focus on how children are taught mathematics, rather than on what mathematics they are taught, is needed.

Changing perspectives in this way involves implications for teaching approaches, the way in which mathematical dialogue is 'controlled' by teachers, the role attached to questioning, and the impact of all these considerations on teachers' planning.

Implications for teaching approaches

Research into effective teaching and teachers of numeracy (Askew *et al.*, 1997) highlighted that one factor involved in effective teaching was the emphasis placed on child/teacher discussion. In a school deemed to be one of the most effective in the teaching of numeracy there was a consistent expectation through Key Stage 1 and Key Stage 2 that children would develop skills in explaining their thinking processes: lessons in this school were characterised by dialogue in which teacher and children had to listen carefully to what was being said by others. Significant to this approach was a teacher belief, described as a *connectionist belief*, which views mathematics teaching and learning as something based on a dialogue between teacher and children and is characterised by extensive use of focused discussions in practice. Such a belief has connections with social constructivist perspectives on social and cultural dimensions to learning in which it is recognised that children can learn effectively from others including their peers. Chapter 1 discusses these ideas further.

One concern here for trainee teachers and experienced teachers alike could be the possibility of peer discussion and/or peer collaboration compounding existing mathematical errors and misconceptions through persuasive dialogue. However Anghileri (2000) refutes the notion that common errors or misconceptions will be 'spread' among children through discussion: rather, she suggests that such activities will encourage children to review their thinking, leading to self-correction. Pound's research in Early Years settings supports this and found that peer discussion in play situations provided opportunities for rehearsing misconceptions. Through such rehearsals – providing that there were no interjections from adults – children develop better understandings as they *are able to challenge their own and other children's misconceptions* (Pound, 2008, page 70).

The value in listening to explanations and the reasoning of others is viewed not only in the benefits to the restructuring of the specific and immediate mathematical idea, but also in the overall contribution to the development of individual mathematical thinking. This would suggest that the skills involved in using logic, reasoning, communication and problem-solving – the very skills inherent in children's ability to use and apply mathematics – are actively developed by teaching beliefs and approaches which are deemed as *connectionist*.

Tanner and Jones (2000) suggest that restructuring thinking to accommodate new knowledge is not easy. In Piagetian terms this presents the children with *uncomfortable learning*, as previously assimilated knowledge has to be revisited, reshaped and challenged. In order for this to happen the authors suggest that:

- children need to accept and appreciate that their response is not quite right;

- the learning process and environment need to be of sufficient importance to the children in order for them to make the effort to restructure and change their thinking;

- teachers need to accept that just explaining the misconception is not enough – the children will need help in the restructuring process.

The above is referred to as teaching for *cognitive conflict*: this describes children presented with examples and problems which lead to illogical outcomes. An example could be addition of fractions $^1/_2 + {}^1/_4\ldots$: if the strategy of 'add across top and bottom' is applied, this result ($^2/_6$) can be compared to a demonstration of a bar of chocolate where $^1/_2$ is given to pupil A and $^1/_4$ is given to pupil B – how much is left? ($^1/_4$). The two different answers to the same example create conflict between existing conceptual understanding (to add fractional values just 'add across') and new information which challenges this existing framework. This conflict can be resolved through peer discussion, sharing of ideas, justifying responses, listening to others and teacher questioning. *Accommodation* can only occur when restructuring takes place within one's schema to deal with this cognitive conflict.

Ryan and Williams (2007, page 13) argue that misconceptions are often *intelligent constructions that should be valued by learners and teachers alike* and as such suggest that what is needed is a *related teaching design or strategy that engages or conflicts with the underlying misconception and reasoning directly* (page 16).

Mathematical dialogue in classrooms

Swan (2001, page 150) believes that mistakes and misconceptions *should be welcomed, made explicit, discussed and modified* if long-term learning is to take place. He suggests that this is unlikely to happen unless the teacher and children negotiate the *social nature of the classroom* and establish a classroom ethos based on trust, mutual support and value of individual viewpoints: there is a recognition that this is not easy and could result in teacher loss of confidence through apparent reduction in 'control', reduction in amount of 'work' produced on paper as more emphasis is placed on discussion, and noisier classrooms.

While some of this research was undertaken in junior-aged classes, it has to be acknowledged that the majority of research undertaken in this area has been with Key Stage 3 and Key Stage 4 children. The issue of a child's maturity level to be able to deal with conflicting points of view, or engage in mathematical dialogue, is an important one and may lead teachers in Foundation Stage settings and Key Stage 1 classrooms to believe such an approach 'unworkable'. It is interesting to note, however, that effective learning in mathematics appears to be connected with a school policy on an expectation that all children within the primary school will explain their mathematical ideas and methods (Askew *et al.*, 1997). The notion of provoking cognitive conflict is not alien to a young child's mathematical learning experiences: consider the 'conflict' caused by noticing that a 'small' object appears to be heavier than a 'big' object, a 'tall' container holds less water than a 'short' container or that the digit 4 can be 'worth' different amounts depending on the position of that digit in, for example, two- or three-digit numbers. The following chapters provide further discussion on this.

The development of a *learning culture* within classrooms is fundamental for teachers and children alike to explore how challenge can be an opportunity for new learning to take place. Hughes and Vass (2001) suggest that teacher language needs to be supportive in this respect: they identify the types of teacher language which would be helpful in supporting and motivating children to take risks in their learning. For example:

- the language of success – I know you can;

- the language of hope – you can do it and what help do you need to do it?;

- the language of possibility – supporting a climate of greater possibility by the choice of response comment – yes, you did get it a bit mixed up but let's see which bit is causing you problems.

Ryan and Williams (2007, page 27) take this further by suggesting that teachers and pupils should view themselves as belonging to a *community of enquiry* in which the notion of *persuasion with coherent reasoning* is the norm. In such a community pupils are encouraged to share responsibility for sustaining the dialogue.

A key factor appears to be the 'control' and use made of teacher/pupil and pupil/pupil mathematical dialogue. Effective teachers of numeracy (Askew *et al.*, 1997) encourage both types of dialogue, allow it to be sustained, and use the results to help establish and emphasise connections and address misconceptions.

The role of questioning

Watson and Mason (1998, page 37) describe the learning of mathematics taking place within a social situation of talk, comprising of discussion, questions, prompts and answers in which the teacher and children are as much a part of mathematical activity as what is in a textbook, on the worksheets, or on the board. Teacher and/ or child questioning is viewed as questioning to enhance and develop learning rather than questioning to see if the 'correct' answer has been achieved. While there is some need for the latter, if it becomes the focus for teacher questioning there is a danger that children will develop a model of mathematical behaviour which gives the responses they think acceptable; it avoids suggesting alternatives and hides queries/ areas of confusion. Relying on answers alone, therefore, will not alert teachers to any underlying misconceptions. Worse still, simply correcting mathematical 'errors' without explanation, or engaging with reason, could lead to a pupil regarding mathematics as meaningless.

A Qualifications and Curriculum Authority (QCA) report into using assessment to raise achievement in mathematics (QCA, 2001) identified the need for teacher questioning to make greater use of *probing questions* to extend into dialogue which builds upon pupil responses in order to elicit the child's thinking and develop the child's understanding further. Ofsted (2003) noted that one characteristic of mathematics lessons they deemed unsatisfactory was a tendency for teachers to do most of the talking. This resulted in children having *too few opportunities to try out their ideas orally, testing their thinking against that of others*. Where teachers used oral work well, they were more likely to:

- *discover and deal with errors or misconceptions and adjust their teaching in the light of these*

- *help children to reflect on and sort out ideas and confirm their own understanding.*

(Ofsted, 2003, page 18)

Listening to children's questions also provides opportunities to gain insights into levels of understanding, errors in use of terminology and underlying misconceptions. Providing children with a diet of closed questions or tasks is therefore unlikely to allow teachers to ascertain children's errors or misconceptions.

Skilful questioning can have the additional benefit of providing opportunities for children to engage in creative thinking and responses in mathematics (Briggs and Davis, 2008).

Reflection

The National Strategies placed emphasis on child interaction and participation, particularly in the whole-class elements of each lesson, and encouraged discussion and co-operation between children in group/paired work. The guidance provided recommended that teachers should use effective questioning techniques which allow children thinking time, encourage explanation of methods and reasoning, and probe reasons for incorrect answers. Much of the advice in this area focused on how best to develop mathematical language and reasoning through guided group work. Mathematical language was defined in the guidance as *not just vocabulary but children's ability to confidently explain their methods and solutions, choices, decisions and reasoning* and the guidance advocates *interaction and sustained discussion as opposed to a single question and moving on* (DfES, 2007, page 8).

However, Ofsted (2009, page 5) continues to report that in primary mathematics *most lessons do not emphasise mathematical talk enough; as a result, pupils struggle to express and develop their thinking* and that teachers *did not show enough urgency in checking whether each pupil had started the work correctly, had shown any of the expected misconceptions or was being challenged enough* (page 19). In contrast, they identify that *the best teachers focus on pupils' errors as a learning point. They spot the significant misconceptions which are illuminated by pupils' mistakes* (page 41).

Creating more time for reflection, dialogue, interpretations and assessment of errors and misconceptions would clearly lead to less mathematical 'content' being taught, but, as research demonstrates, more deep-rooted, long-term mathematical learning taking place. Kafai and Harel (1991b) refer to reflection as an *incubation phase* and Ackermann (1991) identifies a *cognitive dance* where children necessarily 'dive in' and 'step back' from a situation to create balance and understanding. Freudenthal (1991, page 127) explains how reflection is an integral part of children *expanding their reality* or *expanding common sense*. Similarly, Ackermann (1991) believes that children's mathematical development is achieved through the *progressive widening of fields of experience* and Pratt and Noss (2002) refer to the *broadening of contextual neighbourhood*. However it is referred to, it appears that reflection enables the development of children's mathematical understanding.

Implications for planning

> *Misconceptions are a natural outcome of intelligent mathematical development involving connections, generalisations, and concept formation ... they signal a learning opportunity or zone and so, potential for development – for example – through targeted teaching.*
>
> (Ryan and Williams, 2007, page 270)

It appears that effective teaching of mathematics involves planning to expose and discuss errors and misconceptions in such a way that children are challenged to think, encouraged to ask questions and listen to explanations, and helped to reflect upon these experiences. This suggests that the more aware teachers and trainee teachers are of the common errors and possible misconceptions associated with a topic, the more effective will be the planning to address and deal with such.

Ofsted (2009, page 4) identify that a good teacher of mathematics recognises *quickly when pupils already understand the work or what their misconception might be. They extend thinking through building on pupils' contributions, questions and misconceptions to aid learning, flexibly adapting to meet needs and confidently departing from plans.*

The role of questioning, dialogue and discussion is significant if children are to shift their perspectives on only contributing if they think they have a 'correct' answer, or the answer they believe is wanted by their teacher.

Swan (2003, pages 119–122) discusses types of activities which are helpful to generate discussions likely to uncover children's misconceptions: the use of cards which have equivalent representations of the same concept, or statement cards which have to be sorted as always true, never true or sometimes true and placing children in situations where choices have to be justified or counter-examples provided.

It seems that a growing emphasis on children participating in meaningful mathematical dialogue which assists in the exposure of 'alternative' constructions has implications for the amount of time teachers should plan to teach new content.

Summary

The research demonstrates that teaching to avoid children developing misconceptions is unhelpful and could result in misconceptions being hidden from the teacher (and from the children themselves).

There needs to be a greater recognition from teachers that mathematical misconceptions are much more deeply rooted than errors and that it takes time for children and other learners to resolve long-held misconceptions. This implies that a shift in mindset is needed for teachers to move from planning mathematical lessons to avoid errors/misconceptions occurring, to actively planning lessons which will confront children with carefully chosen examples that allow for challenge, dialogue and restructuring of thinking.

Misconceptions are a natural part of a child's conceptual development and consequently, greater time in mathematical lessons should be given to encouraging children to make connections between aspects of mathematical learning and their own meanings. The time needed for children's reflection, examination of their own ideas, and comparison with those of other children and the mathematical situation presented, challenges the amount of mathematical content often covered in primary schools. The amount of time spent on revision for the National Tests continues to distort the curriculum (Ofsted, 2009) and is unhelpful in encouraging all teachers of mathematics to adopt teaching practices which would focus more on exploring and diagnosing misconceptions.

Regardless of the time allocated to mathematical discussion or activity, the culture of the classroom has to be one in which children are 'rewarded' for having the courage to test out their mathematical ideas in order for errors and misconceptions to be aired, discussed and resolved. If getting the right answer is the aim of the activity, or presenting the work in a neat way, or completing a set of exercises in a given time, then probing children's misunderstandings and misconceptions may prove difficult and counter-productive to effective mathematical learning.

3 Number: number and place value

Many number concepts are taught in a hierarchical sequence because the ability to understand and engage with more difficult concepts relies upon a sound understanding of ideas met earlier in the curriculum. Place value, for example, underpins much of the number curriculum, as does counting. Teachers, therefore, might consider how the use of a spiral curriculum (Bruner, 1960; see also Chapter 1) may support the teaching and learning of number in the primary curriculum. In the Early Years Foundation Stage (DfE, 2012, page 6) practitioners are expected to provide *children with opportunities to develop and improve their skills in counting, understanding and using numbers*. The principal focus of mathematics teaching in Key Stage 1 (Years 1 and 2) is to ensure that children develop confidence and mental fluency with whole numbers, counting and place value. This sets them up to increase their understanding of place value in lower Key Stage 2 (Years 3 and 4) to support their fluency in whole numbers and the four operations. By upper Key Stage 2 (Years 5 and 6) children will extend their understanding of the number system and place value to include larger numbers.

In primary school, children are introduced to number sequences from Reception onwards. Counting in number sequences (e.g. from 0 in twos) forms the basis of understanding number patterns which can be thought of as the building blocks for formal algebra. Nickson (2000, page 117) suggests that the shift of ideas from arithmetic to algebraic is a difficult transition for children and one in which *children tend to carry with them the perspectives and processes established in arithmetic to fall back on*. You can read more about algebra-related errors in Chapter 7.

Counting

Counting is one of the earlier mathematical concepts that children learn. Children learn to count both formally and informally through interaction with others and their environment. Amazingly, by six years of age, the average child attending an educational setting has an understanding of number which took man several thousands of years to discover. Dauben and Scriba (2002) explore the development of counting systems in great detail. Our decimal system has only developed over the last 5000 years and there are still places in the world today where the indigenous population cannot count beyond two. Interestingly, seminal research undertaken by American psychologists Gelman and Gallistel shows that learning to count mirrors the historical development of counting. Gelman and Gallistel (1986, 2004) spent six years researching children's cognitive development in number and formulated five principles of counting. These principles are outlined below.

The Gelman and Gallistel *'how-to-count'* principles

The one–one principle – a child understanding the one–one principle understands that each item to be counted has a name and that we only count each item once during the counting process. The child needs to make a physical or mental *tag* of the items to be counted and the counted items and keep them separate.

The stable-order principle – a child understanding the stable-order principle knows that every time we use number names to count a set of items, the order of the number names does not change. In English the order of the number names is always one, two, three, four, etc., every time a set of objects is counted.

The cardinal principle – a child understanding the cardinal principle knows the answer to 'how many?' The child knows that the last number counted represents the number of items in the set of objects.

The abstraction principle – a child understanding the abstraction principle knows that 'anything' can be counted and that not all the 'anythings' need to be of the same type.

The order-irrelevance principle – a child understanding the order-irrelevance principle knows that we can start to count with any object in a set of objects; we don't have to count from left to right, for example (adapted from Gelman and Gallistel, 1986, pages 77–83).

The importance placed on the findings of Gelman and Gallistel is reflected in the Early Years Foundation Stage Statutory Framework (DfE, 2012), in which the *'how-to-count'* principles are embedded.

In Key Stage 1 children are expected to understand all the *how-to-count* principles. Munn (2008) describes the typical responses of young children to a range of counting activities and she describes what a typical child understands at particular ages. Munn researched children's beliefs about counting and found *preschool children appear to have little or no understanding of the adult purpose of counting* (page 17). The interesting point about Munn's research is that the children believed they could count because they understood counting as saying the words in the right order. No doubt readers have heard friends and relatives boasting that their child could count at only three years old. Teachers need to be aware that children who can apparently count fluently may, in fact, just be 'reeling off' the number names by rote. The danger here is that the child might be introduced to more complex concepts before s/he understands what is meant by counting.

Since counting underpins early arithmetic concepts (Donlan, 2003), it is important that teachers are able to provide appropriate counting activities to support a child's learning. Having an awareness of the *how-to-count* principles will enable practitioners to understand the nature of counting and the potential difficulties that children may face during their journey to successful counting.

You can read more about how counting develops into the four rules of arithmetic in Chapters 4 (addition and subtraction) and 5 (multiplication and division).

Place value

The term 'place value' is used to describe the method by which numbers are represented in written form. The modern place-value system is based on the Hindu-Arabic method, which only became consistently used in Europe from the fifteenth century. The Hindu-Arabic system is a pure place-value system which is the most effective method of representing numbers, particularly if we wish to perform calculations with them. Given that it took such a long time to develop the modern place-value system, it is not surprising that many children find place-value concepts difficult. There are several underpinning structures to place value which children need to understand if they are to progress from counting, to representing numbers, to written calculations. The key principles are given below.

Digits – there are only ten digits in the system (0, 1, 2, 3, 4, 5, 6, 7, 8 and 9).

Position – the columnar position of a digit determines its value.

Base 10 – in our system we use base 10. Columns represent increasing/decreasing powers of 10.

Zero – we use zero to represent an empty column (0 as a place holder).

Grouping and exchange – once we have ten objects in a column, we can exchange them for one object in the next column to the left and vice versa.

If we stop to consider that there are so many principles to learn and understand, it enables us to reflect upon the challenges that this presents for children. The first obstacle faced by young children is that numerals are abstract concepts. When children learn to count, they usually do so by being introduced to concrete objects that can be moved, touched and seen. Numerals themselves bear no relation to the objects with which children are familiar. Baroody *et al.* (2006) discuss the work of Ginsburg from the 1970s. They identify how a key source of learning difficulties is the gap between children's existing knowledge and the teaching they receive at school. There are two main causes for this gap. These are: (a) *unconnected formal instruction*, and (b) *spotty or inadequate informal knowledge* (page 198). Others, such as Dickson *et al.* (1984, page 206) also use Ginsburg's (1977) seminal work. They explain how Ginsburg suggested that there are three stages to understanding place value.

Stage 1 – the child can write a number correctly but cannot explain why.

Stage 2 – the child can recognise when a number has been written down incorrectly.

Stage 3 – the child can understand what each digit in a number represents.

In summary, the teaching and learning of mathematics that depends on understanding place value is complex. To support children, teachers need to be able to accurately diagnose children's place value errors. They should not attempt to re-teach poorly understood methods, but return to earlier stages of understanding of place-value concepts.

You can read further about how place value supports calculation in Chapters 4 (addition and subtraction) and 5 (multiplication and division).

3.1 Consistent counting

The teacher asks the children how many teddies altogether have come to the picnic (see Figure 3.1).

Figure 3.1: One child says, 'One, two, three, four, six, nine, ten'

The errors

The child has made two errors. He has counted one teddy twice and he has omitted *five, seven* and *eight* in his counting sequence.

Why this happens

The child's first error has occurred because he does not understand the one–one principle. He has 'counted' one of the bears twice. This may be because he cannot remember which teddy he 'counted' first. The child is unable to separate the 'counted' objects from the 'to be counted' objects. The child's second error is that he is unfamiliar with the counting sequence. He does not understand the stable-order principle. He knows by heart the number sequence, *one, two, three, four*, but then chooses any number he has 'heard' for the rest of the sequence. Children need to know the English counting sequence before they can count effectively.

Curriculum links

EYFS	Children count reliably with numbers from 1 to 20, place them in order and say which number is one more or one less than a given number
Year 1	Count to and across 100, forwards and backwards, beginning with 0 or 1, or from any given number
Year 1	Count, read and write numbers to 100 in numerals; count in multiples of twos, fives and tens
Year 1	Identify and represent numbers using objects and pictorial representations including the number line, and use the language of: equal to, more than, less than (fewer), most, least

3.2 Abstraction and order irrelevance

The teacher asks a child how many things he has collected altogether (Figure 3.2). He is hesitant. The teacher knows that the child can count up to ten buttons or cars without any difficulty in the nursery. She asks him again. He empties out his bucket and groups his pinecones, rocks and leaves.

Figure 3.2

The error

The child has not counted all the objects together and therefore cannot find the total.

Why this happens

The child is not using the abstraction principle. He does not understand that we can count a mixed set of objects. He thinks that all the objects have to be of the same type or class. Another possible reason for the child's hesitation is that he is unable to understand the order-irrelevance principle and so could only count the objects when they were laid out in a line. The child, at this stage, needs to count the objects from one side to another; he doesn't realise that we can start the count with any object. His decision to lay out the objects in a line may also be related to difficulties with partitioning the 'counted' and 'to be counted' objects in an irregular array.

Curriculum links

EYFS	Children count reliably with numbers from 1 to 20, place them in order and say which number is one more or one less than a given number
Year 1	Count to and across 100, forwards and backwards, beginning with 0 or 1, or from any given number
Year 1	Count, read and write numbers to 100 in numerals; count in multiples of twos, fives and tens
Year 1	Identify and represent numbers using objects and pictorial representations including the number line, and use the language of: equal to, more than, less than (fewer), most, least

3.3 Conservation of number: more or less?

The teacher asks a child to look at two groups of counters and tell her which one contains more (see Figure 3.3). She states that the group with four large counters has more than the group with six small counters.

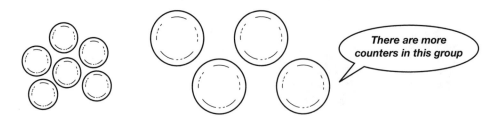

Figure 3.3

The error

The child has used a visual cue to deem that the group with four large counters has more than the group with six small counters.

Why this happens

Visual cues are often more convincing than other cues. The child may have even counted the objects in both sets and known that there were six and four respectively, but because the four counters take up more area, this has an overriding impact on the child's understanding of knowing the total number of counters in each group. This is known as conservation, a notion introduced by Piaget.

Curriculum links

EYFS	Children count reliably with numbers from 1 to 20, place them in order and say which number is one more or one less than a given number
Year 1	Identify and represent numbers using objects and pictorial representations including the number line, and use the language of: equal to, more than, less than (fewer), most, least

3.4 Using 'digit' and 'number'

A teacher overhears a child in his class saying to his friend, *Write down the number 6 and the number 3. That makes sixty-three.*

The error

The child is using the term 'number' incorrectly. In this situation, the number contains two digits.

Why this happens

Perhaps the child has heard others saying that four add two make six and he has borrowed some of the language to explain to his friend how to write 63. He has understood that four and six are numbers, but he has yet to understand that 0, 1, 2, 3, 4, 5, 6, 7, 8 and 9 should be referred to as digits when they are used in numerals. So, 5 is a one-digit number, written using the digit '5', and '5' is also a numeral. Similarly, 327 is a three-digit number, written using the digits '3', '2' and '7'. It is a numeral, where the digit '2' in the tens column has a value of 20.

Curriculum links

EYFS	Children count reliably with numbers from 1 to 20, place them in order and say which number is one more or one less than a given number
Year 1	Count, read and write numbers to 100 in numerals; count in multiples of twos, fives and tens
Year 1	Read and write numbers from 1 to 20 in numerals and words

(Continued)

(Continued)

Year 2	Recognise the place value of each digit in a two-digit number (tens, ones)
Year 3	Recognise the place value of each digit in a three-digit number (hundreds, tens, ones)
Year 4	Recognise the place value of each digit in a four-digit number (thousands, hundreds, tens, and ones)
Year 5	Read, write, order and compare numbers to at least 1 000 000 and determine the value of each digit
Year 6	Read, write, order and compare numbers up to 10 000 000 and determine the value of each digit

3.5 Zero (1)

A child believes that 0 is the lowest number. He says, 'Zero is the smallest number'.

The error

The child believes zero is the lowest number.

Why this happens

The child's experience to date may have included no experience of negative numbers, or if he has met negative numbers (such as cold temperatures in winter) he may not have associated the negative numbers as less than zero.

Curriculum links

Year 1	Count to and across 100, forwards and backwards, beginning with 0 or 1, or from any given number
Year 2	Count in steps of 2, 3, and 5 from 0, and in tens from any number, forward and backward
Year 3	Identify, represent and estimate numbers using different representations
Year 3	Count backwards through zero to include negative numbers
Year 4	Count backwards through zero to include negative numbers
Year 5	Interpret negative numbers in context, count forwards and backwards with positive and negative whole numbers, including through zero
Year 6	Use negative numbers in context, and calculate intervals across zero

3.6 Zero (2)

The teacher asks the children where 0 will go on the number line. One child says, 'Zero isn't a real number because you can't count zero things'.

The error

The child is correct that zero is not a counting number, but 0 sits on the number line between −1 and 1.

Why this happens

The child's experience to date may have included counting, in which case zero may not have been used. Zero is used as a place holder within numbers and therefore some people consider zero as being a symbol of a digit but not a number. However, mathematicians do see zero as a real number, on the number line between −1 and 1.

Curriculum links

Year 1	Count to and across 100, forwards and backwards, beginning with 0 or 1, or from any given number
Year 1	Identify and represent numbers using objects and pictorial representations including the number line, and use the language of: equal to, more than, less than (fewer), most, least
Year 2	Identify, represent and estimate numbers using different representations, including the number line
Year 2	Compare and order numbers from 0 up to 100; use <, > and = signs
Year 3	Identify, represent and estimate numbers using different representations
Year 3	Count backwards through zero to include negative numbers
Year 4	Count backwards through zero to include negative numbers
Year 5	Interpret negative numbers in context, count forwards and backwards with positive and negative whole numbers, including through zero
Year 6	Use negative numbers in context, and calculate intervals across zero

3.7 Reading and writing whole numbers

The teacher writes the number 609 on the board and asks the children to say the number (Figure 3.4). A child says it is the number sixty-nine.

Figure 3.4

The error

The child has read the digits as 60 and 9. The child does not recognise that the 6 is worth 6 hundreds (600) because it is in the hundreds column.

Why this happens

This type of error occurs because the child does not understand that the position of a digit determines its value. The child may be unaware of the principles of grouping and exchange. Children need to have practical experience of grouping sets of objects into tens and then exchanging each group of ten for another object which represents a 'ten' and so on for hundreds, thousands, etc.

Similarly, when asked to write '**six hundred and nine**', a child may write '**6009**', i.e. 600 and (then) 9. Again this error occurs because the child does not understand that the position of a digit determines its value and they write what they hear.

Curriculum links

Year 1	Count, read and write numbers to 100 in numerals; count in multiples of twos, fives and tens
Year 1	Read and write numbers from 1 to 20 in numerals and words
Year 2	Recognise the place value of each digit in a two-digit number (tens, ones)
Year 2	Read and write numbers to at least 100 in numerals and in words
Year 3	Recognise the place value of each digit in a three-digit number (hundreds, tens, ones)
Year 4	Recognise the place value of each digit in a four-digit number (thousands, hundreds, tens, and ones)
Year 5	Read, write, order and compare numbers to at least 1 000 000 and determine the value of each digit
Year 6	Read, write, order and compare numbers up to 10 000 000 and determine the value of each digit

3.8 The concept of zero as a place holder

Children are working with multi-base 10 apparatus. A child has a number of items on her table (Figure 3.5). The child is asked by the teacher to record the number represented by the apparatus.

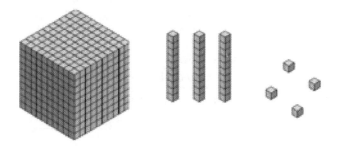

Figure 3.5: A child says 'one thousand and thirty four' but writes: 134

The error

The child does not understand the need to use zero as a place holder.

Why this happens

The child does not understand that if we have no 'hundreds' we must write 0 in the hundreds column so that the recorded digits are given in the correct position, i.e. the 1 in the thousands position, the 3 in the tens position and the 4 in the units position. This error may have occurred because the child does not understand that the position of a digit determines its value.

A similar example of the confusion surrounding the use of zero is the case where a child believes that 0.6 is smaller than 0.600. Here the child does not understand that the zeros in the hundredths and thousandths positions have no significance.

Curriculum links

Year 1	Count, read and write numbers to 100 in numerals; count in multiples of twos, fives and tens
Year 2	Recognise the place value of each digit in a two-digit number (tens, ones)
Year 2	Use place value and number facts to solve problems
Year 3	Recognise the place value of each digit in a three-digit number (hundreds, tens, ones)

(Continued)

(Continued)

Year 4	Recognise the place value of each digit in a four-digit number (thousands, hundreds, tens, and ones)
Year 4	Read Roman numerals to 100 (I to C) and know that over time, the numeral system changed to include the concept of zero and place value
Year 5	Read, write, order and compare numbers to at least 1 000 000 and determine the value of each digit
Year 6	Read, write, order and compare numbers up to 10 000 000 and determine the value of each digit

3.9 Writing the 'teen' numbers

The error

The child has reversed the digits in the number (see Figure 3.6).

I've written the number fourteen!

Figure 3.6

Why this happens

The child has written the numeral 4 first because in the English counting system we say '*four*teen'. The teens numbers often cause this difficulty. In addition, for 11 and 12, children must learn two new number names.

Curriculum links

Year 1	Count, read and write numbers to 100 in numerals; count in multiples of twos, fives and tens
Year 1	Read and write numbers from 1 to 20 in numerals and words
Year 2	Read and write numbers to at least 100 in numerals and in words
Year 3	Read and write numbers up to 1000 in numerals and in words
Year 3	Order and compare numbers beyond 1000

3.10 Number names

The teacher asks the children to count to twenty. One child says, '... seventeen, eighteen, nineteen, twenteen'.

The error

The child says *twenteen* instead of *twenty*.

Why this happens

This is a common error that comes about because children overgeneralise the 'teens' numbers on to twenty. It is also common because twenteen and twenty sound similar and so children do not pick up their error themselves easily.

Curriculum links

EYFS	Children count reliably with numbers from 1 to 20, place them in order and say which number is one more or one less than a given number
Year 1	Count to and across 100, forwards and backwards, beginning with 0 or 1, or from any given number
Year 1	Count, read and write numbers to 100 in numerals; count in multiples of twos, fives and tens
Year 1	Identify and represent numbers using objects and pictorial representations including the number line, and use the language of: equal to, more than, less than (fewer), most, least
Year 1	Read and write numbers from 1 to 20 in numerals and words
Year 2	Read and write numbers to at least 100 in numerals and in words
Year 3	Read and write numbers up to 1000 in numerals and in words

3.11 Spelling numbers

The teacher is concerned when the children are spelling numbers incorrectly, such as those in Table 3.1.

Table 3.1

2: tow	3: free
4: for	8: ate
11: alevin	13: furteen
13: firtene	14: forteen
15: fiveteen	21: twenteewn

The errors

The children have misspelt various numbers incorrectly.

Why this happens

Spelling often improves with exposure to written examples. In these examples the errors are:

- phonetic errors due to the children mispronouncing the number words

- using homophones incorrectly

- using correctly spelt numbers (e.g. five) in the teens numbers

- incorrectly combining letters and digits.

Curriculum links

Year 1	Count, read and write numbers to 100 in numerals; count in multiples of twos, fives and tens
Year 1	Read and write numbers from 1 to 20 in numerals and words
Year 2	Read and write numbers to at least 100 in numerals and in words
Year 3	Read and write numbers up to 1000 in numerals and in words

3.12 Continuing a number pattern

Having counted on and back in 2s with his class, the teacher decides to introduce counting on in 3s (Figure 3.7). He writes the following number sequence on the whiteboard and then asks what the next number will be. One child responds that the next number will be 18.

The error

The child has counted on two instead of three.

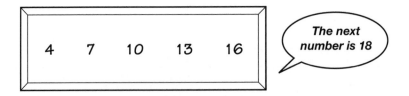

Figure 3.7

Why this happens

There are several possible reasons why the child might have given the wrong answer.

- The child miscounts the numbers. He says to himself: sixteen, seventeen, eighteen, instead of counting from 17.

- The child sees the 16 and thinks the numbers are the even numbers he was learning yesterday. If so, then the next even number would be 18.

- The child is still unable to understand symbolic representations of numbers and has been learning counting on in 2s through listening and rote learning. The child therefore gives a random response which happens to be 18 but could be any other number.

Curriculum links

Year 1	Count, read and write numbers to 100 in numerals; count in multiples of twos, fives and tens
Year 2	Count in steps of 2, 3, and 5 from 0, and in tens from any number, forward and backward
Year 3	Count from 0 in multiples of 4, 8, 50 and 100; find 10 or 100 more or less than a given number
Year 4	Count in multiples of 6, 7, 9, 25 and 1000
Year 5	Count forwards or backwards in steps of powers of 10 for any given number up to 1 000 000

3.13 Consistent counting in number patterns

When counting in threes, a child says, 'One, three, six, twelve, fifteen'.

The errors

The child has made two errors. He has started counting with *one* and he has omitted *nine*.

Why this happens

The child's first error has occurred because he does not understand that counting can start from any number. This is most likely because he will have experienced counting from *one* far more often than any other starting number. The child's second error shows that he is unfamiliar with the counting sequence. He does not understand the stable-order principle. He knows by heart the number sequence, *one, two, three, four,* but this is a new number sequence to learn. It also demonstrates that he is unfamiliar with what the number labels represent if he does not self-correct when he counts from *six* to *twelve*.

Curriculum links

Year 1	Count, read and write numbers to 100 in numerals; count in multiples of twos, fives and tens
Year 2	Count in steps of 2, 3, and 5 from 0, and in tens from any number, forward and backward
Year 3	Count from 0 in multiples of 4, 8, 50 and 100; find 10 or 100 more or less than a given number
Year 4	Count in multiples of 6, 7, 9, 25 and 1000
Year 5	Count forwards or backwards in steps of powers of 10 for any given number up to 1 000 000

3.14 Counting in steps

A class is counting in steps of powers of 10 for any given number up to 1 000 000. The teacher notices that three children are not confidently joining in. Later, she asks them to count from 24 700 in steps of 1000. Two are very slow but can manage it. The third counts: 24 700; 35 700; 45 700; 55 700 …

The error

The child is counting in steps of 10 000 instead of 1000.

Why this happens

In Chapter 1 working and long-term memory were discussed. Here, it appears that the two children who are able to complete the task slowly have had less experience of reciting larger numbers and as a result need more time to process the numbers. They will simply require more exposure and practice to these sorts of numbers, but understand the underpinning place value ideas. The third child is counting in the wrong steps. This may be because (a) she is lacking place value understanding and does not understand the digit or column she should be increasing by 1 each time; (b) she has simply confused 1000 with 10 000 on this occasion; or (c) because it is easier to count in steps changing the first (or last) digit of a number – she may have used this as her default if this is one of the first times she has had to count in steps with larger numbers.

Curriculum links

Year 4	Find 1000 more or less than a given number
Year 5	Count forwards or backwards in steps of powers of 10 for any given number up to 1 000 000

3.15 Finding one more and one less

When asked to find one more than 15, the child writes 151. When asked to find out one less than 21, the child writes 2 and says, 'One more than one five is one, five, one; one less than two one is 2'.

The errors

The child has inserted a digit 1 on to the end of 15. Furthermore, the child has removed the digit 1 from the number 21.

Why this happens

The child appears to be thinking about each of the digits separately, rather than as reading the whole number and seeing the digits as representing parts of the integer. They have simply inserted a single digit 1 rather than thinking about the number that is one greater than 15 and/or removed the digit 1 rather than thinking about the number that is one less than 21. This may also occur because the child misunderstands *one more* to mean *one more one* or misunderstands *one less* as *take one (digit) away*.

Curriculum links

Year 1	Given a number, identify one more and one less
Year 1	Identify and represent numbers using objects and pictorial representations including the number line, and use the language of: equal to, more than, less than (fewer), most, least

3.16 Odd and even numbers

A child in the class can say that the even numbers are 2, 4, 6, 8 ... 20 and can count in twos to 100. The teacher is surprised when he asks the child, 'Is 700 even or odd?' and the child replies 'odd'.

The errors

The child says 700 is an odd number.

Why this happens

It is likely that the child hears the seven in 700 and because they know that seven is an odd number, they state that 700 is odd. The child may have also not realised that the units digit is the identifier for the number.

Curriculum links

Year 1	Count, read and write numbers to 100 in numerals; count in multiples of twos, fives and tens
Year 2	Count in steps of 2, 3 and 5 from 0, and in tens from any number, forward and backward

3.17 Negative numbers

A pair of children are ordering negative numbers on a number line in Figure 3.8.

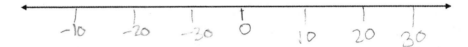

Figure 3.8

The errors

The children have placed the negative numbers in reverse order.

Why this happens

The children may be treating the two parts of the number (the minus sign and the number) separately or they have ignored the minus signs altogether. Either way, they have applied their knowledge of positive integers increasing in size from left to right in this situation.

Curriculum links

Year 4	Count backwards through zero to include negative numbers
Year 5	Interpret negative numbers in context, count forwards and backwards with positive and negative whole numbers, including through zero
Year 6	Use negative numbers in context, and calculate intervals across zero

3.18 Estimating numbers on a number line

The children have been asked to estimate the number on the number line. A child states the number (Figure 3.9) is 50.

Figure 3.9

The error

The child incorrectly estimates the number on the number line.

Why this happens

It is most likely that the child is most experienced using a number line from 0 to 100, so when the number line is from 0 to 200 the child applies her previous knowledge (50 is in the middle) without considering the range of the number line.

Curriculum links

Year 1	Identify and represent numbers using objects and pictorial representations including the number line, and use the language of: equal to, more than, less than (fewer), most, least
Year 2	Identify, represent and estimate numbers using different representations, including the number line
Year 3	Identify, represent and estimate numbers using different representations
Year 4	Identify, represent and estimate numbers using different representations

3.19 Placing numbers on a number line

The children have been asked to place numbers on the number line. A child shows where the number 52 would be placed (Figure 3.10).

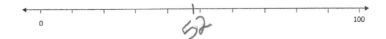

Figure 3.10

The error

The child incorrectly shows where 52 is placed on the number line.

Why this happens

If the arrow was sitting near 42 or 62, it would be most likely that he had miscounted the tens. Given the arrow is near 48, it seems that he may have counted from 100 backwards (demonstrating a lack of knowledge of counting from left to right on the number line) or that he got to 50 and then counted back two more rather than counting on. This type of error cannot be easily explained by looking at the outcome of a child's work and therefore further questioning would ascertain the child's understanding related to the area of mathematics being taught.

Errors on the number line are more likely as the numbers being represented get bigger. Children need to hold a lot more information in their head (i.e. the hundreds, thousands, tens and units) and this provides a high cognitive load for them, thus making them prone to errors.

Curriculum links

Year 1	Identify and represent numbers using objects and pictorial representations including the number line, and use the language of: equal to, more than, less than (fewer), most, least
Year 2	Identify, represent and estimate numbers using different representations, including the number line
Year 3	Identify, represent and estimate numbers using different representations
Year 4	Identify, represent and estimate numbers using different representations

3.20 Rounding

The children are asked to round to the nearest 1000. Table 3.2 shows one pair's answers.

Table 3.2

Original number	Rounded number
1354	1000 ✓
23047	24000 ✗
76789	77000 ✓
102303	102000 ✓
237600	237000 ✗

The error

The pair have applied an incorrect rounding strategy to the numbers.

Why this happens

At first some of these responses appear correct, but on closer analysis it is possible to see that there is a pattern in the strategy used. Both children have paid attention to the units (or ones) digit of the number, rather than the digit to the right of the column that the rounding is concerned with (in this case the hundreds). This demonstrates the children are following an insufficient procedural approach to completing the task, rather than understanding the purpose of rounding to the nearest 1000.

Curriculum links

Year 4	Round any number to the nearest 10, 100 or 1000
Year 5	Round any number up to 1 000 000 to the nearest 10, 100, 1000, 10 000 and 100 000
Year 6	Round any whole number to a required degree of accuracy

3.21 Roman numerals

The children are asked to write numbers using Roman numerals. The worksheet (Table 3.3) shows one pair's answers.

Table 3.3

Number	Roman numeral
4	IIII
9	VIIII
14	XIIII
19	XVIIII
22	XVVII

The error

The pair have not applied the conventions of writing Roman numerals correctly.

Why this happens

Unlike our own base ten system, Roman numerals are not well structured. Until the conventions are learned and understood, Roman numerals can be difficult to read and write. Here the children have used their own system which is logical to them, but they have have not applied the conventions of writing Roman numerals that need to be followed.

Curriculum links

Year 4	Read Roman numerals to 100 (I to C) and know that over time, the numeral system changed to include the concept of zero and place value
Year 5	Read Roman numerals to 1000 (M) and recognise years written in Roman numerals

4 Number: addition and subtraction

In the Statutory Framework for the Early Years Foundation Stage (DfE, 2012, page 6) practitioners are expected to provide children with *opportunities to develop and improve their skills calculating simple addition and subtraction problems*. Children in Key Stage 1 are involved with working with numerals, words and the four operations, including with practical resources (for example, concrete objects and measuring tools). The principal focus in lower Key Stage 2 is to ensure that children become increasingly fluent with whole numbers and the four operations. This should ensure that children develop efficient written and mental methods and perform calculations accurately with increasingly large whole numbers. At upper Key Stage 2 (Years 5 and 6), pupils develop their ability to solve a wider range of problems, including increasingly complex properties of numbers and arithmetic, and problems demanding efficient written and mental methods of calculation.

Counting

Counting forms the building blocks of arithmetic. Imagine there is a set of three objects and a set of four objects and a child wants to find the total number of objects. (To read further about counting, see Chapter 3.) There are five ways they could identify the total. They could:

Count-all: one, two, three, four, five, six, seven;

Count-on: The child counts on from the first set: four, five, six, seven;

Count-on from the larger: five, six, seven;

Count-on from either: four, five, six, seven or five, six, seven (and know that the answer will be the same);

Known facts: The child just knows three plus four equals seven.

What appears to be clear from research (e.g. Carpenter and Moser, 1979; Foster, 1994; Gray and Tall, 1994; Steffe *et al.*, 1982) is that less able children are more likely to rely on concrete counting methods whereas more able children have a more flexible and abstract approach. Orton and Frobisher (2005, page 13) suggest that this may be to do with memory: *the more readily one remembers the easier it is to think ... {and so} less effort is required in pulling essential information to the forefront of the mind* (see Chapter 1 for discussion about working memory and long-term memory to explain this further). Boaler (2009) suggests that children who are involved in talking about different mental calculation strategies are able to see how thinking flexibly about number can help approach problems in different ways.

Hall (2000) explains to us the importance of Piaget's argument that thought is internalised action. According to Piaget, children do not have the ability to start to use *mental actions* until they are about seven years old. If this is the case, then it is not surprising that children have difficulty understanding the concept of abstract numerals. However, research undertaken by Carruthers and Worthington published in a book described as *the most important book on emergent mathematical thought ever written* (Matthews, in Carruthers and Worthington, 2006) identify how children's mark making is the way that they make their own meanings of mathematical ideas, often devising their own representations from a very young age.

Place value in addition and subtraction

Since the late 1990s, children have been encouraged to use quantity value (i.e. 43 is 40 plus 3) rather than column value (i.e. 43 is 4 tens and 3 units) in the early stages of learning how to perform calculations. Orton and Frobisher (2005) describe the findings of several research projects which assess children's understanding of place value. The findings are alarming – only 43 per cent of 15-year-old children could identify what the digit '2' represents in the number 521 400 (Orton and Frobisher, 2005, 98). However, children did 'do better' in questions where they were given a number, for example 7 tens, and asked to ring a number containing 7 tens (Orton and Frobisher, 2005, page 98).

Howat (2006) identified that children who were struggling with arithmetic were often unable to use place value effectively. The children had not conceived 'ten' as being capable of being ten ones or one ten, and this remained the case regardless of her intervention strategies. To read more about the importance of place value in our number system and how children learn place value, read Chapter 3.

4.1 'Take away' and 'difference'

A guided group have been asked what is the difference between 6 and 9. One child responds with, *Well, they look the same if you stand on your head.*

The error

The child has used the everyday meaning for 'difference', identifying that '6' and '9' are essentially the same figure rotated. She has not considered the mathematical difference of these.

Why this happens

The child may have experienced more questions involving 'take away' (*what is nine take away six?*). The term 'difference' may be new and she has fallen back onto the more familiar interpretation she has. Using models to demonstrate how the processes for taking away or finding the difference are quite different may be one way to help understanding.

Curriculum links

EYFS	Using quantities and objects, they add and subtract two single-digit numbers and count on or back to find the answer
Year 1	Solve one-step problems that involve addition and subtraction, using concrete objects and pictorial representations, and missing number problems such as $7 = \Box - 9$.
Year 2	Add and subtract numbers using concrete objects, pictorial representations, and mentally, including: a two-digit number and ones a two-digit number and tens two two-digit numbers adding three one-digit numbers

4.2 Mathematical symbols for addition and subtraction

A teacher asks a guided group to record some number sentences they have made up. Figure 4.1 shows the questions and one child's responses.

$$3 + 4 = 7$$
$$5 - 4 - 9$$
$$13 = 7 - 20$$
$$10 - 3 = 7$$
$$20 + 5 - 15$$

Figure 4.1

The error

The child has confused the $+$, $-$ and $=$ symbols.

Why this happens

Mathematical symbols are abstract representations. In this case they represent mathematical operations. Children may find it difficult to remember what the symbols look like or which symbol is used for which operation. Children need to have a sound understanding of the underlying concepts alongside the introduction of symbols.

4.3 Addition and subtraction facts

A teacher is working with a group of children. One child answers the addition sums correctly, but struggles with answering subtraction questions correctly (Figure 4.2).

$$6 + 4 = 10$$
$$10 - 6 = 5$$
$$2 + 8 = 10$$
$$10 - 8 = 3$$
$$14 + 6 = 20$$
$$20 - 6 = 15$$
$$17 + 3 = 20$$
$$20 - 3 = 18$$

Figure 4.2

The error

The child is giving the wrong answer to subtraction questions.

Why this happens

Often children learn their number bonds to ten and twenty before the related subtraction facts, so it is understandable that subtractions facts are not recalled as quickly at first. If a child is, after some time, still providing incorrect solutions, one reason may be a lack of understanding of the relationship between addition and subtraction. They may not realise that they can use their addition facts to derive the subtraction facts.

In this particular example, the child is counting back from the minuend, but is including it in the counting so is consistently finding answers that are incorrect by one. See error 4.4 below for a similar error in addition – derived addition facts.

Curriculum links

Year 1	Represent and use number bonds and related subtraction facts within 20
Year 2	Recall and use addition and subtraction facts to 20 fluently, and derive and use related facts up to 100
Year 2	Recognise and use the inverse relationship between addition and subtraction and use this to check calculations and solve missing number problems
Year 3	Estimate the answer to a calculation and use inverse operations to check answers
Year 4	Estimate and use inverse operations to check answers to a calculation

4.4 Derived addition facts

Children are working independently on a worksheet where they are using known facts to derive facts.

Teacher: If you know that 14 add 3 is 17, what is 24 add 3?

Child: 24 [counting on] 25, 26, 27

Teacher: Try without counting on. How can you use what you know to work out the answer? If you know that 14 add 3 is 17 and 24 add 3 is 27, what is 34 add 3?"

Child: 34 [counting on] 35, 36, 37

The error

The child is counting on instead of using known facts to derive facts.

Why this happens

The child is using their preferred addition strategy of counting on to find the solution. This strategy is taught initially, but when using larger numbers it can be laborious and error-prone. Children need to be encouraged to use their knowledge of place value to derive the fact because they can more efficiently produce the answers they need to use in problem solving. This child may not be confident in their understanding of place value and how it can support deriving new facts.

Curriculum links

Year 2	Recall and use addition and subtraction facts to 20 fluently, and derive and use related facts up to 100
Year 2	Recognise and use the inverse relationship between addition and subtraction and use this to check calculations and solve missing number problems
Year 3	Solve problems, including missing number problems, using number facts, place value, and more complex addition and subtraction

4.5 Addition and subtraction of single-digit numbers

Two children have been asked to complete number sentences. Two of their answers are given in Figure 4.3.

Number sentences

3 + 4 = [6]

7 − 5 = [3]

Figure 4.3

The error

This is a counting error.

Why this happens

The children have counted the starting number twice in each calculation. For 3 + 4, they have counted: *three, four, five, six*. For 7 − 5, they have counted *seven, six, five, four, three*. Many young children make this error. Encouraging young children to play board games where they count on from the next square may help them to calculate number sentences accurately.

Curriculum links

EYFS	Using quantities and objects, they add and subtract two single-digit numbers and count on or back to find the answer
Year 1	Add and subtract one-digit and two-digit numbers to 20, including zero
Year 2	Recall and use addition and subtraction facts to 20 fluently, and derive and use related facts up to 100

4.6 Adding three one-digit numbers together

A child has been asked to add three one-digit numbers (2 + 5 + 3) together (Figure 4.4).

$$2 + 5 + 3 =$$

253

Figure 4.4

The error

The child places the three one-digit numbers next to each other to create one three-digit number, rather than adding the numbers together.

Why this happens

The child may not understand what the + symbol represents, and therefore thinks that the combining of digits is required or the child may have not met the addition of more than two numbers previously, and been confused by the task.

Curriculum links

Year 2	Add and subtract numbers using concrete objects, pictorial representations, and mentally, including: • a two-digit number and ones • a two-digit number and tens • two two-digit numbers • adding three one-digit numbers
Year 3	Add and subtract numbers mentally, including: • a three-digit number and ones • a three-digit number and tens • a three-digit number and hundreds

4.7 Finding an unknown in a number sentence

A child has been asked to complete the number sentence shown in Figure 4.5.

He writes '7' in the empty box.

$$2 + \boxed{7} = 5$$

Two add five makes seven

Figure 4.5

The error

The child has added 2 to 5 to obtain 7.

Why this happens

The child may be familiar with number sentences of the type $2 + 3 = \square$, so he sees the addition sign and adds the two numbers together. The child may not realise that the question is asking, *How many more are needed to make five?*

Alternatively, a subtraction calculation could be used. It may be that he does not understand that subtraction is the inverse of addition. Using subtraction is difficult for children because it requires children to solve an algebraic equation of the type $32 + x = 57$, and should not be used until they have a good understanding of counting on to find the answer.

Curriculum links

Year 1	Solve one-step problems that involve addition and subtraction, using concrete objects and pictorial representations, and missing number problems such as $7 = \square - 9$.
Year 2	Show that addition of two numbers can be done in any order (commutative) and subtraction of one number from another cannot
Year 3	Solve problems, including missing number problems, using number facts, place value, and more complex addition and subtraction
Year 4	Estimate and use inverse operations to check answers to a calculation

4.8 Adding and subtracting numbers mentally

A child has been asked to calculate $462 - 20$ mentally. She provides the answer 262.

The error

The child incorrectly calculates that $462 - 20 = 262$.

Why this happens

The child appears to have either taken 200 from 462 or she has taken '2' from the '4'. Either way, she has made a place value error. This may be an accidental error or she may have misheard the question. Alternatively she may not be aware of the value of the digits in each number if she has simply calculated '4' – '2' and not realised her mistake. This error is common in mental addition too, and becomes more common as numbers become larger for older children.

Curriculum links

Year 1	Add and subtract one-digit and two-digit numbers to 20, including zero
Year 2	Solve problems with addition and subtraction: • using concrete objects and pictorial representations, including those involving numbers, quantities and measures • applying their increasing knowledge of mental and written methods
Year 2	Add and subtract numbers using concrete objects, pictorial representations, and mentally, including: • a two-digit number and ones • a two-digit number and tens • two two-digit numbers • adding three one-digit numbers
Year 3	Add and subtract numbers mentally, including: • a three-digit number and ones • a three-digit number and tens • a three-digit number and hundreds
Year 5	Add and subtract numbers mentally with increasingly large numbers
Year 6	Perform mental calculations, including with mixed operations and large numbers

4.9 Place-value errors

The following examples illustrates place-value errors related to addition and subtraction.

(a)
$$\begin{array}{r} 72 \\ +\ 5 \\ \hline 92 \end{array}$$

(b)
$$\begin{array}{r} 56 \\ +\ 8 \\ \hline 514 \end{array}$$

(c)
$$\begin{array}{r} 47 \\ +\ 6 \\ \hline 71 \\ \hline 3 \end{array}$$

(d)
$$\begin{array}{r} 47 \\ +\ 82 \\ \hline 29 \end{array}$$

(e)
$$\begin{array}{r} 54 \\ +\ 72 \\ \hline 216 \end{array}$$

(f)
$$\begin{array}{r} 8^13 \\ -\ 27 \\ \hline 66 \end{array}$$

Figure 4.6

The errors

(a) Failure to understand that the position of a digit determines its value. The 5 has been placed in the tens column instead of the units column.

(b) Failure to understand that the position of a digit determines its value. An additional column has been added. The child is unaware that 14 equals 1 ten and 4 units.

(c) Failure to understand that the position of a digit determines its value. The child has reversed the tens and units digits when carrying.

(d) Failure to understand that the hundreds column exists even when no digits reside in it initially.

(e) Failure to understand the value of the digits in the answer. The child has reversed the tens and hundreds digits when writing the answer.

(f) Lack of understanding about decomposition. The child does not understand the principle of exchange, for example exchanging 1 ten for 10 ones.

Why this happens

The number operations errors above usually occur because the child has been introduced to standard written methods which s/he does not understand because s/he does not have a clear understanding of place value. Often children are trying to perform the calculations procedurally, by following poorly understood rules. Answers will remain incorrect or unchecked if children do not use approximation to check their answers.

Curriculum links

Year 3	Add and subtract numbers with up to three digits, using formal written methods of columnar addition and subtraction
Year 3	Solve problems, including missing number problems, using number facts, place value, and more complex addition and subtraction
Year 4	Add and subtract numbers with up to 4 digits using the formal written methods of columnar addition and subtraction where appropriate
Year 5	Add and subtract whole numbers with more than 4 digits, including using formal written methods (columnar addition and subtraction)

4.10 Overgeneralisation errors

The following examples illustrate overgeneralisation errors related to addition and subtraction.

(a)
$$\begin{array}{r} 374 \\ -\,158 \\ \hline 224 \\ \hline \end{array}$$

(b)
$$\begin{array}{r} 4\cancel{5}^1 9 \\ -\,28 \\ \hline 211 \\ \hline \end{array}$$

Figure 4.7

The errors

(a) The child has overgeneralised the commutative law, which applies to addition but not to subtraction.

(b) Overgeneralisation of the need for decomposition.

Why this happens

In example (a) the child has actually found the difference between 4 and 8. When learning number bonds, children are encouraged to find the difference between numbers. Often in our questioning of children we ask, *What is the difference between 8 and 4?* or, *What is the difference between 4 and 8?* We make no distinction between the two questions so children use this logic when performing standard calculations. In example (b) the child is likely to be following 'rules'. S/he may have been introduced to decomposition and is now applying this 'new rule' to all calculations. The child may also have a weak understanding of place value. Answers will remain incorrect if children are not using approximation to check their answers.

Curriculum links

Year 3	Add and subtract numbers with up to three digits, using formal written methods of columnar addition and subtraction
Year 3	Solve problems, including missing number problems, using number facts, place value, and more complex addition and subtraction
Year 4	Add and subtract numbers with up to 4 digits using the formal written methods of columnar addition and subtraction where appropriate
Year 5	Add and subtract whole numbers with more than 4 digits, including using formal written methods (columnar addition and subtraction)

4.11 Undergeneralisation errors

A teacher is introducing her children to mentally calculating the sum of two two-digit numbers. She wants the children to partition the multiples of 10. She shows the children the following examples on the whiteboard (Figure 4.8A). She asks them to practise this idea. Figure 4.8B shows one child's response to two of the calculations.

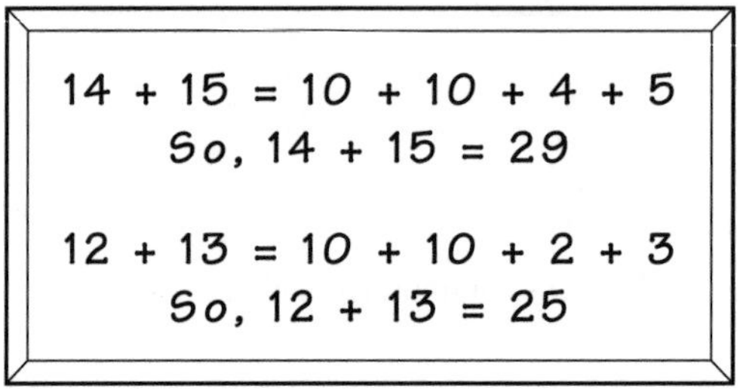

```
14 + 15 = 10 + 10 + 4 + 5
    So, 14 + 15 = 29

12 + 13 = 10 + 10 + 2 + 3
    So, 12 + 13 = 25
```

Figure 4.8A

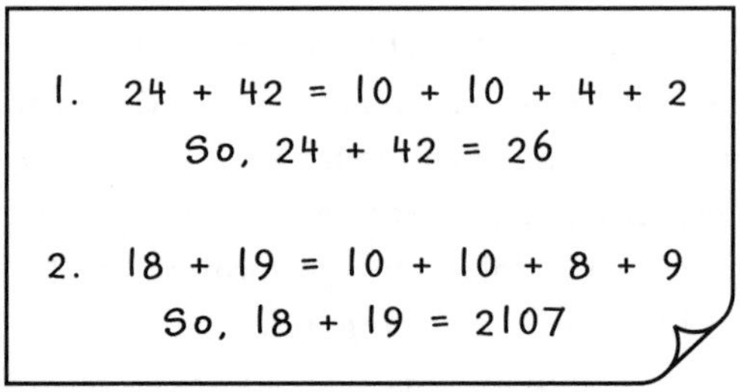

```
1.  24 + 42 = 10 + 10 + 4 + 2
        So, 24 + 42 = 26

2.  18 + 19 = 10 + 10 + 8 + 9
        So, 18 + 19 = 2107
```

Figure 4.8B

The errors

1 The child has copied the teacher's method and partitioned the numbers into one lot of 10 then the units.

2 The child writes down the '2' from the 10 + 10 then works out that 8 + 9 is 17. He partitions the 17 into 10 + 7 and then writes both numbers down next to his '2'.

Why this happens

These errors occur because the child has not encountered sufficient examples of the methods being taught. The child is unable to abstract the underpinning concepts which make the method 'work'. The child then tries to develop his own method to solve the problem.

Curriculum links

Year 3	Add and subtract numbers mentally, including: • a three-digit number and ones • a three-digit number and tens • a three-digit number and hundreds
Year 3	Solve problems, including missing number problems, using number facts, place value, and more complex addition and subtraction
Year 4	Add and subtract numbers with up to 4 digits using the formal written methods of columnar addition and subtraction where appropriate
Year 5	Add and subtract whole numbers with more than 4 digits, including using formal written methods (columnar addition and subtraction)

4.12 'Borrowing' from zero

A guided group are looking at some vertical subtraction equations with their teacher (see Figure 4.9).

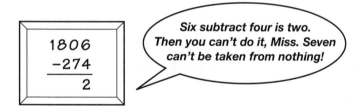

Figure 4.9

The error

The child is using a procedural method of carrying out decomposition, rather than understanding that zero is a place holder in this equation.

Why this happens

Until this lesson, the child has met subtraction algorithms presented in this format that do not require decomposition, and he has learned that to get the answer correct, he needs to 'subtract the digit at the bottom from the digit at the top' each time.

He has been shown how to calculate the answer procedurally, rather than building on from earlier methods he was taught. For example, if he had thought about how 70 could be subtracted from 100 and how that might help him to proceed with the calculation, he might have been more successful. Developing more formal algorithms from intuitive mathematics is a more effective way to develop children's use of algorithms like the one in this example (Anghileri, 2000).

Curriculum links

Year 3	Add and subtract numbers with up to three digits, using formal written methods of columnar addition and subtraction
Year 4	Add and subtract numbers with up to 4 digits using the formal written methods of columnar addition and subtraction where appropriate
Year 5	Add and subtract whole numbers with more than 4 digits, including using formal written methods (columnar addition and subtraction)

4.13 Estimating the answer to a calculation

A teacher is working with some children to encourage them to use estimation to check answers (see Figure 4.10). One child estimates that the sum will be approximately 220.

$$26 + 17 + 36 + 37 + 84 = ?$$

Figure 4.10

The error

The child has rounded up every number in the sum, so that the estimation is too high.

Why this happens

Children are taught a range of strategies for estimating, such as finding pairs that make 10 or 100, and rounding up/down. In this example, the child has rounded all the numbers up, perhaps because in previous examples this has been the preferred method or because the child has not considered how choosing to round up or down appropriately can have a significant effect on the outcome.

Curriculum links

Year 3	Estimate the answer to a calculation and use inverse operations to check answers
Year 3	Solve problems, including missing number problems, using number facts, place value, and more complex addition and subtraction
Year 4	Estimate and use inverse operations to check answers to a calculation
Year 5	Use rounding to check answers to calculations and determine, in the context of a problem, levels of accuracy

4.14 Word problems

Two word problems follow to exemplify the complexity of solving numerical word problems.

Example 1

The children have been presented with the following problem.

> On Joel's birthday he was given a model car worth £9.00. The next week, Joanne received a doll worth £7.00. How much more was spent on Joel?

A child says sixteen.

The error

The child has added seven and nine together instead of subtracting £7.00 from £9.00. Instead of counting on or using subtraction, she has chosen an operator she is comfortable using: addition. She has also not encoded the answer so that it fits in with the original context of money.

Why this happens

There are several reasons why the child might have been unable to solve this problem correctly.

- There is superfluous information in the problem, for example 'Joel's birthday' and 'The next week'. This causes 'interference' in the child's ability to transform the problem into a calculation.

- The names Joel and Joanne are quite similar visually so this may confuse the reader.

- This is a comparison problem, which is more difficult than a 'take away' problem.

- The problem contains gender stereotyping. The child might wonder why Joel gets a car and Joanne a doll. This problem may not match her everyday experiences.

Example 2

A child was asked to solve the following word problem.

> *Helen had some money. She gave away 12p to her brother and now has 37 pence left. How much money did Helen have to start with?*

She says that Helen has 25 pence.

The error

The child has subtracted 12p from 37p. She has selected the wrong operation.

Why this happens

There are several reasons why the child might have been unable to solve this problem correctly.

- The words 'gave away' may imply subtraction. The child may have focused on these words to select the operation.

- The order of the numbers in the problem does not correspond to the chronological order of events.

- This is a complementary subtraction problem which is more difficult than a combination problem.

Curriculum links

Year 3	Solve problems, including missing number problems, using number facts, place value, and more complex addition and subtraction
Year 4	Solve addition and subtraction two-step problems in contexts, deciding which operations and methods to use and why
Year 5	Solve addition and subtraction multi-step problems in contexts, deciding which operations and methods to use and why
Year 6	Solve addition and subtraction multi-step problems in contexts, deciding which operations and methods to use and why

5 Number: multiplication and division

This chapter is closely related to Chapter 3. In the Statutory Framework for the Early Years Foundation Stage (DfE, 2012, page 6) practitioners are expected to provide children with *opportunities to develop and improve their skills in counting, understanding and using numbers*. Children in Key Stage 1 are involved with working with numerals, words and the four operations, including with practical resources (for example, concrete objects and measuring tools). The principal focus in lower Key Stage 2 is to ensure that children become increasingly fluent with whole numbers and the four operations, including number facts. This should ensure that children develop efficient written and mental methods and perform calculations accurately with increasingly large whole numbers. At upper Key Stage 2 (Years 5 and 6), pupils develop their ability to solve a wider range of problems, including increasingly complex properties of numbers and arithmetic, and problems demanding efficient written and mental methods of calculation.

Place value in multiplication and division

Howat (2006) identified that children who were struggling with arithmetic were often unable to use place value effectively. The children had not conceived 'ten' as being able to be ten ones or one ten, and this remained the case regardless of her intervention strategies.

To read more about place value in our number system and how children learn place value, read Chapter 3.

5.1 Multiplicative reasoning

After the Sport Relief Mile weekend, a child explains to the class how she ran one mile and her mother ran three miles.

Teacher:	How many times further did your mum run?
Daughter:	She ran two times further than me, because three miles is two more than one mile

The error

The daughter thinks that her mother is running only twice the distance she is.

Why this happens

The daughter has used additive reasoning here to calculate the difference between one mile and three miles, rather than multiplicative reasoning to calculate that three miles is three times longer than one mile. This is a common misuse of additive reasoning because experiences in school in the earlier years are almost exclusively related to adding or subtracting. The move to using multiplication and division to compare different amounts is difficult and some learners struggle to achieve this, making later mathematics more difficult to learn and understand. See also error 6.4.

Curriculum links

Year 1	Solve one-step problems involving multiplication and division, by calculating the answer using concrete objects, pictorial representations and arrays with the support of the teacher
Year 2	Solve problems involving multiplication and division, using materials, arrays, repeated addition, mental methods, and multiplication and division facts, including problems in contexts

5.2 'Sum'

A teacher overhears two children discussing their answers. One child asks, *'What have you got for that division sum?'*

The error

The child has used 'sum' in an incorrect context. 'Sum' should only be used for addition, and no other operations.

Why this happens

Colloquially, people refer to 'maths sums'. However, to be mathematically correct, a sum is the result of adding two or more numbers (addend + addend = sum), the *summation* of the numbers. In this case, the child could been have asked, *Have you found the quotient?* (dividend ÷ divisor = quotient).

Curriculum links

Year 1	Solve one-step problems involving multiplication and division, by calculating the answer using concrete objects, pictorial representations and arrays with the support of the teacher
Year 2	Solve problems involving multiplication and division, using materials, arrays, repeated addition, mental methods, and multiplication and division facts, including problems in contexts
Year 3	Write and calculate mathematical statements for multiplication and division using the multiplication tables that they know, including for two-digit numbers times one-digit numbers, using mental and progressing to formal written methods

5.3 Mathematical symbols for multiplication and division

A teacher asks a guided group to complete some number sentences. Figure 5.1 shows the questions and one child's responses.

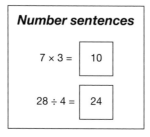

Figure 5.1

The error

The child has confused the × symbol with the + symbol and the ÷ with the – symbol.

Why this happens

Mathematical symbols are abstract representations. In this case they represent mathematical operations. The multiplication and addition symbols are visually similar, as are the division and subtraction symbols. Children may find it difficult to distinguish between each pair of symbols. It may also be that the child has a poor conceptual understanding of multiplication and division so reverts to the more familiar concepts of addition and subtraction. Children need to have a sound understanding of the underlying concepts alongside the introduction of symbols.

Curriculum links

Year 2	Calculate mathematical statements for multiplication and division within the multiplication tables and write them using the multiplication (×), division (÷) and equals (=) signs
Year 3	Write and calculate mathematical statements for multiplication and division using the multiplication tables that they know, including for two-digit numbers times one-digit numbers, using mental and progressing to formal written methods

5.4 Families of facts for multiplication

A teacher asks a guided group to complete some number sentences. Figure 5.2 shows the questions and one child's responses.

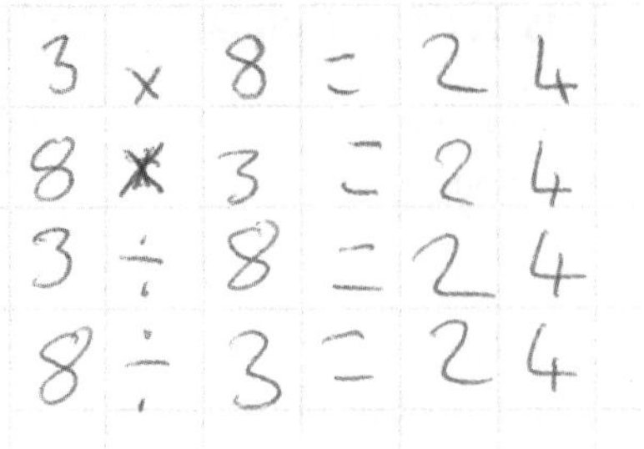

Figure 5.2

The error

The child has incorrectly completed the family of facts.

Why this happens

There are several reasons why the child may have made the errors here. It is most likely that they are trying to recreate a pattern they have seen without thinking about whether or not what they have written makes sense. It may also be that they do not know what the division sign means (see previous error), or that they do not understand the difference between division and multiplication.

Curriculum links

Year 2	Recall and use multiplication and division facts for the 2, 5 and 10 multiplication tables, including recognising odd and even numbers
Year 2	Calculate mathematical statements for multiplication and division within the multiplication tables and write them using the multiplication (×), division (÷) and equals (=) signs
Year 2	Show that multiplication of two numbers can be done in any order (commutative) and division of one number by another cannot
Year 3	Recall and use multiplication and division facts for the 3, 4 and 8 multiplication tables
Year 3	Write and calculate mathematical statements for multiplication and division using the multiplication tables that they know, including for two-digit numbers times one-digit numbers, using mental and progressing to formal written methods
Year 4	Recall multiplication and division facts for multiplication tables up to 12 × 12
Year 6	Multiply and divide numbers mentally drawing upon known facts

5.5 Finding a missing number

A child has been asked to complete the number sentence shown in Figure 5.3.

$$6 \times \square = 30$$

Figure 5.3

He writes '180' in the empty box.

The error

The child has multiplied 6 x 30 to obtain 180.

Why this happens

The child may be familiar with number sentences of the type 2 x 3 = □, so he sees the multiplication sign and simply multiplies the two numbers he sees together. The child may not realise that the question is asking, *How many times do we multiply six to make thirty?*

Alternatively, a division calculation could be used. It may be that he does not understand that division is the inverse of multiplication. Using division is difficult for children because it requires children to solve an algebraic equation of the type $30 \div x = 6$, which looks different to the original questions being asked, so it should not be used until children confidently understand what they are being asked.

Curriculum links

Year 3	Solve problems, including missing number problems, involving multiplication and division, including positive integer scaling problems and correspondence problems in which n objects are connected to m objects

5.6 Multiplying by 10: 'adding a zero'

The class is learning the 10 times table. One child says: Miss, this is easy! You can just add a nought: 3 × 10 is 30, 9 × 10 is 90, so 12 × 10 must be 120.

The error

The child believes that to multiply by 10, a zero is 'added' to the end of the number.

Why this happens

In mathematics we encourage children to spot patterns and rules. The child has spotted such a pattern. The problem with the child's pattern is that it is not generalisable because the rule only works for whole numbers. While the teacher might praise the child for recognising the pattern, s/he needs to address this misconception to discourage the child from applying this rule to decimal numbers. The child may not understand that when numbers are multiplied by 10 all the digits move one place to the left because they become ten times bigger. The 0 is acting as a place holder in the units/ones column. This can also be seen in other contexts, such as converting between different units of measurement.

Curriculum links

Year 2	Recall and use multiplication and division facts for the 2, 5 and 10 multiplication tables, including recognising odd and even numbers
Year 4	Use place value, known and derived facts to multiply and divide mentally, including: multiplying by 0 and 1; dividing by 1; multiplying together three numbers
Year 5	Multiply and divide whole numbers and those involving decimals by 10, 100 and 1000. Recognise and use square numbers and cube numbers, and the notation for squared (²) and cubed (³)

5.7 Multiplication and division by powers of ten: 'moving the decimal point'

Two children have been asked to convert measures in metres to centimetres (see Figure 5.4).

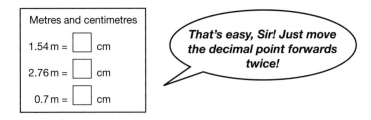

Figure 5.4

The teacher checks their answers and notes that they are all correct. He then asks the children how they calculated their answers. The children tell the teacher that they moved the decimal point 'forwards' twice. They proudly tell the teacher that they remembered to 'add some noughts' onto the 0.7 (i.e. 0.700000) before moving the decimal point.

The error

The children believe that the decimal point moves rather than the digits.

Why this happens

This error may happen because children are constructing their own 'rules' based upon their observations. The children need to understand that the digits move (not the decimal point). The children may not have a clear understanding that the position of a digit determines its value, or the effect multiplying a number by ten has on making it ten times bigger, so we see each digit move to the left one column.

Curriculum links

Year 5	Multiply and divide whole numbers and those involving decimals by 10, 100 and 1000. Recognise and use square numbers and cube numbers, and the notation for squared (^{2}) and cubed (^{3})

5.8 Dividing by 100

The teacher writes $500.82 \div 100$ on the board and asked for a child to write up the answer. One child writes 5.82.

The error

The child divides the whole number, but ignores the decimal number, giving an answer of 5.82 rather than 5.0082.

Why this happens

The child may believe that it is only possible to divide whole numbers or they may only know how to divide the whole number. In this case they are treating the whole number and decimal number as separate entities, rather than focusing on making the original number 100 times smaller by moving the digits along to the right.

Curriculum links

Year 5	Multiply and divide whole numbers and those involving decimals by 10, 100 and 1000. Recognise and use square numbers and cube numbers, and the notation for squared (^{2}) and cubed (^{3})

5.9 Dividing by zero

The class have been working on multiplying by 0 and 1. The teacher overhears one child saying, '12 divided by 0 is 0'.

The error

The child thinks it is possible to divide by zero.

Why this happens

Multiplying by 0 and 1 can be difficult for young children to understand, particularly in the way that they tend to be taught multiplication (by repeated addition). Here, the child has overgeneralised the multiplication rule of 'anything multiplied by 0 is 0' into division. The child has not considered that it is impossible to divide 12 into 0 sets, or that if $12 \div 0 = \square$ then $\square \times 0 = 12$, which is nonsense.

Curriculum links

Year 4	Use place value, known and derived facts to multiply and divide mentally, including: multiplying by 0 and 1; dividing by 1; multiplying together three numbers
Year 5	Multiply and divide numbers mentally drawing upon known facts

5.10 Factor pairs

The children have been identifying factor pairs. Two children list the factor pairs but notice their lists are different (Figure 5.5).

Child A:	Child B:
12	12
1, 12, 2, 6, 3, 4, 4, 3, 6, 2, 12, 1	1, 3, 4, 6, 12

Figure 5.5

The errors

Child A has duplicated factors and Child B has omitted some factors.

Why this happens

Child A has been systematic in the way she has listed the factors but has not realised when she could have stopped. Child B has been less systematic and as a result he has omitted 2 x 6. This might be due to the children not understanding what factor pairs are, or how factors pairs can be used. Another reason might be the way the teacher has expected the children to list the factor pairs. Using a factor tree or arrays might have been more appropriate for these children.

When checking to see if a number is prime, it is a common error for children to overlook some factors.

Curriculum links

Year 4	Recognise and use factor pairs, and commutativity in mental calculations
Year 5	Identify multiples and factors, including finding all factor pairs of a number and common factors of two numbers
Year 5	Identify multiples and factors, including finding all factor pairs of a number and common factors of two numbers
Year 5	Establish whether a number up to 100 is prime and recall prime numbers up to 19
Year 6	Use their knowledge of the order of operations to carry out calculations involving the four operations
Year 6	Solve problems involving multiplication and division including using their knowledge of factors and multiples, squares and cubes

5.11 Recording the results of calculations

Two children enthusiastically perform several calculations using short multiplication. Here is one of their calculations (Figure 5.6).

$$
\begin{array}{r}
236 \\
\times\ \ 8 \\
\hline
1834 \\
\hline
{\scriptstyle 2\ 8}
\end{array}
$$

Figure 5.6

The error

The children have placed the digits in incorrect columns.

Why this happens

The children have correctly calculated that 8 multiplied by 6 is 48 but have placed the '40' in the units/ones column and the 8 in the tens column. They may not understand that the position of a digit determines its value. The children may need to return to expanded methods of multiplication which use quantity value instead of column value. Alternatively, the error may have happened because the children are trying to use a standard algorithm (written method) which they do not understand. They are possibly attempting to solve the problem by following a set of rules.

Curriculum links

Year 3	Write and calculate mathematical statements for multiplication and division using the multiplication tables that they know, including for two-digit numbers times one-digit numbers, using mental and progressing to formal written methods
Year 4	Multiply two-digit and three-digit numbers by a one-digit number using formal written layout
Year 5	Multiply numbers up to 4 digits by a one- or two-digit number using a formal written method, including long multiplication for two-digit numbers

5.12 Place-value errors

The following examples illustrate place-value errors.

(a)
$$\begin{array}{r} 24 \\ \times\ 3 \\ \hline 612 \\ \hline 1 \end{array}$$

(b)
$$\begin{array}{r} 36 \\ \times\ 3 \\ \hline 08 \\ \hline 1 \end{array}$$

(c)
$$\begin{array}{r} 47 \\ \times\ 23 \\ \hline 141 \\ 94 \\ \hline 235 \\ \hline \end{array}$$

(d)
$$\begin{array}{r} 33 \\ 3\overline{)909} \end{array}$$

Figure 5.7

The errors

(a) Failure to understand the position of a digit determines its value. The carrying digit has been inserted in the answer in the tens column. The answer to 3 × 20 has been placed in the hundreds column instead of the tens column.

(b) Failure to understand the position of a digit determines its value. The child has not created a hundreds column.

(c) Failure to understand the position of a digit determines its value. The child has treated the tens digit multiplication as if it were a units digit multiplication. The child does not understand that the '2' in 23 is actually two tens or 20.

(d) Lack of understanding of the role of zero as a place holder. The child doesn't realise that 0 must be used to preserve the place value in the answer.

Why this happens

The number operations errors above usually occur because the child has been introduced to standard written methods which s/he does not understand because s/he does not have a clear understanding of place value. Often children are trying to perform the calculations procedurally, by following poorly understood rules. Answers will remain incorrect or unchecked if children do not use approximation to check their answers.

Curriculum links

Year 4	Multiply two-digit and three-digit numbers by a one-digit number using formal written layout
Year 5	Multiply numbers up to 4 digits by a one- or two-digit number using a formal written method, including long multiplication for two-digit numbers
Year 6	Multiply multi-digit numbers up to 4 digits by a two-digit whole number using the formal written method of long multiplication

5.13 Overgeneralisation errors

The following examples illustrate overgeneralisation errors related to multiplication and division.

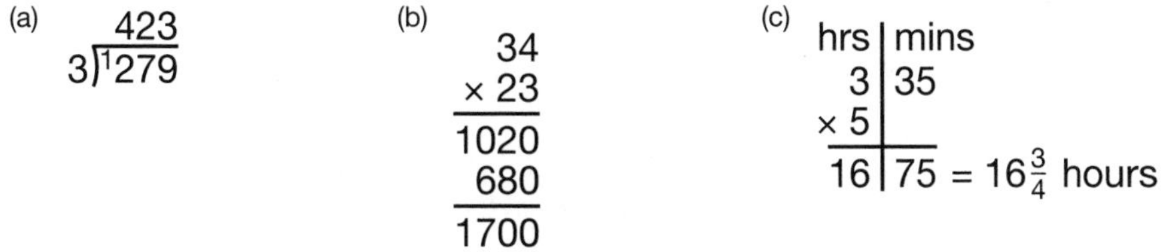

(a)
$$\begin{array}{r} 423 \\ 3\overline{)1279} \end{array}$$

(b)
$$\begin{array}{r} 34 \\ \times\ 23 \\ \hline 1020 \\ 680 \\ \hline 1700 \end{array}$$

(c)
$$\begin{array}{r|l} \text{hrs} & \text{mins} \\ \hline 3 & 35 \\ \times\ 5 & \\ \hline 16 & 75 = 16\frac{3}{4}\ \text{hours} \end{array}$$

Figure 5.8

The errors

(a) The child has overgeneralised the 'rule' for short multiplication. S/he has divided the units/ones digits first then the tens and finally the hundreds. The child has worked right to left instead of left to right.

(b) The child has overgeneralised the rule 'put down a zero' for multiplication by the tens digit. The child has placed a zero in the units multiplied by units row.

(c) The child has overgeneralised base-ten methods of calculation. S/he has used base ten methods for the multiplication of minutes. The child has seen the calculation as a 'decimal' calculation.

Why this happens

In all of the cases above the child has learned a 'rule' and then applied it inappropriately. This probably occurs because the child has a poor understanding of the methods to which s/he has been introduced. Answers will remain incorrect if children are not using approximation to check their answers.

Curriculum links

Year 4	Multiply two-digit and three-digit numbers by a one-digit number using formal written layout
Year 5	Multiply numbers up to 4 digits by a one- or two-digit number using a formal written method, including long multiplication for two-digit numbers
Year 6	Multiply multi-digit numbers up to 4 digits by a two-digit whole number using the formal written method of long multiplication
Year 6	Divide numbers up to 4 digits by a one-digit number using the formal written method of short division and interpret remainders appropriately for the context

5.14 Two-step word problems

Two children have been asked to solve the following problem.

> *Stephen already has £42 in his bank savings account. He wants to buy a dog. How much money will he have if he earns 75p every day for 6 weeks?*

They say he will have £492.

The errors

The children have calculated that 75 × 6 is 450 and then assumed this is £450, which they have added to the £42 pounds that Stephen already has. The children have made two errors. Firstly they have not calculated that there are 42 days in 6 weeks so they have just multiplied 75 by 6. Secondly, they have not changed the answer in pence into pounds before adding it to the original amount.

Why this happens

There are several reasons why the children may have been unable to solve this problem correctly.

The problem is a two-step problem which is more complex. It contains a mix of operations: multiplication and addition.

- There is a mix of units (£ and pence). This means that the children have to either multiply decimal numbers (0.75) or remember to represent their answer in pounds not pence.

- There is superfluous information in the question, for example, 'He wants to buy a dog'.

- The children may not recognise (or may forget) that the phrase 'every day' implies multiplying by 7 (the number of days in a week) because the number 7 cannot be seen in the problem.

- The children may have assumed their answer is correct when they compare their answer with their everyday knowledge of the price of buying a dog.

Curriculum links

Year 4	Solve problems involving multiplying and adding, including using the distributive law to multiply two digit numbers by one digit, integer scaling problems and harder correspondence problems such as n objects are connected to m objects
Year 5	Solve problems involving addition, subtraction, multiplication and division and a combination of these, including understanding the meaning of the equals sign
Year 6	Use their knowledge of the order of operations to carry out calculations involving the four operations

5.15 Dividing a small dividend by a large divisor

A teacher asks the children the following question:

A five-metre-long pole was divided into 15 equal parts. What is the length of each part?

The children responded with a solution of '3'.

The error

The children have incorrectly solved the problem by thinking it is asking for 15 divided by 5 (instead of the correct 5 divided by 15).

Why this happens

The children are most familiar with division problems where the dividend is always larger than the divisor, and the quotient (solution) is always smaller. Therefore, instead of taking the context of the word problem into consideration, they have jumped to the conclusion that they should be answering $15 \div 5$ instead of $5 \div 15$.

Curriculum links

Year 5	Divide numbers up to 4 digits by a one-digit number using the formal written method of short division and interpret remainders appropriately for the context
Year 6	Divide numbers up to 4 digits by a two-digit whole number using the formal written method of long division, and interpret remainders as whole number remainders, fractions, or by rounding, as appropriate for the context
Year 6	Solve problems involving addition, subtraction, multiplication and division, and a combination of these, including understanding the meaning of the equals sign

5.16 Interpreting calculator displays after division

The teacher asks the class to work out the number of 33-seater buses that are needed for the school trip if there are 63 children and 8 adults are going. The children are allowed to use a calculator to work out the answer (see Figure 5.9).

> Child 1: We need two point one five buses
> Child 2: You can't get two point one five buses! We need two buses

The errors

Both children have not paid attention to the context of the problem. Child 1 has not considered that it is not possible to get 0.15 of a bus! Child 2 rounded down, without considering the context will mean not everyone would be accommodated.

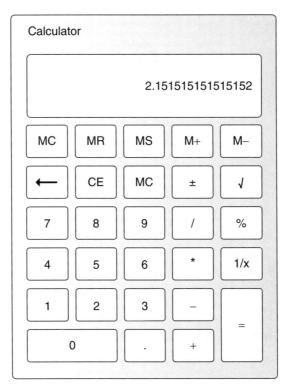

Figure 5.9

Why this happens

Children can dismiss or even forget the context of the initial problem as they focus on the calculations they are carrying out. In a problem where the context would not have been a consideration, both children would have been correct.

Curriculum links

Year 6	Divide numbers up to 4 digits by a two-digit number using the formal written method of short division where appropriate, interpreting remainders according to the context

5.17 Combination problems

The children have been shown 3 hats and 4 coats and been asked how many different outfits can be made. One child says that there are 24 different outfits.

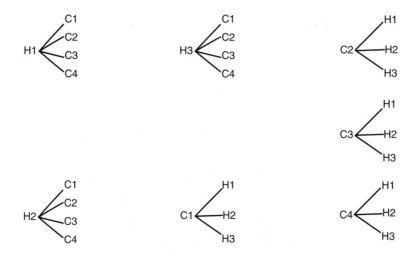

Figure 5.10

The error

The child thinks there are 24 combinations of outfits.

Why this happens

Although the child has been logical in his approach, he has overlooked the pairings he is making. Often children make similar errors (usually not finding all the combinations) because they have not thought through the task systematically.

Curriculum links

Year 3	Solve problems, including missing number problems, involving multiplication and division, including positive integer scaling problems and correspondence problems in which n objects are connected to m objects

5.18 BODMAS

The children have been given $8 + (5 \times 3^2 + 6)$ to calculate. There are several answers given:

a) 123

b) 83

c) 59

The errors

The children have given different answers.

Why this happens

All the children did not use the correct order of operations, known as BODMAS. For example, (a) worked out $(8 + 5) \times 9 + 6$ and (b) worked out $8 + (5 \times (9 + 6))$. Interestingly, (c) gives the correct answer, but the child has added 8 and 6 first, then multiplied 5 and 9 (from 3^2). Although this strategy has produced the correct solution, the child does not understand that the numbers inside the bracket have to stay together (unless they are being multiplied out).

Curriculum links

Year 5	Solve problems involving addition, subtraction, multiplication and division, and a combination of these, including understanding the meaning of the equals sign
Year 6	Use their knowledge of the order of operations to carry out calculations involving the four operations

5.19 Scaling by fractions

The error

The child believes that it is impossible to multiply the sides of Square A to make Square B as Square B is smaller and multiplying makes the answer bigger (Figure 5.11).

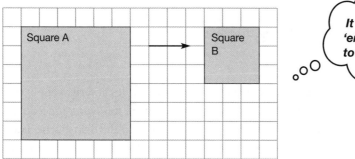

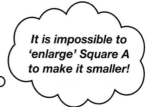

It is impossible to 'enlarge' Square A to make it smaller!

Figure 5.11

Why this happens

As in number, there is a common misunderstanding that multiplication always makes numbers bigger. Of course we can enlarge square A by a scale factor of 0.5 to make square B, just as multiplying by a half makes a number half the size. Some teachers confuse children by talking about 'reducing' a shape by half. This demonstrates the conflict between the technical use of the word 'enlargement' and its use in ordinary English which can often be identified in mathematics.

Curriculum links

Year 6	Solve problems involving multiplication and division, including scaling by simple fractions and problems involving simple rates

5.20 Overgeneralisation of the distributive law

After exploring the distributive law with his children using examples like the one in Figure 5.12,

$$3 \times 14$$
$$= 3 \times (10 + 4)$$
$$= (3 \times 10) + (3 \times 4)$$
$$= 30 + 12$$
$$= 42$$

Figure 5.12

the teacher noticed the error in Figure 5.13 creeping in to later work.

$$6 + 17$$
$$= 6 + (10 \times 7)$$
$$= (6 + 10) \times (6 + 7)$$
$$= 60 \times 13$$
$$= 780$$

Figure 5.13

The error

The child has erroneously extended the distributive law.

Why this happens

It is common for children to incorrectly generalise or extend rules and then apply them to other areas of mathematics. When this happens, children are following procedures without understanding. In this example, the child has extended the distributive law $a \times (b + c) = (a \times b) + (a \times c)$ to addition: $a + (b \times c) = (a + b) \times (a + c)$ and actually made a rather simple question much more difficult!

Curriculum links

Year 6	Perform mental calculations, including with mixed operations and large numbers

6 Number: fractions, decimals and percentages

In the Early Years Foundation Stage (DfE, 2012, page 6) practitioners are expected to provide children with opportunities to develop and improve their skills in counting, understanding and using numbers, calculating simple addition and subtraction problems, and describing shapes, spaces and measures. Problems with simple fractions are often met in these contexts. In Key Stage 1 (Years 1 and 2) children are introduced to early notions of fractions through finding simple fractions of objects, numbers and quantities. During lower Key Stage 2 (Years 3 and 4) children develop their ability to solve a range of problems, including some with simple fractions and decimal place value. Children will develop the connections between multiplication and division with fractions, decimals, percentages and ratio in upper Key Stage 2 (Years 5 and 6). By the end of Year 6, children should be fluent in working with fractions, decimals and percentages.

Fractions

It is important to remember that most children will have met fractions informally in an everyday context before coming to school and teachers need to be aware of the potential for misconceptions arising from these encounters. For example, a parent may encourage a child to choose the 'biggest half' of a food item they are sharing. However, this is incorrect as mathematically, the halves should be equal.

Lamon (2001) argues that *traditional instruction in fractions does not encourage meaningful performance* (page 146). She researched the effect of teaching fractions for understanding and found that where learning was underpinned by understanding, children were able to solve problems involving more complex fractions. Similarly, Critchley (2002) describes how a *real* problem-solving activity involving the use of fractions supported a child's ability to understand and use them.

There are many different interpretations of fractions and it is important that teachers are both aware of and understand these interpretations so they can introduce them to children in a meaningful way. Teachers also need to be aware that some interpretations of fractions are conceptually more difficult than others. The relative conceptual difficulty of particular interpretations of fractions is widely recognised by mathematics educators (Charalambous and Pitta-Pantazi, 2005). The interpretations (Lamon, 1999) are:

Part of a whole: here an object is 'split' into two or more equal parts.

Part of a set of objects: what part of the set of objects has a particular characteristic?

Number on a number line: numbers which are represented *between* whole numbers.

Operator: the result of a division.

Ratio: comparing the relative size of two objects or sets of objects.

The first interpretation in this list is that a fraction is part of a whole. Charalambous and Pitta-Pantazi's (2005) research identified that while this way of teaching fractions was necessary, it was not appropriate to use this as the only way in to teaching the other interpretations of fractions. They explained that it was necessary for teachers *to scaffold students to develop a profound understanding of the different interpretations of fractions, since such an understanding could also offer to uplift students' performance in tasks related to the operations of fractions* (Charalambous and Pitta-Pantazi, 2005, page 239).

Fractions are among the most difficult mathematical concepts that children come across at primary school (Charalambous and Pitta-Pantazi, 2005). In fact, analysis of children's errors in fractions has been investigated for many years (see e.g. Brueckner, 1928; Morton, 1924). Nickson (2000) suggests that children have difficulty applying their knowledge of fractions to problem-solving situations because there are several interpretations of fractions and therefore children do not know which interpretation to use. Lamon (2001, pages 147–148) explains that even students who are studying for a degree in mathematics may have a limited understanding of fractions.

Decimals

Decimal numbers are an extension of the whole-number place-value system. Bailey and Borwein (2010) argue that the modern system of decimal notation with zero, together with basic computational schemes, was the greatest discovery in mathematics. This happened over 1500 years ago in India, around 500 BC.

Decimal numbers are symbolic representations of units less than one (rational numbers) in the same way that the whole-number place-value system represents quantities of objects. The conceptual ideas underpinning decimals are the same as those underpinning fractions, for example part of a whole, part of a set, and so on (see the discussion in the 'Fraction' section above). In effect, decimals are simply another way of representing fractions in written form. The implication of this is that children need to have a sound understanding of fractions in order to use abstract decimal notation to represent fractions. Pagni (2004) argues that fractions and decimals should not be taught separately. Since fractions and decimals are representations for the same numbers, Pagni suggests teachers should show the connection between them by placing equivalent fractions and decimals on a number line.

Errors in the use of decimals are likely to have two sources of misunderstanding: place value and fractions (Moloney and Stacey, 1997). Where such errors occur, teachers might consider returning to much earlier concepts to ensure the child has sufficient understanding of these ideas to be able to use decimal notation.

According to Sadi (2007), more children have difficulties with decimals than any other number concept. He suggests that this is because of the gap in understanding between the natural numbers and decimal numbers.

Percentages

The term 'per cent' means literally 'for every hundred'. Percentages are conceptually equivalent to the part-of-a-set interpretation of fractions – if our set contains 100 objects then we can easily see that if 50 of the objects have a particular attribute then 50 per cent (%) of the set can be said to have the attribute. Equally, we can relate percentages to the part–whole representation of fractions in that 'the whole' represents 100%. Percentages are used widely in 'everyday' life and children will have an understanding that 30% off in the sale means that the item is reduced in price. This does not mean that children understand the mathematics of percentages, just as a young child who can 'reel off' the numbers to 20 may not be able to count. Like decimals, percentages are a method of representing rational numbers, so children need to have a sound understanding of fractions before being formally introduced to percentages.

In primary school, the focus should be on helping children to understand the notion of per cent and relating this to simple fractional amounts, for example halves, quarters and tenths. It is tempting to think that we might introduce children to a mathematical formula in order to solve more complex percentage problems, but this should be avoided – it might be argued that teaching in this way leads to weak understanding and negative attitudes towards percentages. Instead, just as reported earlier in the 'Decimals' section, it is useful to introduce equivalent fractions, decimals and percentages together. Van den Heuvel-Panhuizen (2003) explores a Dutch Realistic Mathematics Education (RME) learning trajectory in which Grade 5 children were taught percentages through a process drawing on the children's own experiences of using percentages, decimals and fractions, reporting that it was *remarkable how easily the children got to work so easily … everything happened very naturally, and it was clear from the way in which the children discussed {the assignment}… that they knew what the percentages represented* (page 20).

White *et al.* (2007) discuss how the multiplicative relationship of percentages causes children difficulties. They cite Misailidou and Williams (2003), who showed how 10–14-year-olds often used inappropriate additive strategies.

Another difficulty is with the terms 'of' and 'out of' – both of which represent an operator which needs explaining:

'of' represents the multiplication operator, for example 50% of 80 means 0.5×80;

'out of' represents the division operator, for example 40 out of 80 means $40 \div 80$.

A key aspect of teaching percentages in the primary school is to help children to understand the relationship between fractions and percentages. Children need to understand that 50% is equivalent to one-half and 25% is equivalent to one-quarter. This enables children to solve simple percentage problems using a conceptual model based on their understanding of fractions, thus avoiding 'the formula'. If teachers wish to explore more complex problems with some children, they can then use the conceptual model to derive 'the formula' for 'of' problems, so that becomes a natural progression in understanding. Some children will find the concept of percentages very difficult. This may be because their understanding of fractions is weak. In these cases, teachers will need to return to earlier concepts relating to fractions, including concrete representations of part of a set and part of a whole.

Ratio and proportion

Ratio and proportion are no longer an explicitly taught aspect in the new national curriculum for England. However, in the non-statutory notes and guidances, ratio and proportion are contextualised in other problems, such as scale drawings, similar shapes, recipes and comparing quantities.

Lamon (2008) explores how the key to understanding fractions, decimals, percentages, ratio and proportion is discussion during reasoning activities. Her book, developed after years of research on this area, develops teacher confidence by asking the same sorts of questions that teachers may ask children. She explains how ratio is a comparison of any two quantities and that it expresses an idea that cannot be expressed by a single number. Additionally, a key premise of the book is about using proportion as a powerful mathematical tool. For example, to know that when two quantities are related to each other and one changes, the other also changes in a precise way, and knowing that the relationship does not change but that the quantities may increase or decrease, this aids the development of proportional reasoning.

You may find these practical examples helpful.

> **Ratio:** 'for every' – there are three pencils for every child in the class.

> **Proportion:** 'in every' – there are two red pencils in every pot of pencils.

Much research in the area of proportional reasoning identifies that solving ratio and proportion problems is a very difficult task for most children and student teachers (Misailidou and Williams, 2002). Similarly to the research discussed above on percentages, Ryan and Williams (2007) also identify multiplicative versus additive strategies as a barrier to solving ratio and proportion problems. They explain how, on occasion, additive strategies can work (for example in the case of 1:2 or 1:n, it is possible to count on in order to solve the problems) but that most problems in any ratio m:n cannot work by using additive strategies. Their research identifies how many children prefer to add or subtract numbers in problems, and avoid multiplication, division and particularly fractions.

6.1 Fractions as part of a shape

The teacher asks the children to divide a semicircle into quarters. One child's response is given in Figure 6.1.

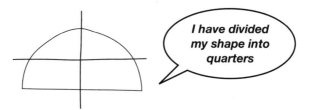

Figure 6.1

The error

The child has not divided the semicircle into four equal parts.

Why this happens

The child does not understand that all the parts must be equal. He may not have had sufficient experience of dividing physical objects into equal parts where the parts can be directly compared to each other. Additionally, he may be used to dividing squares, oblongs and circles so he thinks the methods he has used for these shapes works for all shapes. In effect, he incorrectly generalises the methods he has used for squares, oblongs and circles.

Curriculum links

EYFS	They solve problems, including doubling, halving and sharing
Year 1	Recognise, find and name a half as one of two equal parts of an object, shape or quantity
Year 1	Recognise, find and name a quarter as one of four equal parts of an object, shape or quantity
Year 2	Recognise, find, name and write fractions $^1/_3$, $^1/_4$, $^2/_4$ and $^3/_4$ of a length, shape, set of objects or quantity

6.2 Fractions as part of a set of objects

The teacher asks two children what fraction of the set in Figure 6.2 is black. They say one-third.

Figure 6.2

The error

The children have failed to take the complete set of objects as the whole unit.

Why this happens

The children have compared the one black cube against the three white cubes and concluded that one-third of the set of objects is black. This misconception may be common in children up to about seven years of age and may be related to Piaget's findings from his class-inclusion task. Piaget found that if children are presented with a set of say five red objects and two blue objects and asked if there are more red objects or more 'objects', children will say there are more red objects. This is because they compare the red objects with the blue objects instead of comparing the red objects with the total number of objects in the set.

Curriculum links

EYFS	They solve problems, including doubling, halving and sharing
Year 2	Recognise, find, name and write fractions 1/3, 1/4, 2/4 and 3/4 of a length, shape, set of objects or quantity
Year 3	Recognise, find and write fractions of a discrete set of objects: unit fractions and non-unit fractions with small denominators

6.3 Fractions as numbers on a number line

The teacher is using a counting stick in the oral/mental part of the daily mathematics lesson (Figure 6.3). She tells children that one end of the counting stick represents 0 and the other end of the counting stick represents 10. She asks one child to place '½' on the counting stick. He places his card in the centre of the counting stick.

The error

The child has placed his card halfway along the counting stick instead of halfway between 0 and 1.

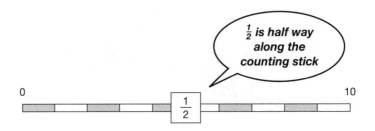

Figure 6.3

Why this happens

When children are introduced to fractions they are introduced to unit fractions such as one-half or one-quarter. They sometimes believe that a fraction is a number smaller than one, i.e. between 0 and 1. Children can usually successfully identify fractions on a number line between 0 and 1. The difficulty arises when the number line is extended to include numbers greater than 1. It is likely that the child's previous experience has involved halving shapes, and when a shape had been halved, there has been a line drawn in the middle. The child has applied this knowledge to the number line, instead of treating ½ as a number in its own right with a specific place on the number line half way between 0 and 1.

Curriculum links

Year 3	Recognise and use fractions as numbers: unit fractions and non-unit fractions with small denominators

6.4 Fractions as ratios

The teacher asks the class to compare two sets of objects, A and B (Figure 6.4).

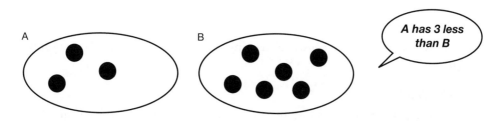

Figure 6.4

One child tells the teacher that set A is 3 less than set B.

The error

The child has used additive comparison instead of multiplicative comparison.

Why this happens

The correct response should be that set A has half as many dots as set B. The child is drawing on her knowledge of addition and subtraction from earlier in her education – when comparing the size of two sets of objects involved using addition/subtraction. She may do this because she does not fully understand the nature of the task. This type of error may also arise when we are comparing lengths. For example, a child may say that object A is 12cm longer than object B instead of saying that object A is 5 times as long as object B. See also error 5.1.

Curriculum links

Year 6	Solve problems involving unequal sharing and grouping using knowledge of fractions and multiples

6.5 Reading fractions (1)

Two children are working with their teacher shading in parts of shapes (see Figure 6.5). The teacher asks them what fraction of the shape has been shaded. One of them tells the teacher that one-'twoth' of the shape has been shaded.

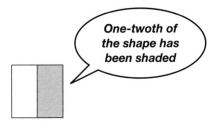

One-twoth of the shape has been shaded

Figure 6.5

The error

The child is trying to apply a consistent naming system to a system which is not fully consistent.

Why this happens

The child is actually thinking logically. Furani (2003) explores how naming and misnaming involve logic and rules, and are often an aid to supporting children's mathematical learning. Unfortunately, there are inconsistencies in the English conventions of naming fractions and this can confuse children. Indeed, in American English, one-quarter is referred to as 'one fourth'. The child needs to learn that we use the term 'half' to represent 1 out of 2. Another common error with naming fractions is the use of 'one whole'. Sometimes children interpret this as 'one hole'.

Curriculum links

Year 2	Write simple fractions, for example: $^1/_2$ of 6 = 3 and recognise the equivalence of $^2/_4$ and $^1/_2$

6.6 Reading fractions (2)

The child writes $^2/_{10}$ and says 'two tens'.

Figure 6.6

The error

The child uses whole numbers, rather than the fraction's name, when reading it.

Why this happens

The child may simply not have the vocabulary of 'tenth' to read the fraction accurately. It is likely that she sees the numbers in the fraction as two unrelated whole numbers separated by a line, rather than as a (fractional) number in its own right.

Curriculum links

Year 2	Write simple fractions for example, $^1/_2$ of 6 = 3 and recognise the equivalence of $^2/_4$ and $^1/_2$

6.7 Reading fractions (3)

The children are working together as a class and the teacher is asking them to read the fractions he displays. One child says 2/3 is 'two and three' and another says 'two slash three'.

The error

The children are using whole numbers, rather than the fraction's name, when reading it.

Why this happens

The child may simply not have the vocabulary of 'third' to read the fraction accurately. It is likely that they see the numbers in the fraction as two unrelated whole numbers separated by a line, rather than as a (fractional) number in its own right.

Curriculum links

Year 2	Write simple fractions for example, $^1/_2$ of 6 = 3 and recognise the equivalence of $^2/_4$ and $^1/_2$

6.8 Representing fractions

The children are drawing fractions using shapes (see Figure 6.7). The teacher asks one of them what fraction she has drawn and she tells the teacher that it shows one-third.

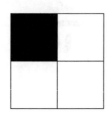

Figure 6.7

The error

The child sees one part shaded and three parts not shaded as the fraction 1/3.

Why this happens

There are several reasons why the child has made this error. The most likely reason is that the child doesn't see the four parts as all part of the whole. Understanding the whole and that fractions are a part of the whole is very important, but here, the child may have focused on the individual parts of the square. Another reason is that the child may have only just begun to focus on thirds at school. In this case she may be overgeneralising her knowledge of fractions (as quarters and halves only) to draw the square, divide it, and try to make an unfamiliar fraction in some logical manner. Finally, the child may be thinking of 1/3 as a ratio – 1:3 – and therefore showing a ratio of one to three which, in the fraction context, is incorrect.

Curriculum links

Year 1	Recognise, find and name a half as one of two equal parts of an object, shape or quantity
Year 2	Recognise, find and name a quarter as one of four equal parts of an object, shape or quantity
Year 3	Recognise, find, name and write fractions $^1/_3$, $^1/_4$, $^2/_4$ and $^3/_4$ of a length, shape, set of objects or quantity

6.9 Writing and using fractions

When asked to write a story using the fraction *one-third*, this child produced a story using *one-third* and *one-quarter* interchangeably.

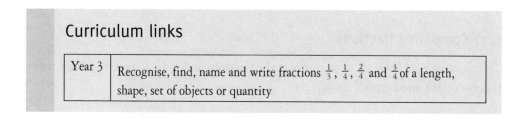

Figure 6.8

The error

The child has used *one-third* and *one-quarter* interchangeably in their story.

Why this happens

The child may have done this because the words 'quarter' and 'third' do not suggest the numbers 4 and 3 and therefore they have not realised that the two fractions (that they have heard used in other contexts) have different meanings.

Curriculum links

Year 3	Recognise, find, name and write fractions $\frac{1}{3}$, $\frac{1}{4}$, $\frac{2}{4}$ and $\frac{3}{4}$ of a length, shape, set of objects or quantity

6.10 Ordering fractions

The children have been given some cards with unit fractions written on them (Figure 6.9). The teacher asks the children to look at the two cards and say which is the biggest.

Figure 6.9

The error

The child believes that one-third is bigger than one-half because the denominator of one-third is larger than the denominator of one-half.

Why this happens

The child is using his knowledge of whole numbers to order the fractions. He is over- generalising whole-number concepts. The child does not understand the written notation of fractions. He needs to know what the notation means – that we have one part **out of** three equal parts. The child probably does not have a clear understanding of the concept of fractions in a practical sense.

Associated with this idea, children also need to realise that 'the line' in a fraction represents division. So ¾ means 3 **out of** 4, which is also 3 **divided by** 4.

Curriculum links

Year 3	Compare and order unit fractions, and fractions with the same denominators
Year 6	Compare and order fractions whose denominators are all multiples of the same number

6.11 Comparing fractions

The children have been asked to compare the fractions and write a sentence about them (Figure 6.10A and Figure 6.10B).

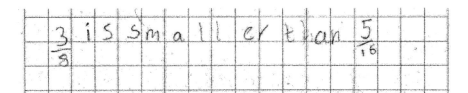

Figure 6.10A

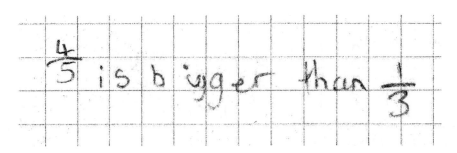

Figure 6.10B

The errors

Child A states that $^3/_8$ is smaller than $^5/_{16}$. Child B states that $^4/_5$ is bigger than $^1/_3$.

Why this happens

It is likely that Child A is focusing only on the numerator and dismissing the denominator, to show that 3 is smaller than 5, and that Child B is focusing only on the denominator to show that 4 is greater than 1. Both children are showing a lack of understanding of fractions, treating the two parts of each fraction as a whole number. The children need to know what the notation means – that we have x parts (the numerator) **out of** y equal parts (the denominator).

Associated with this idea, children also need to realise that 'the line' in a fraction represents division. So ¾ means 3 **out of** 4, which is also 3 **divided by** 4.

Curriculum links

Year 3	Compare and order unit fractions, and fractions with the same denominators
Year 6	Compare and order fractions whose denominators are all multiples of the same number

6.12 Converting mixed numbers to proper fractions

A child writes:

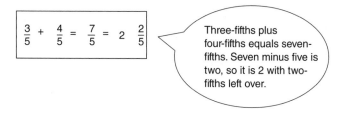

$$\frac{3}{5} + \frac{4}{5} = \frac{7}{5} = 2\frac{2}{5}$$

Three-fifths plus four-fifths equals seven-fifths. Seven minus five is two, so it is 2 with two-fifths left over.

Figure 6.11

The error

The child states that $^7/_5$ is equivalent to $2\,^2/_5$.

Why this happens

Here the child has used subtraction instead of division to work out the mixed number. This can happen when children think of the numerator and denominator as whole numbers, rather than parts of a fraction.

Curriculum links

Year 5	Recognise mixed numbers and improper fractions and convert from one form to the other and write mathematical statements > 1 as a mixed number [for example, $^2/_5 + {}^4/_5 = {}^6/_5 = 1\,{}^1/_5$]
Year 6	Add and subtract fractions with different denominators and mixed numbers, using the concept of equivalent fractions

6.13 Equivalent fractions (1)

While using a computer program called 'Fractions Lab' (see link.lkl.ac.uk/FractionsLab) a child said, '$^2/_6 = {}^1/_{12}$. The computer is wrong because $2 \times 6 = 1 \times 12$'.

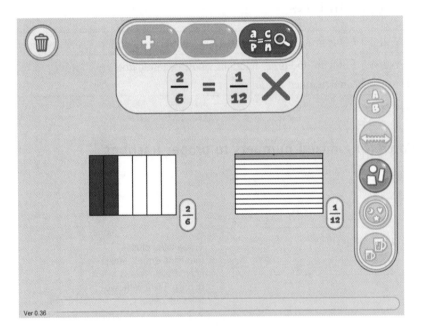

Figure 6.12

The error

The child states the computer is wrong because $2 \times 6 = 1 \times 12$.

Why this happens

Here the child is treating the numerator and denominator as if they were whole numbers. He knows that 2 multiplied by 6 is equal to 1 multiplied by 12, and is treating the vinculum (the fraction bar) as a multiplier.

Curriculum links

Year 2	Recognise, find, name and write fractions $\frac{1}{3}$, $\frac{1}{4}$, $\frac{2}{4}$ and $\frac{3}{4}$ of a length, shape, set of objects or quantity
Year 3	Recognise and show, using diagrams, equivalent fractions with small denominators
Year 4	Recognise and show, using diagrams, families of common equivalent fractions
Year 5	Identify, name and write equivalent fractions of a given fraction, represented visually, including tenths and hundredths
Year 6	Use common factors to simplify fractions; use common multiples to express fractions in the same denomination

6.14 Equivalent fractions (2)

A child explains, '$\frac{6}{7} = \frac{8}{9}$ because 7 take 6 is one and 9 take 8 is one'.

The error

The child states that $\frac{6}{7}$ is equivalent to $\frac{8}{9}$ because the two parts have a difference of 1.

Why this happens

Here the child is treating the numerator and denominator as if they were whole numbers. She knows that the difference between 6 and 7 is 1, and the difference between 8 and 9 is also 1. Therefore, she has concluded that they are equivalent.

Curriculum links

Year 2	Recognise, find, name and write fractions $\frac{1}{3}$, $\frac{1}{4}$, $\frac{2}{4}$ and $\frac{3}{4}$ of a length, shape, set of objects or quantity
Year 3	Recognise and show, using diagrams, equivalent fractions with small denominators
Year 5	Identify, name and write equivalent fractions of a given fraction, represented visually, including tenths and hundredths

6.15 Equivalent fractions (3)

A child does not believe that 'Fractions Lab' (link.lkl.ac.uk/FractionsLab) is right when it shows that $\frac{6}{8}$ and $\frac{9}{12}$ are equal.

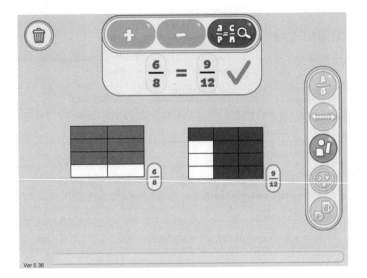

Figure 6.13

The error

The child says, '6 + 6 = 12, but 8 + 8 ≠ 9'.

Why this happens

Here the child is treating the numerator and denominator as if they were whole numbers and using addition to try and explain the relationship between the two fractions, which is unhelpful. This is common, and children should be encouraged to think about using multiplicative structures to explain relationships between fractions rather than additive structures.

Curriculum links

Year 2	Recognise, find, name and write fractions $^1/_3$, $^1/_4$, $^2/_4$ and $^3/_4$ of a length, shape, set of objects or quantity
Year 3	Recognise and show, using diagrams, equivalent fractions with small denominators
Year 4	Recognise and show, using diagrams, families of common equivalent fractions
Year 5	Identify, name and write equivalent fractions of a given fraction, represented visually, including tenths and hundredths
Year 6	Use common factors to simplify fractions; use common multiples to express fractions in the same denomination

6.16 Converting fractions to decimals (1)

The children have been asked to complete a series of conversions of fractions to decimals.

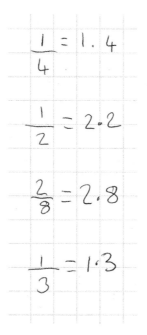

$$\frac{1}{4} = 1.4$$

$$\frac{1}{2} = 2.2$$

$$\frac{2}{8} = 2.8$$

$$\frac{1}{3} = 1.3$$

Figure 6.14

The error

The child has replaced the vinculum (the fraction bar) with a decimal point.

Why this happens

The child does not appear to understand that the conventions for writing fractions and decimals are not interchangeable. The child appears to have focused on the numbers in the fractions as whole numbers and has not demonstrated an understanding of fractions or decimal numbers as part of a whole.

Curriculum links

Year 4	Recognise and write decimal equivalents to $^1/_4$, $^1/_2$ and $^3/_4$
Year 5	Read and write decimal numbers as fractions [for example, $0.71 = ^{71}/_{100}$]
Year 6	Associate a fraction with division and calculate decimal fraction equivalents [for example, 0.375] for a simple fraction [for example, $^3/_8$]

6.17 Converting fractions to decimals (2)

A child is asked to find the decimal equivalent of $^7/_2$. The child responds, 'Seven halves are 3.1 because there are three wholes and one left over' and draws the representation shown in Figure 6.15.

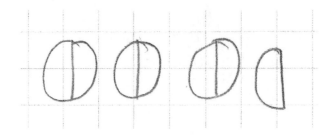

Figure 6.15

The error

The child has correctly identified that there are three wholes, but has misinterpreted the 'one left over' as 0.1.

Why this happens

The child has not used 0.5 for ½. This may be because using remainders in whole number division is more familiar to the child and they have applied that knowledge in this situation. The child may not know that ½ = 0.5 (or that 0.1 = $^{1}/_{10}$) in this context, and settles on what they deem to be the most sensible solution: that 0.1 represents one left over.

Curriculum links

Year 4	Solve problems involving increasingly harder fractions to calculate quantities, and fractions to divide quantities, including non-unit fractions where the answer is a whole number
Year 5	Read and write decimal numbers as fractions [for example, 0.71 = $^{71}/_{100}$]
Year 6	Associate a fraction with division and calculate decimal fraction equivalents [for example, 0.375] for a simple fraction [for example, $^{3}/_{8}$]

6.18 Converting fractions to decimals (3)

The teacher is working with a focus group and asked them to write in decimal form: 756 + $^{4}/_{100}$.

The children discuss various answers, including:

(a) 756.004

(b) 756.25

The errors

The children have

(a) incorrectly calculated the 4/100 is 0.004

(b) calculated that 100 divided by 4 gives 1/25 or 0.25

Why this happens

In (a) the children may have focused on the number of zeros in 100, rather than on the effect of dividing by 100. In (b) the children may have simplified the fraction and then concluded that 0.25 = $^1/_{25}$. Alternatively, the children are most familiar with division problems where the dividend is larger than the divisor, and the quotient (solution) is smaller. Therefore, they have jumped to the conclusion that they should be answering 100 ÷ 4 instead of 4 ÷ 100 and placed 0.25 at the end of the number.

Curriculum links

Year 3	Count up and down in tenths; recognise that tenths arise from dividing an object into 10 equal parts and in dividing one-digit numbers or quantities by 10
Year 4	Count up and down in hundredths; recognise that hundredths arise when dividing an object by one hundred and dividing tenths by ten.
Year 4	Recognise and write decimal equivalents of any number of tenths or hundredths
Year 4	Find the effect of dividing a one- or two-digit number by 10 and 100, identifying the value of the digits in the answer as ones, tenths and hundredths
Year 5	Read and write decimal numbers as fractions [for example, 0.71 = $^{71}/_{100}$]
Year 6	Associate a fraction with division and calculate decimal fraction equivalents [for example, 0.375] for a simple fraction [for example, $^3/_8$]

6.19 Converting fractions to decimals (4)

The teacher notices that a number of children are writing incorrect answers on their whiteboards during a whole-class interactive teaching session (Figure 6.16).

$$\frac{23}{100} = 0.0023$$

$$\frac{64}{100} = 0.0064$$

$$\frac{7}{100} = 0.007$$

Figure 6.16

The error

The children have provided answers that relate to thousandths, not hundredths.

Why this happens

The children may have focused on the number of zeros in 100 and inserted them after the decimal point. The children may have thought that the third digit to the left of the decimal point is in the hundreds column, so the third column to the right must be the hundredths. They may have also been working with converting thousandths and confused them with hundreths.

Curriculum links

Year 3	Count up and down in tenths; recognise that tenths arise from dividing an object into 10 equal parts and in dividing one-digit numbers or quantities by 10
Year 4	Count up and down in hundredths; recognise that hundredths arise when dividing an object by one hundred and dividing tenths by ten.
Year 4	Recognise and write decimal equivalents of any number of tenths or hundredths
Year 4	Find the effect of dividing a one- or two-digit number by 10 and 100, identifying the value of the digits in the answer as ones, tenths and hundredths
Year 5	Read and write decimal numbers as fractions [for example, $0.71 = {}^{71}/_{100}$]
Year 5	Recognise and use thousandths and relate them to tenths, hundredths and decimal equivalents
Year 6	Identify the value of each digit in numbers given to three decimal places and multiply and divide numbers by 10, 100 and 1000, giving answers up to three decimal places

6.20 Adding fractions using a common denominator

The following examples illustrate only a selection of errors seen that are related to children adding fractions where a common denominator should be found.

a) $\frac{1}{2} + \frac{2}{3} = \frac{2}{5}$; $\frac{1}{2} + \frac{1}{4} = \frac{1}{6}$
b) $\frac{1}{2} + \frac{2}{3} = \frac{3}{6}$
c) $\frac{1}{2} + \frac{2}{3} = \frac{2}{6}$
d) $\frac{1}{2} + \frac{2}{3} = \frac{3}{5}$; $\frac{1}{2} + \frac{1}{4} = \frac{2}{6}$
e) $\frac{1}{2} + \frac{2}{3} = 1 + 2$
f) $\frac{1}{2} + \frac{2}{3} = {}^{(1+2)}/_{8}$, $\frac{1}{2} + \frac{1}{4} = {}^{(1+1)}/_{8}$
g) $\frac{1}{2} + \frac{1}{4} = \frac{8}{4}$

Figure 6.17

The errors

(a) The numerators are multiplied and the denominators are added.

(b) The numerators are added and the denominators are multiplied.

(c) The numerators and the denominators are multiplied, respectively.

(d) The numerators and the denominators of the given fractions are added, respectively.

(e) The numerators are added and the denominators are ignored.

(f) A common denominator is obtained by adding all denominators and numerators; the numerators remain untouched and are added to each other at the end.

(g) The common denominator is obtained correctly; the new numerators are obtained by adding the numerator and denominator in each fraction, respectively, i.e. $\frac{1}{2} + \frac{1}{4} = \frac{(3+5)}{4}$.

Why this happens

In these examples, the children have not used a common denominator accurately to find the solution. This may be due to the child having learnt the algorithm but forgetting to use it in these instances. It might also be that they do not realise the need to find a common denominator to make the sum easier to calculate. For (c), the child may have confused the multiplication algorithm. For (d) the child has attempted to find a common denominator, by adding all the numerators and denominators. Finally, the children all lack understanding of fractions and what the numerator and denominator represent.

Curriculum links

Year 3	Add and subtract fractions with the same denominator within one whole [for example, $\frac{5}{7} + \frac{1}{7} = \frac{6}{7}$]
Year 4	Add and subtract fractions with the same denominator
Year 5	Recognise mixed numbers and improper fractions and convert from one form to the other and write mathematical statements > 1 as a mixed number [for example, $\frac{2}{5} + \frac{4}{5} = \frac{6}{5} = 1\frac{1}{5}$]

6.21 Adding fractions with unlike denominators

The child has added ¼ + ½ and written the answer as $\frac{2}{6}$ (Figure 6.18).

$$\frac{1}{4} + \frac{1}{2} = \frac{2}{6}$$

Figure 6.18

The error

The child has added the two numerators and then the two denominators to calculate the sum.

Why this happens

The child may have been shown the procedure for multiplying fractions (with the same denominator), and has overgeneralised it to addition. They may not know that to add fractions with different denominators, it is often easier to find equivalent fractions to add together. Whatever the specific reason, it is clear that the child is not aware of what the fractions represent and is carrying out the equation without understanding.

Curriculum links

Year 5	Recognise mixed numbers and improper fractions and convert from one form to the other and write mathematical statements > 1 as a mixed number [for example, $^2/_5 + {}^4/_5 = {}^6/_5 = 1\,{}^1/_5$]
Year 6	Add and subtract fractions with different denominators and mixed numbers, using the concept of equivalent fractions

6.22 Dividing fractions by whole numbers

The teacher has been showing a group of children how to divide fractions by a whole number. When the children are working individually, one child says to the teacher, 'My answer can't be right. One sixth is bigger than one third!'

$$\frac{1}{3} \div 2 = \frac{1}{6}$$

Figure 6.19

The error

The child has achieved a correct answer, but can't believe it is correct because he incorrectly thinks $^1/_6$ is bigger than $^1/_3$.

Why this happens

The child is following a procedure to find the solution, rather than demonstrating any conceptual understanding of the task. He is looking at the denominator of the quotient and thinks that because it is larger than the dividend then it must be wrong. Actually the quotient is smaller but he has not realised this. Experience with cutting up fractions to divide them will support his conceptual understanding.

Curriculum links

Year 5	Multiply proper fractions and mixed numbers by whole numbers, supported by materials and diagrams
Year 6	Divide proper fractions by whole numbers [for example, $\frac{1}{3} \div 2 = \frac{1}{6}$]

6.23 Multiplying and dividing by fractions

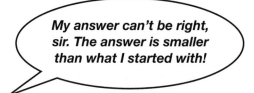

Figure 6.20

The error

The child has achieved a correct answer, but can't believe it is correct because he holds the belief that the result of a multiplication is always a larger number, and the result of a division is always a smaller number.

Why this happens

The child has created an overgeneralisation from previously working with whole numbers. Earlier work in mathematics about multiplication as repeated addition (where the answer always gets bigger) and division as repeated subtraction (where the answer always reduces) can also compound this misconception (although number-line work with fractions can still be used to explain these answers). Additionally, in everyday language, we talk about animals multiplying (increasing in number), which may cause confusion.

Curriculum links

Year 5	Multiply proper fractions and mixed numbers by whole numbers, supported by materials and diagrams
Year 6	Multiply simple pairs of proper fractions, writing the answer in its simplest form [for example, $\frac{1}{4} \times \frac{1}{2} = \frac{1}{8}$]

6.24 Reading and ordering decimal numbers

The teacher writes two numbers on the whiteboard (see Figure 6.21). The children are asked to discuss and then identify the largest number. One group claim that 8.35 is the largest number.

Figure 6.21

The error

When asked why, the group says that 8.35 is larger because 35 is larger than 5 so 8.35 must be larger than 8.5.

Why this happens

The group have read the digits after the decimal point as if they were whole numbers. They may have read the numbers as 'eight point thirty five' and 'eight point five' respectively. They do not understand the relative value of successive groupings of ten in the place-value system for numbers to the right of the decimal point. They need to know that for each place to the right of the decimal point, the numbers are successively smaller by powers of ten. Additionally, some children believe that numbers are larger if there are more decimal digits. Teachers should ensure that children correctly name decimals to help to overcome this difficulty, i.e. 'eight point three five' and 'eight point five'. This type of error may occur because children have been using money as a context for decimals. In money it is quite legitimate to say 'eight, thirty-five'. This is a potential drawback of the use of money to explore the concept of decimals.

Curriculum links

Year 6	Identify the value of each digit in numbers given to three decimal places and multiply and divide numbers by 10, 100 and 1000 giving answers up to three decimal places

6.25 Reading and writing decimals

The children are planning how to spend some additional school funds for their classroom. One group decides they want to buy a new carpet for the carpet area of their classroom.

The children measure and then calculate the area of the carpet area. It is 12 square metres. Their calculations are shown in Figure 6.22.

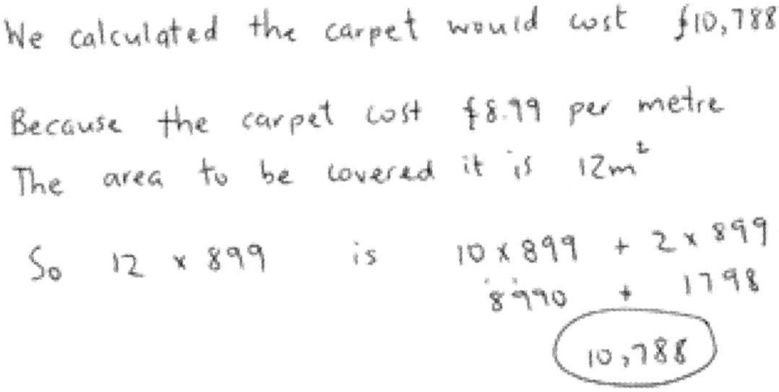

Figure 6.22

The error

The group have read 8.99 as 899.

Why this happens

The children do not understand the significance of the decimal point in the place value system. This error is linked to the children's understanding of place value. The children do not understand what each digit in the number 8.99 represents; that we have £8 and 99 hundredths of a pound. Of course, this error might be simply a careless slip, but they have not used estimation strategies in order to consider the reasonableness of their answer.

Curriculum links

Year 5	Read, write, order and compare numbers with up to three decimal places
Year 5	Solve problems involving number up to three decimal places

6.26 Ordering decimals

The teacher writes the following numbers on the board and asks the children to place them in order from smallest to largest: 0.15, 1.3, 0.095, 2.8 (see Figure 6.23).

A child writes the following on her whiteboard:

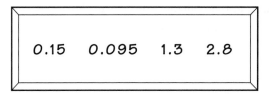

0.15   0.095   1.3   2.8

Figure 6.23

The error

The child thinks that 0.095 is larger than 0.15.

Why this happens

The child knows that 2.8 is bigger than 1.3 because she knows that 2 is larger than 1 from her understanding of whole numbers. However, when comparing two decimal numbers between 0 and 1, she does not understand which digit is most significant. She does not realise she must look to the tenths column first then to the hundredths column and finally to the thousandths column. The child does not have a clear understanding of the decimal place-value system. The child may also have read the numbers as 'nought point fifteen' and 'nought point ninety-five' and concluded that since 95 is larger than 15, that 0.095 is larger than 0.15. (See also place-value sections in this chapter and Chapter 4.)

Curriculum links

Year 4	Compare numbers with the same number of decimal places up to two decimal places
Year 5	Read, write, order and compare numbers with up to three decimal places
Year 6	Compare and order fractions, including fractions > 1

6.27 Rounding decimals

The children are asked to round to the nearest whole number. The worksheet (Figure 6.24) shows one pair's answers.

Original number	Rounded number
3.04	3 ✓
23.07	24 ✗
76.79	77 ✓
102.03	102 ✓
237.61	237 ✗

Figure 6.24

The error

The children have applied an incorrect rounding strategy to the numbers.

Why this happens

At first some of these responses appear correct, but on closer analysis it is possible to see that there is a pattern in the strategy used. Both children have paid attention to the units (or ones) digit of the number, rather than the digit in the tenths column. This demonstrates the children are following an insufficient procedural approach to completing the task, rather than understanding the purpose of rounding to the nearest whole number.

Curriculum links

Year 4	Round decimals with one decimal place to the nearest whole number
Year 5	Recognise and use thousandths and relate them to tenths, hundredths and decimal equivalents

6.28 Decimal systems and non-decimal systems

A class is going on a day trip to London. Two children use an internet site to check how long it will take them to get from Birmingham to London on the train (see Table 6.1).

They calculate that regardless of which train they get, the duration of the train journey will be the same: 1:24.

When the teacher asks them how long the journey will take, they say it will take *one point two four hours*.

Table 6.1   Train timetable

Leaving	From	To	Arriving
08:10	Birmingham New Street [BHM]	London Euston [EUS]	09:34
08:30	Birmingham New Street [BHM]	London Euston [EUS]	09:54
08:50	Birmingham New Street [BHM]	London Euston [EUS]	10:14
09:10	Birmingham New Street [BHM]	London Euston [EUS]	10:34
09:30	Birmingham New Street [BHM]	London Euston [EUS]	10:54

The error

The children have interpreted their answer as if it were a decimal rather than a length of time.

Why this happens

The children have completed their calculation using an algorithm for base-10 numbers and so they have interpreted their answer in base 10. They have not realised that their answer means 1 hour 24 minutes rather than 1.24 (one point two four) hours.

Curriculum links

Year 4	Solve simple measure and money problems involving fractions and decimals to two decimal places
Year 5	Solve problems involving number up to three decimal places

6.29 Decimal calculations

Two children's answers are shown in Figure 6.25 for a worksheet they were given by their teacher.

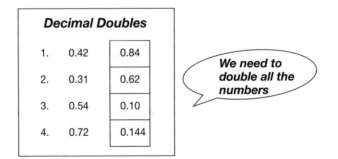

Figure 6.25

The error

The children have doubled all their numbers but failed to take into account that they are decimal numbers.

Why this happens

The children have overgeneralised the rule for doubling which can be applied to whole numbers. They have not taken into account the decimal value of each number. For example, they have calculated that 72 plus 72 is 144 and written 0.144 down. They have not realised what each digit in their answer represents, i.e. 1 unit, 4 tenths and 4 hundredths. This error may be due to a limited understanding of the decimal place-value system.

Similarly, research undertaken by Rees and Barr (cited by Sadi, 2007) found that there were *100 different answers* provided by ten-year-olds for the question 16.36 + 1.9 + 243.075. The most common involved adding the digits before the decimal points and then adding the digits after the decimal point, then combining them to form an answer.

Curriculum links

Year 5	Solve problems involving number up to three decimal places

6.30 Multiplying decimals (1)

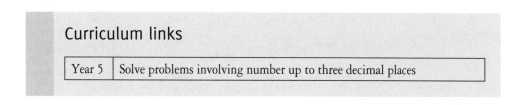

60 × 0.4 = 24
10 ÷ 0.1 = 100

My calculator is broken. These answers are wrong!

Figure 6.26

The error

The child has found the correct calculation using the calculator, but thinks the answers are wrong.

Why this happens

The child has created an overgeneralisation from previously working with whole numbers. In everyday language, we talk about animals multiplying (increasing in number). Earlier work in mathematics about multiplication as repeated addition (where the answer always gets bigger) and division as repeated subtraction (where the answer always reduces) can also compound this misconception (although number-line work with decimals can still be used to explain these answers).

Curriculum links

Year 6	Identify the value of each digit in numbers given to three decimal places and multiply and divide numbers by 10, 100 and 1000 giving answers up to three decimal places

6.31 Multiplying decimals (2)

The children complete a worksheet multiplying decimals (see Figure 6.27).

1. 0.2 x 0.8 = <u>0.16</u>

2. 0.5 x 0.5 = <u>0.25</u>

3. 0.7 x 0.8 = <u>0.56</u>

4. 0.3 x 0.24 = <u>0.72</u>

5. 0.8 x 0.21 = <u>1.68</u>

Figure 6.27

The error

The child is multiplying the digits as if they are whole numbers and then adjusting two decimal places.

Why this happens

The child is not demonstrating an understanding of place value and she is using known whole-number facts, then applying a learned rule (adjust two places) incorrectly.

Curriculum links

Year 6	Identify the value of each digit in numbers given to three decimal places and multiply and divide numbers by 10, 100 and 1000, giving answers up to three decimal places

6.32 Equivalence of percentages, fractions and decimals (1)

The teacher asks her class to colour in 50 squares in a 100 square. She tells the children that they have coloured in 50% of the 100 square. She asks the children what they notice. They children appear to grasp the idea that one half of the square has been coloured in. Mrs Smith then asks the children to colour in 25 squares of the 100 squares and is again pleased to note that the children seem to understand that 25% is the same as one-quarter. The following day she extends the activity. This time she asks the children to colour in 50% of a different number square. One child's response to the task is shown in Figure 6.28.

1	2	3	4	5	6	7	8	9	10
11	12	13	14	15	16	17	18	19	20
21	22	23	24	25	26	27	28	29	30
31	32	33	34	35	36	37	38	39	40
41	42	43	44	45	46	47	48	49	50
51	52	53	54	55	56	57	58	59	60
61	62	63	64	65	66	67	68	69	70
71	72	73	74	75	76	77	78	79	80

I have coloured in 50% of the numbers

Figure 6.28

The error

The child has coloured in 50 squares instead of 50% of the squares.

Why this happens

This may have happened because the child thinks that percentages are always linked to 100 objects. She has not understood that 50% is equivalent to one-half and that we do not always need to have 100 objects. The child may need to return to the 100 square and check for herself what part of the square is coloured for 50%, 25% and so on. Children may not progress effectively with percentages unless they understand the equivalence between percentages and fractions. Children also need to understand the relationship between fractions, decimals and percentages. Lamon (2008, page 217) suggests that shading grids is not a particularly helpful way to teach percentages because children can achieve the answer more quickly in their heads.

Curriculum links

Year 5	Recognise the per cent symbol (%) and understand that per cent relates to 'number of parts per hundred', and write percentages as a fraction with denominator 100, and as a decimal
Year 5	Solve problems which require knowing percentage and decimal equivalents of $^1/_2$, $^1/_4$, $^1/_5$, $^2/_5$, $^4/_5$ and those fractions with a denominator of a multiple of 10 or 25.
Year 6	Solve problems involving the calculation of percentages [for example, of measures, and such as 15% of 360] and the use of percentages for comparison

6.33 Equivalence of percentages, fractions and decimals (2)

A child is matching some cards to show percentage and decimal equivalents (Figure 6.29).

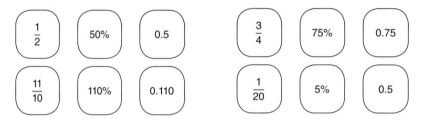

Figure 6.29

The errors

The child has matched the top two sets correctly but 110% has been incorrectly paired with 0.110 and 5% has been incorrectly paired with 0.5.

Why this happens

The child is confident with grouping the fractions, percentages and decimals that she is familiar with. Working with fractions, decimals and percentages greater than 1 is more difficult. It is also common to see children pairing 5% with 0.5 even though they have previously stated that 0.5 = 50%. This happens because children are not yet making all the connections required between the different types of numbers and their equivalents.

Curriculum links

Year 5	Recognise the per cent symbol (%) and understand that per cent relates to 'number of parts per hundred', and write percentages as a fraction with denominator 100, and as a decimal
Year 5	Solve problems which require knowing percentage and decimal equivalents of $^1/_2$, $^1/_4$, $^1/_5$, $^2/_5$, $^4/_5$ and those fractions with a denominator of a multiple of 10 or 25

6.34 Percentages as a proportion (1)

The class is calculating percentage discounts. One question requires the children to calculate the cost of two bikes, both having a 10% discount applied. One pair decides to find the total of the full cost of the bikes, and then deduct 20% from the total.

The error

The pair has decided to deduct 20% from the total, instead of 10%.

Why this happens

The children are combining the percentages as absolute amounts (and use inappropriate additive strategies), rather than as a proportion of the price.

Curriculum links

Year 6	Solve problems involving the calculation of percentages [for example, of measures, and such as 15% of 360] and the use of percentages for comparison

6.35 Percentages as a proportion (2)

The class is calculating percentage increases. One question is 'A computer costs £235 including 17.5% VAT. VAT goes up to 20%. Calculate the new price'. The results of one pair of children are shown in Figure 6.30.

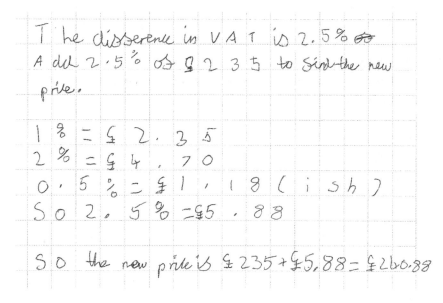

The difference in VAT is 2.5% so
Add 2.5% of £235 to find the new price.

1 % = £2.35
2 % = £4.70
0.5 % = £1.18 (ish)
So 2.5 % = £5.88

So the new price is £235 + £5.88 = £260.88

Figure 6.30

The error

One pair has decided to add 2.5% to the total, instead of finding the original price (£235) and then finding 20% of that.

Why this happens

The children have not realised that by simply adding a further 2.5% on to the existing price they are inadvertantly increasing the price of the original item value by more than 20%. They are not demonstrating an understanding of the multiplicative nature of percentages and proportion.

Curriculum links

Year 6	Solve problems involving the calculation of percentages [for example, of measures, and such as 15% of 360] and the use of percentages for comparison

6.36 Ratio and proportion

A child is looking at a collection of ribbons. She counts 20 blue ribbons and 10 red ribbons. The teacher asks: *What proportion of the ribbons are red?* She says: *Ten out of twenty.*

The error

The child has confused ratio and proportion.

Why this happens

The difference between ratio and proportion is difficult for children, and sometimes for adults, to understand. The child needs to know that ratio compares **part** with **part** in a set of objects but proportion compares **part** with the **whole** in a set of objects. The proportion of red ribbons is 10 out of 30 or one-third ($^1/_3$), whereas the ratio of red ribbons to blue ribbons is 10 to 20 or one to two (1:2). The children need to become familiar with the language of ratio and proportion: For ratio they should use '*for every*'. For proportion they should use '*in every*'. Using the language of ratio and proportion regularly will help children to distinguish between these two concepts.

Curriculum links

Year 6	Solve problems involving the relative sizes of two quantities where missing values can be found by using integer multiplication and division facts
Year 6	Solve problems involving unequal sharing and grouping using knowledge of fractions and multiples

6.37 The multiplicative nature of direct proportion

A group of children want to bake a cake for four people. They have found a recipe for two people, so they need to calculate the ingredients they will require to bake a cake for four people. The recipe and the children's amendments are shown in Figure 6.31.

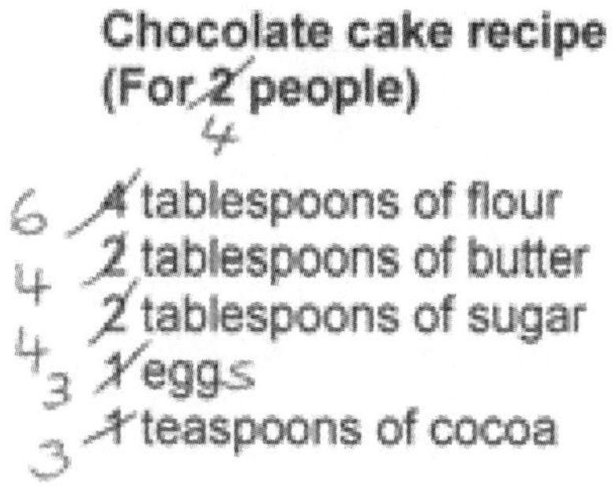

Chocolate cake recipe
(For 2 people)
4

6   4 tablespoons of flour
4   2 tablespoons of butter
4   2 tablespoons of sugar
3   1 eggs
3   1 teaspoons of cocoa

Figure 6.31

The error

The children have added two more of each ingredient to the recipe for two people.

Why this happens

The children do not understand the multiplicative nature of direct proportion. (See also '6.4 Fractions as ratios'.) The children have used an additive rule instead of a multiplicative rule. They have done this because they think that if we have two more people then we need two more of each ingredient. This is a common difficulty with direct proportion.

Curriculum links

Year 6	Solve problems involving the relative sizes of two quantities where missing values can be found by using integer multiplication and division facts

6.38 Scale factor

The error

The child believes that when they double the size of a shape, the area will also double.

111

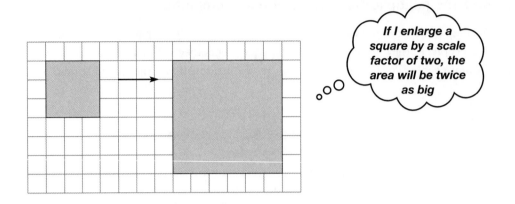

Figure 6.32

Why this happens

In number operations, whatever happens to one side of an operation usually happens to the other. Therefore, it is common for children to believe that if they double the length of the sides on a shape, the area will also double.

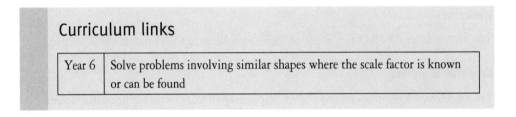

Curriculum links

Year 6	Solve problems involving similar shapes where the scale factor is known or can be found

7 Algebra

Although algebra appears later in the primary years, it is possible to identify pre-algebraic experiences such as continuing and making patterns with shapes in the Early Years Foundation Stage and Key Stage 1. Algebra first appears formally in the national curriculum in upper Key Stage 2 where children are introduced to the language of algebra as a means for solving a variety of problems. However, there are a many pre-algebra experiences that children will meet prior to this stage. These include becoming familiar with number patterns and sequences (you will find errors related to these in Chapter 3, 'Number and place value').

In primary school, children are introduced to number sequences from Reception onwards, though this may not be explicit in curriculum documentation. Counting from 1 to 10 or in 2s forms the basis of understanding number sequences. Number patterns and sequences may be thought of as the building blocks for formal algebra. Nickson (2000, page 117) suggests that the shift of ideas from arithmetic to algebraic is a difficult transition for children and one in which *children tend to carry with them the perspectives and processes established in arithmetic to fall back on.*

Algebra is often difficult to learn, as children need to master the language to be able to use it. However, Warren (2005) suggests a reason why 12–13-year-old children may find it difficult to identify the functional relationship between growing patterns and their position, and use this generalisation to generate other visual patterns for other positions. She suggests that prior pattern development in primary schools is simply related to growing patterns. Her research suggests that *young children are not only capable of thinking about the relationship between two data sets but also of expressing this relationship in a very abstract form* (page 311).

Koedinger and Nathan (2004) identified how children were more successful solving simple algebra story problems than solving mathematically equivalent equations. They explained that the reason for this was that children had difficulties comprehending the formal symbolic representations but were able to use the situated knowledge to facilitate their problem-solving performance.

Ainley *et al.* (2009, page 417) suggest further activities that primary-aged children can undertake to prepare them for formal algebra. These are:

- structuring and generalising: analysing, describing and continuing patterns and structures in geometric and algebraic contexts;

- representing: using actions, gestures, signs and artefacts to bridge the gap to using alphanumeric symbols.

Ainley *et al.* (2005) report that spreadsheets are an effective tool to support children's algebraic development. They explain how the careful design of tasks that are purposeful for children, and contain an opportunity to appreciate the utility of algebra, can support the transition of children from Key Stage 2 to Key Stage 3.

7.1 Continuing a simple pattern

The teacher asks the children to complete a pattern (see Figure 7.1).

The error

The child has not continued the pattern that the practitioner began.

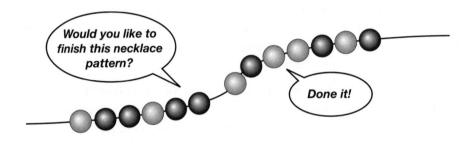

Figure 7.1

Why this happens

There are several possible reasons why the child might have done this.

- The child may not have understood the practitioner's question.

- The child may not know that a pattern continues to repeat.

- The child may have wanted to create their own 'pretty' necklace, finding their own design more appealing than the practitioner's.

- The child may have run out of the darker beads, and then later found some.

Curriculum links

Year 6	Generate and describe linear number sequences

7.2 Expressing formulae algebraically

The class have been calculating the perimeter of a number of different rectangles and the teacher has asked them if they can make a general statement that explains their calculations. The children offer the following responses:

(a) 2a + 2b

(b) a + b + a + b

(c) 4a (when the shape is a square)

The error

The children have been able to identify a general expression, but they are not as precise as they could be.

Why this happens

It may be that the children have simply not seen the algebraic convention of 2(a + b) before. They may not realise that 2(a + b) (following algebraic convention) is equivalent to 2a + 2b and a + b + a + b.

Curriculum links

Year 6	Use simple formulae
Year 6	Generate and describe linear number sequences

7.3 Finding unknown lengths

The class have been calculating the perimeter of a number of different rectangles and the teacher has asked them if they can solve the equation $4 + 2b = 20$ for a rectangle of sides 2cm and $b$cm and a perimeter of 20cm.

One child explains that the other sides are 6 cm.

The error

The child has calculated that the sides of the rectangle are 4cm and 6cm long.

Why this happens

It is likely that the child's previous experience of calculating perimeters using algebraic notation involved the equation $2(a + b)$ or similar. Therefor the child has confused 4 as the length of *each* of the sides a, rather than the *total* of sides a.

Curriculum links

Year 6	Find pairs of numbers that satisfy an equation with two unknowns
Year 6	Enumerate possibilities of combinations of two variables

7.4 Algebraic variables

A guided mathematics group is converting pounds to Euros with the teacher. They complete together Table 7.1, but when they approach the final column, one child states, *That's impossible sir, you can't have n pounds*!

Table 7.1 Conversion task

Pounds	1	2	3	4	5	10	50	n
Euros	1.22	2.44	3.66	4.88	6.10	12.20	61.00	

The error

The child does not understand what '*n*' represents in the question.

Why this happens

The child does not understand the concept of a variable. She does not understand that 'n' can be used to represent any number of pounds. The child is falling back on arithmetic ideas to answer the question. She can understand the question when she can relate it to 'real' money but she is unable to abstract the relationship between the two currencies. The concept that the teacher is asking her to understand may be too complex for her and perhaps introduced in a way which is beyond her experience.

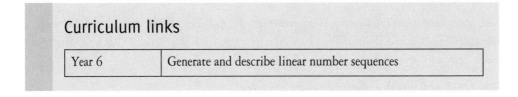

Curriculum links

Year 6	Generate and describe linear number sequences

7.5 Algebraic notation

In a test paper, children were asked to 'Show the number 2 less than k'. The following are some responses:

(a) 2–k

(b) k(2)

(c) k isn't a number

(d) $\frac{k}{2}$.

They were then asked to show 'Double k'. The following are some responses:

(e) You can't have double k because you took 2 away before

(f) k + k

(c)   2 lots of k

(d)   k2.

The errors

In all the errors, the children do not appear to understand that 'k' represents a variable, any number. Furthermore:

(a)   The child has taken k from 2 (incorrect use of commutative law).

(b)   The child has incorrectly used a bracket instead of a subtraction sign.

(c)   The child lacks understanding of the purpose of using 'k' as a variable.

(d)   The child has used division instead of subtraction.

They were then asked to show 'Double k'.

(e)   The child does not realise that this is a new question and that 'k' is being used to represent any number.

(f)   Although this results in the same answer, the child is not representing doubling as multiplication, which is the expectation at this level.

(g)   The child is using colloquial language (lots of) rather than the algebraic convention.

(h)   The child has confused algebraic convention.

Why this happens

Algebraic notation can be a very abstract notion if introduced inappropriately. Understanding that a variable represents any number is essential: teaching children about 'apples' and 'bananas' when adding $a + b$ is unhelpful! Furthermore, there are a number of conventions within algebra that do not necessarily follow any logic, and that just need to be learned.

Curriculum links

| Year 6 | Use simple formulae |
| Year 6 | Generate and describe linear number sequences |

7.6 Satisfying an equation with two unknowns

The class had been exploring what number of cubes could be in two different cups to add up to 20. The teacher thought that all the children understood what was expected and so moved on to ask them to enumerate the possibilities of combinations of two variables: a + b = 20.

Child: I have finished. 8 + 12 = 20.

Teacher: I want you to write all the possibilities

Child: There are no more possibilities because there are two letters so they can only be two numbers.

The error

The child thinks that the variables can only represent one number each.

Why this happens

Because the variable is a particular letter, children often think that the letter can only represent one number. They have not realised that the letter can represent *any* number.

Curriculum links

Year 6	Find pairs of numbers that satisfy an equation with two unknowns
Year 6	Enumerate possibilities of combinations of two variables

7.7 Interpreting variables as objects

A teacher and her group were looking at the statement, 'At Greenbank School there are 20 times as many children as staff'. The group agreed that the algebraic equation that would represent this sentence would be 'C = 20T'. Then the teacher asked the children, 'What does the letter C stand for?'. Three responses ensued:

Child 1:   Children

Child 2:   Teachers

Child 3:   Class

The error

The children have not identified that C represents the *number of children*.

Why this happens

Because the variable chosen is often related to the object, children form the misconception that the variable is the object or item, rather than the *number* of objects or items. Teachers also exhibit this misconception!

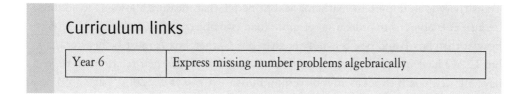

Curriculum links

Year 6	Express missing number problems algebraically

7.8 Equality

The children were given the equation $x + 3 = 7$ to solve. There were several solutions offered, including:

(a) $x = 7 + 3$

(b) $x + 3 + 7 = 0$

(c) $3x = 7$

The error

The children have provided incorrect solutions for $x + 3 = 7$.

Why this happens

In all the incorrect solutions, the children have not grasped the notion of equality, i.e. that the equals sign shows that the quantities on each side have the same value. The children may not have known how to keep both sides of the equation equal and so they have not added/subtracted equally from both sides of the equal sign. Furthermore, children often assume that the solution is always on the right of the equals sign.

Curriculum links

Year 6	Express missing number problems algebraically

8 Measurement

In the Early Years Foundation Stage (DfE, 2012, page 6) practitioners are expected to provide children with opportunities to develop and improve their skills in counting, understanding and using numbers, calculating simple addition and subtraction problems, and in describing shapes, spaces and measures. In Key Stage 1 (Years 1 and 2) teaching involves using a range of measures to describe and compare different quantities such as length, mass, capacity/volume, time and money. During lower Key Stage 2 (Years 3 and 4) children use measuring instruments with accuracy and make connections between measure and number. In upper Key Stage 2 (Years 5 and 6) measures consolidate and extend children's knowledge developed in number.

Measurement has always played a vital role in helping our society function. It is easy to see that measurement is an extension of number and allows us opportunities to develop skills within that area. However, there is a clear distinction between number and measures. Measurement is a real-life application for number, but number can be abstract. Additionally, a number can be precise, but a measurement will only ever be an approximation to the unit being measured.

Transitivity and *conservation* are principles that relate to all aspects of measurement. Transitivity is an important mathematical principle that measure allows us to address because it enables us to order a set of more than two objects. If we know that box A is heavier than box B and box B is heavier than box C, then box A must be heavier than box C. We have been able to compare boxes A and C through their relations to B. We have allowed box B to act as an intervening measure (Cross *et al.*, 2009, page 359). Logical reasoning, such as transitivity, was shown by Nunes *et al.* (2007) to have a causal link in children's mathematical understanding. They trained children in logical reasoning, and found that they made more mathematical progress than a control group who had not received the training. This demonstrates that children's mathematical development is dependent on them understanding the underlying logic. Earlier, Nunes and Bryant (1996, page 76) explained how *no one can have the slightest idea how a ruler works unless he or she can also make and understand such inferences.*

Piaget identified *conservation* as an ability in logical reasoning. He explained how it is a key indicator to a child's intelligence and is a vital component of the understanding of measurement. Knowing that the volume of water in a tall glass does not change when it is poured into a short glass, or that the two pieces of a torn piece of paper have the same surface area as before, is knowing that the transformation has had no effect on the equivalence. However, around the same time as Piaget's work was being published, Smedslund (1961) researched children's acquisition of conservation of substance and weight. Smedslund's findings challenge Piaget's explanation of conservation acquisition as a process of inner equilibrium and instead suggest that the concepts are more likely to be established through external reinforcement (teaching and learning). Perhaps Castle and Needham's (2007) research offers a way forward. They researched Grade 1 children's understanding of measurement. One key recommendation from their work was that teachers should focus on what it means to measure, rather than on how to measure. Teachers need to consider carefully how these key ideas are to be met and how to use the possible misconceptions that arise from these as opportunities to develop their pupils. This is echoed in Clements and Sarama's (2009, page 164) statement that *measuring is a difficult skill, but it also involves many concepts.*

Length

Length is one of the simpler measures to introduce to children because it is one-dimensional and young children learn notions of direct comparisons early. However, there are many concepts within the notion of linear measurement. These are:

- lengths span fixed distances (attribute);

- as objects move, their fixed length does not change (conservation);

- if A is longer than B, and B is longer then C, then A is longer than C (transitivity);

- an object can be sliced up into smaller sections – this is important for understanding that a measurement, for example 5cm, is not simply a mark on a ruler but can be cut up into units (equal partitioning);

- the length of a unit is a part of the length of the object being measured – and therefore those units can be placed end on end to identify the length of the object (units and unit iteration);

- as a unit is iterated, the counting word stated on each iteration represents the length covered by all the units (accumulation of distance and additivity);

- any point on a measuring scale can be used as the origin (origin);

- items that are counted refer to continuous units (relation between number and measurement) (adapted from Clements and Sarama, 2009).

If children do not understand these concepts, misconceptions and errors can arise. For example, if the need for a 'baseline' is not understood, objects are not accurately matched and compared.

Piaget (1970) observed children's perception that the length of an object can be altered by a change in position. The concept of conservation (that an object is the same length whatever its orientation) is one that children need many examples of to aid their understanding. Indeed, Barrett and Clements (2003) showed that for children to further their understanding of the concept of linear measurement, they required activities beyond the measurement of straight lines. Experience involving tasks such as measuring perimeter and the sides of polygons appeared to promote a more abstract understanding of length.

Area and perimeter

Children as young as six months of age can detect a difference in area representing a 1:2 change in the area (Brannon *et al.*, 2006). However, it is widely accepted that the relationship between area and perimeter is complex (Yeo, 2008).

Area is the quantity of surface within a specified closed boundary. As area is a two-dimensional measure, direct comparison can be very difficult. See Figure 8.1 (A and B).

It is not difficult to see in Figure 8.1A which shape has the largest area – we are able to compare visually because we recognise that the shortest sides on both rectangles are the same.

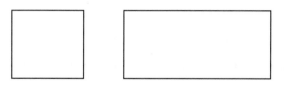

Figure 8.1A

However, in Figure B the shortest sides on both rectangles are not the same, so the answer is more difficult to work out.

Figure 8.1B

When we arrive at the problem of comparing irregular shapes, it can become virtually impossible by visual comparison. The difference between one-dimensional and two-dimensional measures when dealing with area also causes confusion when children are asked to look at perimeter, as they both involve looking at the boundary of the shape. Haylock (2001) points out that the relationship between perimeter and area provides us with a counter-example of the principle of conservation. Rearranging an imaginary perimeter fence around a field to change its shape, without changing the overall perimeter, does not conserve the area (see Haylock, 2001, pages 188–190). Yeo (2008) identified that it is difficult for children to understand how two lines (the length and the width) can produce an area when they are multiplied. Indeed, Yeo cites Menon's (1998) research on student teachers' understanding of area and perimeter, where they found that the student teachers have a procedural understanding of area and perimeter rather than a conceptual and relational understanding.

Volume and capacity

Volume is the third aspect within the logical progression from length (1D), area (2D) and volume (3D) in terms of the amount of space being measured.

Sáiz and Figueras (2009) highlight how confusion between volume and capacity occurs because people tend to use the two terms interchangeably. Additionally, volume was defined three ways by Piaget *et al.* (1970), and Sáiz (2003) identified five meanings from the research literature. Essentially, volume is the amount of 3D space which is occupied by an object. Capacity, on the other hand, can be defined as a measure of the space with which a 3D container can be filled. This distinction is often confused as we talk about interior volume and exterior volume. In the main we tend to use the term 'volume' for shapes that are solid. If we fill something with liquid we then use the term 'capacity' and in Key Stage 1 the term can be used to explore the ability to fill containers (Haylock, 2001). In reality, as internal volume and capacity are measuring the same thing the distinction is not crucial. It becomes crucial, however, when we are referring to the *external* volume or the volume of the material the container is made from.

Sáiz and Figueras (2009) conducted a literature review of the errors and misconceptions that children experience with volume. These include children:

- exhibiting difficulties with 2D representations of 3D objects, particularly if they are required to 'count' cubes that are not visible;

- not distinguishing between weight and volume;

- believing that enlarging the linear measurement of the object x times makes the volume x times larger;

- not distinguishing between volume and capacity;

- not distinguishing between surface area and volume;

- believing that two objects with the same surface area will have the same volume;

- relating the rise of displaced liquid to weight of an object rather than volume.
  (Adapted from Sáiz and Figueras, 2009, pages 148–149.)

Children's vocabulary should be developed through practical tasks involving the use of a range of different sized containers. Words such as 'full' and 'empty' can be developed into 'holds more' and 'holds less'. Comparisons of containers being filled and emptied (pouring one into another) will enable the children to compare more than two containers. By Year 5, approximately 80 per cent of children will have a good understanding of conservation of liquid (Twidle, 2006), so around one child in five is likely to experience difficulties in the upper primary years. Children need a lot of experience of using a variety of arbitrary units before they realise that comparisons require the same unit. At this point they can move on to deciding the most suitable unit to use and look at standard measuring devices such as beakers and measuring cylinders. It is important that children are aware of the link between capacity and volume to help them with displacement problems. This is a much more difficult concept for children to understand (Twidle, 2006).

Discovering that 1 litre of water has the same volume as 1000 cubic centimetres (and also has a mass of 1kg) is a vital concept for children to grasp. Using centimetre cubes to find the volume of regular shapes also helps develop links between the measurement of volume and capacity.

Mass and weight

The vocabulary that we use in our everyday lives leads to a confusion about how we teach 'mass' and 'weight'. The scientific and mathematical meanings of the words are not the same as those used by many people. The terms we actually use are inappropriate, as mass is the amount of matter within an object whereas weight is the force of gravity acting upon an object. When we use the word 'weight' we often mean mass and when we say 'weigh' we mean 'find the mass' (Haylock, 2001).

The scales we use cannot measure mass directly, only the force of gravity upon the object we are measuring. This is possible due to the fact that mass and weight are directly proportional. In Key Stage 1 children can be allowed to treat mass and weight as the same, but in Key Stage 2 they will learn the distinction between the two.

Unlike length, mass cannot be appreciated visually, as Haylock and Cockburn (1997) state *you cannot perceive it, count it, smell it or feel it* and, without the use of a balance, direct comparison of the mass of objects is impossible. Early experiences can be acquired through holding items in each hand and comparing them, although it must be remembered the children are experiencing weight, not mass. Children can also find this a problem due to the fact that the area of contact of the object they are holding varies.

Collecting and using a wide range of non-uniform and non-standard units develops the idea of units for mass. These need to be used with a balance, which does compare mass. Using vocabulary that suggests an object has the same mass as 15 pebbles can be progressed through to the same idea using uniform, non-standard units such as multilink, marbles, pennies, etc. When children are introduced to standard units for mass, work can be done on finding items heavier than and lighter than a given mass.

Haylock (2001) suggests referring to the standard units we use in the classroom as 'masses' rather than weights.

The *transitivity* principle and the *conservation* principle discussed earlier in this chapter can also cause difficulties for children when dealing with mass and weight. The opportunity to place three or more objects in order using the appropriate type of measure should be frequently offered to the children. Effective questioning when these activities are taking place will help to embed these principles in the children's learning.

Time

Children need to understand two aspects of time. Firstly, there is a 'passage of time' (for example, the time taken to run 100m, the time between breakfast and dinner or the time between Christmas and Easter). These time intervals are measured in seconds, minutes, hours, days, weeks and so on. Secondly, there is a 'recorded time' (for example, the time when something happens). For this we use analogue or digital time such as 'o'clock' and the 24-hour system. Neither of these aspects should be taught as isolated topics but need to be raised with the children whenever possible within a variety of cross-curricular contexts (Haylock, 2001). Putting time into meaningful contexts gives children the opportunity to begin to understand cyclical patterns (for example, days of the week, seasons). Using the vocabulary of 'today', 'tomorrow' and 'yesterday' in a story, for example, should complement activities that look at the passage of time.

While time passes at a constant rate, it often doesn't feel like that as a direct experience. Five minutes at the dentist might feel a lot longer than five minutes at a party! Cockburn (1999) uses the analogy of 'a long time for a historian' and 'a long time for a child' when looking at some of the problems in teaching the passing of time. Indeed, no one currently understands how we can psychologically estimate the duration of time (Karmarkar and Buonomano, 2007). Children are often only aware of the recent past or near future and so it is important that early tasks do not incorporate long periods of time.

When starting to learn about the measurement of time (as opposed to the passage of time) it is important to note that telling the time is really a scale-reading task. Hopkins *et al.* (2004) suggest that the dial of an analogue clock is a linear scale wrapped round into a circle. They go on to say that *the complexity of the scale used on the analogue clock is not always recognised* (2004, page 207). Children will go through a process of learning specific times of the day, for instance dinnertime, through recognising hours, parts of the hour, minutes and seconds. Their understanding of time is not helped by the fact that time is not metric and has many different units to get to grips with. There are a number of ways that we can tell the time, for example:

- twenty-five to nine;

- eight thirty-five;

- twenty-five to nine in the evening;

- eight thirty-five in the evening;

- eight thirty-five p.m.;

- twenty thirty-five.

These conventions all add to the confusion – as does the use of phrases like *I won't be a second* or *just a minute*. Not being able to watch the hour hand move also confuses children into thinking that the hour hand and the minute hand move independently.

Money

Given the recent and ongoing international financial context we are faced with, introducing how to manage money into education is a growing concern in a number of countries (e.g. National Institute for Budget Advice, 2009; Personal Finance Education Group, 2010). Teachers need to consider if the money problems that they present to children do encourage them to make decisions.

Increased use of bank cards is reducing children's opportunities to observe money being handled, so it is crucially important that teachers introduce children to 'real' money in the classroom so that children can learn the currency. *Mummy, why is the shopkeeper paying you for your shopping?* This classic misconception is common among young children. It occurs when the parent or carer hands over a note and is given several coins change. The child may simply 'see' the coins and notes as objects and is drawing his knowledge of number concepts to frame his question. Furthermore, Cole (2009) reflects on how the increasingly cashless society is impacting on children's understanding of money:

> There was a time, not so long ago, when the obligation to pay hard cash for school dinners, bus fares and weekly Brownie subs brought money into a child's life gently and naturally. Now parents are more than likely to pay for these things by direct debit, and primary school children are much more likely to be ferried around by car than to take a bus. When public transport does become part of growing up, cashless Oyster cards are likely to give them their ticket to ride. When I was a young lad my mum gave me a couple of 2p coins for my secret inside pocket in case I needed to use a phone box. My 11-year-old daughter, in contrast, has a (cheap) mobile phone that I bought her, topped up with credits buzzed over from my branchless bank account.

Dickson *et al*. (1984) explain that Gibson (1981) identified three key ideas that children need to understand money.

Coin recognition – children need to be able to identify all the coins and notes in the currency.

Equivalence – children need to know that two 5-pence coins are the same as one 10-pence coin.

Practical situations – children need to be able to make decisions relating to buying and selling.

Keat and Wilburne (2009) explored the impact of using story books on young children's ability to recognise and use coins. They found that using children's literature encouraged the children to set and solve their own problems, reason answers, and correctly identify the value of coins. The children had previously been unable to do this through more 'traditional' styles of teaching.

8.1 Conservation of length

The practitioner observes a young child's actions and makes a note of their conversation:

> Saima held a stick in her hand. I asked her what she noticed about the stick. Holding it vertically, she said, 'It is long, long'. She ran her hand along the stick. I agreed. Then she turned it horizontally and looked at it. I asked what she was thinking. She said, 'It isn't as long now'. I asked, 'Why not?' and Saima said, 'Cos it is longer that way' as she rotated it 90^0.

The error

The child thinks that the same stick is longer when it vertical and shorter when it is horizontal.

Why this happens

Saima does not understand the concept of conservation and has not realised that the length of the stick is invariant. She may also be comparing the height of the stick when it is vertical with the height (the stick's width) when it is horizontal.

Curriculum links

EYFS	Children use everyday language to talk about size, weight, capacity, position, distance, time and money to compare quantities and objects and to solve problems
Year 1	Compare, describe and solve practical problems for: lengths and heights [for example, long/short, longer/shorter, tall/short, double/half]
Year 4	Estimate, compare and calculate different measures, including money in pounds and pence

8.2 Conservation of area

The teacher asks the children to cut up a piece of rectangular card and rearrange the pieces to make a different shape (Figure 8.2). A child is then asked if the area of the shape has changed.

Figure 8.2

The error

The child responds by doing the task and replying that the area has changed because the shape has changed.

Why this happens

Children often look at the amount of space a shape takes up and come to the conclusion that the more spread out a shape is, the more area it must take. A parallelogram is often looked at as having a bigger area than a rectangle because it appears to be more spread out.

Curriculum links

Year 4	Find the area of rectilinear shapes by counting squares
Year 5	Calculate and compare the area of rectangles (including squares), and including using standard units, square centimetres (cm²) and square metres (m²) and estimate the area of irregular shapes
Year 6	Recognise that shapes with the same areas can have different perimeters and vice versa
Year 6	Recognise when it is possible to use formulae for the area and volume of shapes

8.3 Conservation of mass

The teacher suggests that two balls of modelling clay have the same mass. The child agrees that the two identical balls do indeed have the same mass. The teacher rolls out one of the balls and asks if they both still have the same mass (Figure 8.3).

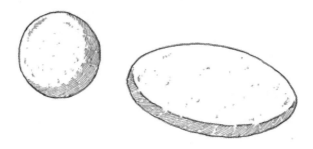

Figure 8.3

The error

The child thinks that because the modelling clay has changed shape, then the mass will have changed.

Why this happens

Children have difficulties with the *conservation* principle. Children often believe that changing the shape of an object will change its mass. This can also be witnessed when children break up a ball of modelling clay into smaller pieces or convert smaller pieces into one large piece. The transformation of the original shape leads some children to believe the total mass must be different.

Curriculum links

EYFS	Children use everyday language to talk about size, weight, capacity, position, distance, time and money to compare quantities and objects and to solve problems
Year 1	Compare, describe and solve practical problems for: mass/weight [for example, heavy/light, heavier than, lighter than]
Year 4	Estimate, compare and calculate different measures, including money in pounds and pence

8.4 Conservation and capacity

The children watch their teacher pour some water from one container into another and are then asked if the amount of water has changed (Figure 8.4).

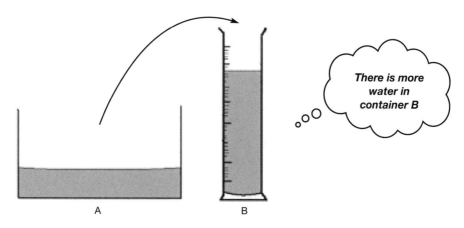

Figure 8.4

The error

It appears that there is more water in the second container. The children believe that the amount of water must have changed.

Why this happens

The children looking at the second container see that the depth of the water has changed and thus the amount of water must have changed. This is a conservation problem. Children often believe that taller containers contain more than shorter containers. The children could also struggle to deal with more than one variable in terms of the height and the cross-section of the containers.

Curriculum links

EYFS	Children use everyday language to talk about size, weight, capacity, position, distance, time and money to compare quantities and objects and to solve problems
Year 1	Compare, describe and solve practical problems for: capacity and volume [for example, full/empty, more than, less than, half, half full, quarter]
Year 4	Estimate, compare and calculate different measures, including money in pounds and pence

8.5 Mass determined by volume

The teacher shows a class of children two boxes: one is very large but light; the other is smaller but heavier (Figure 8.5). The teacher asks the children to decide, just by looking, which is the heavier box.

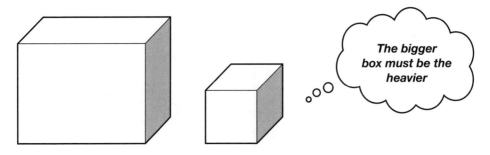

Figure 8.5

The error

The children answer that the bigger box is the heavier.

Why this happens

This comes from the children's belief that the mass of an object is determined by its volume. The bigger an object, the heavier it must be. It is important for the children to realise that visual image does not reflect weight.

Curriculum links

EYFS	Children use everyday language to talk about size, weight, capacity, position, distance, time and money to compare quantities and objects and to solve problems
Year 1	Measure and begin to record the following: mass/weight
Year 4	Estimate, compare and calculate different measures, including money in pounds and pence
Year 5	Estimate volume [for example, using 1 cm^3 blocks to build cuboids (including cubes) and capacity [for example, using water]
Year 6	Calculate, estimate and compare volume of cubes and cuboids using standard units, including cubic centimetres (cm^3) and cubic metres (m^3), and extending to other units [for example, mm^3 and km^3]

8.6 Direct comparison of two objects

The teacher gives the child two objects to compare. He places them on the desk as in Figure 8.6.

The grey stick is longer

Figure 8.6

The error

The child has not matched the ends of the objects together, giving a false impression of the largest and smallest.

Why this happens

Children sometimes fail to understand that in order to give a fair comparison it is important that two ends are carefully put at the same level. Having little previous experience on which to base a mental comparison, a child's answer can be confused by the position of the objects. The visual image of one object looking longer than the other can be avoided by the use of a line the children could use to match the ends first.

This error can also be observed in mass/weight, capacity and volume.

Curriculum links

EYFS	Children use everyday language to talk about size, weight, capacity, position, distance, time and money to compare quantities and objects and to solve problems
Year 1	Compare, describe and solve practical problems for: lengths and heights [for example, long/short, longer/shorter, tall/short, double/half]
Year 1	Compare, describe and solve practical problems for: mass/weight [for example, heavy/light, heavier than, lighter than]
Year 1	Compare, describe and solve practical problems for: capacity and volume [for example, full/empty, more than, less than, half, half full, quarter]
Year 2	Compare and order lengths, mass, volume/capacity and record the results using >, < and =
Year 4	Estimate, compare and calculate different measures, including money in pounds and pence

8.7 Comparing a straight line and a crooked line

The teacher draws two lines on the whiteboard, one straight and one crooked (Figure 8.7). The teacher then asks which line is longer.

Figure 8.7

The error

The child looks at the lines and decides that they are the same length.

Why this happens

Some children do not realise that a crooked line is longer than a straight line between the same two points. In considering only end points or destination, the points in between do not matter. The child has looked at the two starting points and the two end points and has not visualised the lines in terms of an ordered system of points and intervals.

This error can also be observed in mass/weight, capacity and volume.

Curriculum links

EYFS	Children use everyday language to talk about size, weight, capacity, position, distance, time and money to compare quantities and objects and to solve problems
Year 1	Compare, describe and solve practical problems for: lengths and heights [for example, long/short, longer/shorter, tall/short, double/half]
Year 1	Compare, describe and solve practical problems for: mass/weight [for example, heavy/light, heavier than, lighter than]
Year 1	Compare, describe and solve practical problems for: capacity and volume [for example, full/empty, more than, less than, half, half full, quarter]
Year 4	Estimate, compare and calculate different measures, including money in pounds and pence

8.8 Using rulers and tape measures

The teacher gives the class some identical objects to measure (Figures 8.8A, B, C, D, E).

The error

The children return with lots of different answers even though they were measuring identical objects.

Why this happens

(a) The children start to measure from the edge of the ruler (when zero does not start at the end of the ruler they are using). The children do not understand the *origin* concept.

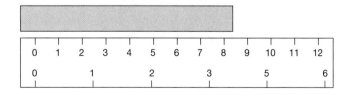

Figure 8.8A

(b) The children start to measure from 1cm instead of 0cm. The children do not understand the origin concept. This is a common error because children start counting from one.

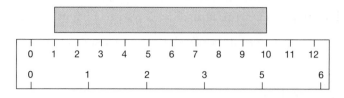

Figure 8.8B

(c) The children have read the number from the scale on the other edge of the ruler (or tape measure) when it has scales on both edges (progressing in different directions).

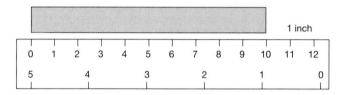

Figure 8.8C

(d) The children have measured the object from the wrong end of the ruler.

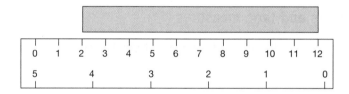

Figure 8.8D

(e) In using the tape measures the children have failed to take account of the metal end on some of the tapes given. The children whose tape measures started from the end avoided this error.

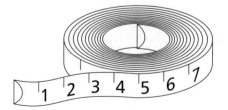

Figure 8.8E

Other errors include:

- The children have failed to mark accurately before moving the ruler/tape measure along when measuring lengths longer than the ruler.

- The children have failed to measure in a parallel direction.

Curriculum links

Year 1	Measure and begin to record the following: lengths and heights
Year 2	Choose and use appropriate standard units to estimate and measure length/height in any direction (m/cm); mass (kg/g); temperature (°C); capacity (litres/ml) to the nearest appropriate unit, using rulers, scales, thermometers and measuring vessels
Year 3	Measure, compare, add and subtract: lengths (m/cm/mm); mass (kg/g); volume/capacity (l/ml)
Year 4	Estimate, compare and calculate different measures, including money in pounds and pence
Year 6	Use, read, write and convert between standard units, converting measurements of length, mass, volume and time from a smaller unit of measure to a larger unit, and vice versa, using decimal notation to up to three decimal places

8.9 Using trundle wheels

The teacher has asked groups of children to measure the perimeter of the playground and playing field. They choose a trundle wheel as the most appropriate piece of equipment to use.

The error

The groups all have different answers on their return.

Why this happens

- Some of the children failed to start the trundle wheel in the correct position. The wheel must start with the 0cm or 0m mark touching the ground before they start to move.

- On moving around the playground, some of the children miscounted the number of clicks made by the wheel.

- When reaching the end of the measurement, the children just counted the clicks and did not account for the fraction of a turn left on the wheel.

- The children made errors in reading the scale itself.

- The children were unable to get the wheel into corners or right up to walls or fences and they did not account for the difference.

Curriculum links

Year 1	Measure and begin to record the following: lengths and heights
Year 2	Choose and use appropriate standard units to estimate and measure length/height in any direction (m/cm); mass (kg/g); temperature (°C); capacity (litres/ml) to the nearest appropriate unit, using rulers, scales, thermometers and measuring vessels
Year 3	Measure, compare, add and subtract: lengths (m/cm/mm); mass (kg/g); volume/capacity (l/ml)
Year 3	Measure the perimeter of simple 2-D shapes
Year 4	Measure and calculate the perimeter of a rectilinear figure (including squares) in centimetres and metres
Year 4	Estimate, compare and calculate different measures, including money in pounds and pence
Year 5	Measure and calculate the perimeter of composite rectilinear shapes in centimetres and metres

8.10 The relationship between length and area

The teacher asks the child what would happen to the area of a rectangle if the length and width were doubled (Figure 8.9).

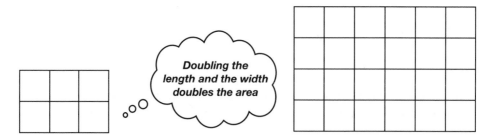

Doubling the length and the width doubles the area

Figure 8.9

The error

The child answers that if you double the width and the length, then the area will be doubled.

Why this happens

The child has incorrectly extrapolated that by multiplying the length of the sides, the same scale factor would apply to the area as was applied to the length and the width.

Curriculum links

Year 4	Find the area of rectilinear shapes by counting squares

8.11 Area and perimeter interdependence

The teacher asks the children if changing the perimeter of a shape changes the area (Figure 8.10).

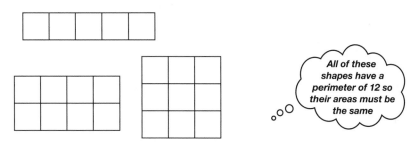

Figure 8.10

The error

The children agree that the shapes have all changed but all have a perimeter of 12 units so the areas must be the same.

Why this happens

The children have not had enough opportunities to realise that changing either the area or the perimeter may or may not cause a change in both cases. There is no direct link or relationship between the changing of area and its effect on the perimeter, and vice versa.

Curriculum links

Year 3	Measure the perimeter of simple 2-D shapes
Year 4	Measure and calculate the perimeter of a rectilinear figure (including squares) in centimetres and metres
Year 4	Find the area of rectilinear shapes by counting squares
Year 5	Measure and calculate the perimeter of composite rectilinear shapes in centimetres and metres

8.12 Calculating the area of parallelograms

The children have worked on finding the area of rectangles for some time and the teacher explains that to find the area of a parallelogram uses the same formula. One child responds, 'There is no way that can be right!'

The error

The child does not believe that calculating the area of a parallelogram uses the same formula as calculating the area of a rectangle.

Why this happens

Here the teacher has not given the children any opportunities to realise that the formula is the same for themselves (e.g. cutting one triangle off an end and matching it to the other to form a rectangle). Therefore, the child has focused on what the parallelogram *looks like*, without considering how the area could be the same as a rectangle (see 8.2 'Conservation of area'). The same errors are exhibited with triangles.

Curriculum links

Year 6	Recognise when it is possible to use formulae for area and volume of shapes
Year 6	Calculate the area of parallelograms and triangles

8.13 Use of inappropriate units

The child is asked to find the area of a rectangle. The child's response is as shown in Figure 8.11.

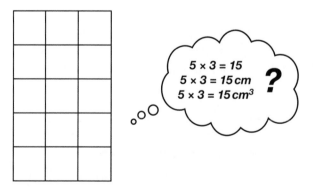

Figure 8.11

The error

The child is unsure which unit to use.

Why this happens

After calculating the area, which is done correctly using the formula required, the child does not understand the importance of answering using the correct units. They are not sure of the need for a unit and this could be indicative of a child's lack of understanding of what they are measuring in the first place.

Curriculum links

Year 6	Use, read, write and convert between standard units, converting measurements of length, mass, volume and time from a smaller unit of measure to a larger unit, and vice versa, using decimal notation to up to three decimal places
Year 6	Recognise when it is possible to use formulae for area and volume of shapes

8.14 Errors when reading measuring scales

The teacher asks the children to write down the weight of an object (Figure 8.12). They discuss their readings:

Child A: It is one kilogram

Child B: No, you can be more accurate. It is 1.2 kgs

Child C: Uh huh. It is 12 kilos.

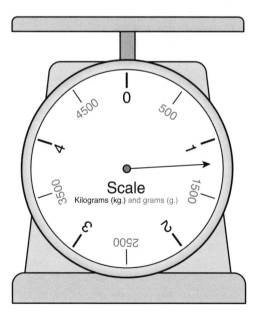

Figure 8.12

The error

The children have come up with a range of different answers.

Why this happens

It appears that all the children may not understand that the increments each represent 100g. Child A may not have been reading the scale at the same level and therefore thought that the needle was pointing to the 1. Child B seems to have treated the increments in the same way as previous experience with mm on the ruler, knowing that 2 increments relates to 0.2cm and generalised this to the scales. Child C has counted the increments in whole numbers.

Curriculum links

Year 1	Measure and begin to record the following: mass/weight
Year 2	Choose and use appropriate standard units to estimate and measure length/height in any direction (m/cm); mass (kg/g); temperature (°C); capacity (litres/ml) to the nearest appropriate unit, using rulers, scales, thermometers and measuring vessels
Year 3	Measure, compare, add and subtract: lengths (m/cm/mm); mass (kg/g); volume/capacity (l/ml)
Year 4	Estimate, compare and calculate different measures, including money in pounds and pence
Year 6	Use, read, write and convert between standard units, converting measurements of length, mass, volume and time from a smaller unit of measure to a larger unit, and vice versa, using decimal notation to up to three decimal places

8.15 Errors when using measuring cylinders

The teacher asks the children to write down the amount of liquid that has been poured into a cylinder (Figures 8.13A, B, C).

The error

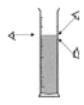

Figure 8.13A   **Figure 8.13B**   **Figure 8.13C**

The children write down a range of different answers.

Why this happens

- Some children pick the cylinder up and then fail to keep it vertical when reading the scale.

- Some children read the scale by looking at the value at the top of the meniscus instead of at the base.

- Some children read the scale from different heights so that parallax errors occur.

- Some children make errors in reading the scale itself.

Curriculum links

Year 1	Measure and begin to record the following: capacity and volume
Year 2	Choose and use appropriate standard units to estimate and measure length/height in any direction (m/cm); mass (kg/g); temperature (°C); capacity (litres/ml) to the nearest appropriate unit, using rulers, scales, thermometers and measuring vessels
Year 3	Measure, compare, add and subtract: lengths (m/cm/mm); mass (kg/g); volume/capacity (l/ml)
Year 4	Estimate, compare and calculate different measures, including money in pounds and pence
Year 6	Use, read, write and convert between standard units, converting measurements of length, mass, volume and time from a smaller unit of measure to a larger unit, and vice versa, using decimal notation to up to three decimal places

8.16 Sequencing events

A young child tells her teacher that she went to visit Grandma and Granddad 'yesterday'. The teacher knows that she was at school yesterday and talks with her about how she visited her grandparents last week, rather than yesterday.

The error

The child refers to an event that happened last week but refers to the event happening 'yesterday'.

Why this happens

Children take a long time to be able to understand the passing of time and correctly use language to explain the passing of time or the position of an event in time. It is also possible to observe this when children are talking about the future, confusing, for example 'in a minute', 'tomorrow' with 'next week', 'next month', or 'next year', etc.

Curriculum links

Year 1	Sequence events in chronological order using language [for example, before and after, next, first, today, yesterday, tomorrow, morning, afternoon and evening]

8.17 Vocabulary related to time

The children are reciting the names of the months in order. Several children confuse the order, e.g. 'January, February, June, April, ...'.

The error

The children do not recite the names of the months in the correct order.

Why this happens

In mathematics, children are encouraged to think systematically and logically about the problems they solve. However, there is no particular logic to the order of the months (or the days of the week). For example they are not alphabetical and they are not ordered according to the number of letters they have. The only order is their chronological order, which is imposed. It takes children some time to learn these; learning songs can help.

Curriculum links

Year 1	Recognise and use language relating to dates, including days of the week, weeks, months and years

8.18 Analogue clocks

The teacher asks the class what time it is on the classroom clock (Figure 8.14).

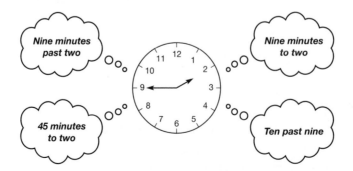

Figure 8.14

The error

The children respond with a range of answers.

Why this happens

- Some of the children misinterpret the hour hand as the minute hand and vice versa. For example, they may read the clock as 'ten past nine'.

- Some of the children use the hour numbers on the clock to read the minutes also (i.e. the clock could read 'nine minutes past two' or as 'nine minutes to two').

- The children get confused because we impose two scales – hours and minutes.

- The children make errors when they identify the time between two known values.

- The children get confused about which side of the clock is 'to' the hour and which side is 'past' the hour.

- The children get confused over the use of fractions on an analogue clock. For example, the clock in Figure 8.14 can be read as 'a quarter to two'. In addition to the minutes not being specifically labelled, the fractions of the hours aren't either.

Curriculum links

Year 1	Tell the time to the hour and half past the hour and draw the hands on a clock face to show these times
Year 2	Tell and write the time to five minutes, including quarter past/to the hour and draw the hands on a clock face to show these times
Year 3	Tell and write the time from an analogue clock, including using Roman numerals from I to XII, and 12-hour and 24-hour clocks
Year 3	Estimate and read time with increasing accuracy to the nearest minute; record and compare time in terms of seconds, minutes and hours; use vocabulary such as o'clock, a.m./p.m., morning, afternoon, noon and midnight

8.19 Digital and 24-hour clocks

The teacher asks the class what time it is on the digital clock (Figure 8.15).

Figure 8.15

The error

The children respond with a range of answers.

Why this happens

- Mixing up the hours and the minutes. The children may read the clock in Figure 8.15 as saying 'eleven minutes past ten'.

- The children can get confused by mixing up digital minutes and decimals. They might read 'ten past eleven' as 'eleven point one'.

- The 12- and 24-hour clock causes confusion without 'p.m.' or 'a.m.' on the digital clock. 'Eighteen forty-five' is unusual language for a child.

- Confusion can arise out of the colloquial use of 'fourteen hundred', which could be expressing the time 14:00. The children can think that the two zeros mean a hundred.

Curriculum links

Year 3	Tell and write the time from an analogue clock, including using Roman numerals from I to XII, and 12-hour and 24-hour clocks
Year 3	Estimate and read time with increasing accuracy to the nearest minute; record and compare time in terms of seconds, minutes and hours; use vocabulary such as o'clock, a.m./p.m., morning, afternoon, noon and midnight

8.20 Comparing the duration of events: reading stopwatches

The children were asked to run a short distance and compare their times. Two children looked at their stopwatches. Child A's read 1:03.26 and Child B's read 58.22.

Child A: I was faster that you. I did it in one and you did it in 58.

Child B: No, I beat you. You did it in one hour and I did it in 58 minutes.

The errors

The children are reading the stopwatch incorrectly.

Why this happens

Reading a stopwatch can be confusing for children because it includes hundredths of seconds on it. When children have been used to reading hours, minutes and seconds it is common for them to mistakenly assign minutes, seconds and hundredths of seconds to the more well-known values. Child A has looked at the first number and applied his whole-number knowledge that the digit on the left is the most significant. In this case he needed to consider the context and read the times in minutes and seconds. Child B has not considered the passing of time when he made the comment about one hour.

Curriculum links

Year 1	Measure and begin to record the following: time (hours, minutes, seconds)
Year 2	Compare and sequence intervals of time
Year 3	Compare durations of events {for example, calculate the time taken by particular events or tasks}

8.21 Problem solving using time

The children are working on a problem (Figure 8.16):

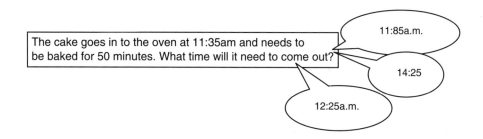

Figure 8.16

The error

Two children give the wrong answer.

Why this happens

One child has applied whole-number knowledge to time which uses a different base, so she has simply added 50 to 35 and provided the answer 11:85a.m. which makes no sense in the context of time. It is essential that the child understands that there are 60 seconds in one minute and how this is a different base system to our decimal system where there are 100 cm in one metre, for example. Another child has attempted to use the 24-hour clock, and knowing that the new time moves into the afternoon, as added two onto 12. He has overgeneralised a rule he has taught himself: 'If it is three in the afternoon add two to the three to make the five and add ten'. The third child has correctly found 12:25 but has not used the appropriate convention of p.m. for this time of day. This convention often seems counter-intuitive to children because they are unfamiliar with the 24-hour clock when they are introduced to am and pm. So, although the time at noon jumps from 11:59 a.m. to 12:00p.m. and at midnight changes from 11:59p.m. to 12:00a.m., the child has assumed that p.m. begins when we get to 1p.m. rather than 12 'because that's when the numbers change'.

Curriculum links

Year 2	Know the number of minutes in an hour and the number of hours in a day
Year 3	Estimate and read time with increasing accuracy to the nearest minute; record and compare time in terms of seconds, minutes and hours; use vocabulary such as o'clock, a.m./p.m., morning, afternoon, noon and midnight
Year 5	Solve problems involving converting between units of time
Year 6	Use, read, write and convert between standard units, converting measurements of length, mass, volume and time from a smaller unit of measure to a larger unit, and vice versa, using decimal notation to up to three decimal places

8.22 Days in a year

The teacher asks the children how many days are in a year. One child responds, 'There are 360 days in a year because $12 \times 30 = 360$'.

The error

The child thinks that there are 360 days in a year.

Why this happens

The child is unable to recall the fact that there are 365 days in a year (or 366 in a leap year). This is a fact that just needs to be learned by rote – there is no easy calculation that can be done, even though the child has tried to multiply the number of months in a year by 30. Many children struggle to recall the number of days in a year, simply because it is not revisited freqently and there is little call for it to be used in everyday contexts very often.

Curriculum links

Year 3	Know the number of seconds in a minute and the number of days in each month, year and leap year

8.23 The value of money

A child is shown the following coins by his teacher (Figure 8.17). The teacher asks him how much money he has. He says he has four pennies.

Figure 8.17

The error

The child has counted the number of coins instead of finding the total value of the coins.

Why this happens

The child does not understand that coins have value. He has counted the coins as if they were objects. This error is common with young children because they may still be learning to count. They may just be reaching the stage where they can understand the concept of cardinality, so do not understand the idea of items having a numerical value more than one.

Curriculum links

EYFS	Children use everyday language to talk about size, weight, capacity, position, distance, time and money to compare quantities and objects and to solve problems
Year 1	Recognise and know the value of different denominations of coins and notes
Year 4	Estimate, compare and calculate different measures, including money in pounds and pence

8.24 The relative value of money (1)

The teacher asks a child which of the coins in Figure 8.18 is worth the most. She points to the 2-pence piece and says this coin is worth the most.

The biggest coin is worth the most

Figure 8.18

The error

The child has identified the wrong coin.

Why this happens

The child believes that the bigger the object, the more it is worth. She may believe this because of her experiences in relation to measures, where generally the bigger an object is, the more numerical value can be attributed to it. The child does not understand that the value of a coin is not directly proportional to its size.

This child does not understand the concept of equivalence and may also have a limited knowledge of currency. Teachers need to ensure that children have considerable opportunities to handle 'real' money in role-play contexts before moving on to more complex and, essentially abstract, pencil and paper money problems.

Curriculum links

EYFS	Children use everyday language to talk about size, weight, capacity, position, distance, time and money to compare quantities and objects and to solve problems
Year 1	Recognise and know the value of different denominations of coins and notes
Year 4	Estimate, compare and calculate different measures, including money in pounds and pence

8.25 The relative value of money (2)

The teacher introduces a problem-solving activity to his class. He asks the children to find and record as many ways as possible of making 26p. One child draws the solutions shown in Figure 8.19.

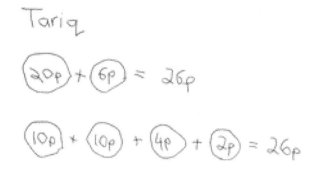

Figure 8.19

The error

The child has included coins that do not exist in our currency.

Why this happens

He has used his knowledge of numbers to find solutions to the problem. The child is not aware that some coin values do not exist in our currency. The child may have insufficient experience of handling 'real' money.

Curriculum links

Year 2	Recognise and use symbols for pounds (£) and pence (p); combine amounts to make a particular value
Year 2	Find different combinations of coins that equal the same amounts of money
Year 4	Estimate, compare and calculate different measures, including money in pounds and pence

8.26 Giving change

The teacher is helping the children with how to give change by counting back the coins. One child counts back the change received from using £2.00 to pay for an item that is 23p:

> *23 pence, {gives 5p} 28 pence, {gives 2p} 30 pence, {gives £1} one pound 30, {gives 50p} one pound 80, {gives 20p} two pounds*

The error

The child has not counted back the change according to the convention.

Why this happens

The child has been able to give the correct change, and has counted back the coins error-free. However, the child has not demonstrated an understanding of how counting to the next denomination can support calculating the change. The child may also have a gap in their understanding when calculating addition and subtraction of whole numbers, counting to the next appropriate signpost (e.g. 10, 50 or 100) to support working out.

Curriculum links

Year 2	Solve simple problems in a practical context involving addition and subtraction of money of the same unit, including giving change
Year 3	Add and subtract amounts of money to give change, using both £ and p in practical contexts
Year 4	Estimate, compare and calculate different measures, including money in pounds and pence
Year 6	Use, read, write and convert between standard units, converting measurements of length, mass, volume and time from a smaller unit of measure to a larger unit, and vice versa, using decimal notation to up to three decimal places

8.27 Representing money on a calculator

A child has used a calculator to help solve a problem involving money. The calculator states that the answer is 1.5, so she writes £1.5 and says *One pound and five pence.*

The error

There are two errors made by the child here: (1) She has incorrectly written the answer of £1.50 as £1.5; (2) she has read 1.5 on the calculator as 'One pound and five pence' rather than 'One pound and fifty pence'.

Why this happens

The child may not know that the calculator automatically truncates the answer of 1.50 to 1.5 on the display. Alternatively, she may not have taken into consideration the context of the answer. She has not considered that an answer of 1.5 means 1.5 (or 1½) pounds in this case, which is written as one pound and fifty pence: £1.50. It could also be that she has not used zero as a place holder, but reads the answer as one pound and fifty pence (thus ignoring the zero in the hundreds column) or as one pound and five pence (thus ignoring the need for a zero in the tenths column).

8.28 Converting between different units of measure (1)

The children are completing worksheets converting between metres and kilometres. One child completes the sheet below (Figure 8.20).

1. 4,000 m = __4__ km

2. 23,000 m = __23__ km

3. 800 m = __8__ km

4. 10 km = __1__ m

5. 45 km = __45__ m

6. 0.6 km = __6__ m

Figure 8.20

The error

The child has written a number of incorrect answers.

Why this happens

The child has answered the first two questions correctly and has then overgeneralised that the answer is always the first digit(s) in the question. It is clear that the child has not used their knowledge that there are 1000m in 1km to convert between the lengths. It may be that the child does not know how to find the number one thousand times smaller or larger than another. Furthermore, the child has continued their incorrect reasoning in the second half of the worksheet, demonstrating they did not notice the change of units.

Curriculum links

Year 4	Convert between different units of measure [for example, kilometre to metre; hour to minute]
Year 5	Convert between different units of metric measure (for example, kilometre and metre; centimetre and metre; centimetre and millimetre; gram and kilogram; litre and millilitre)

(Continued)

(Continued)	
Year 6	Solve problems involving the calculation and conversion of units of measure, using decimal notation up to three decimal places where appropriate
Year 6	Use, read, write and convert between standard units, converting measurements of length, mass, volume and time from a smaller unit of measure to a larger unit, and vice versa, using decimal notation to up to three decimal places

8.29 Converting between different units of measure (2)

The teacher give the children the following problem: 'The meat weighs 2.5kg. The cooking instructions state the meat should be cooked for 25 minutes per 500g plus a further 25 minutes. What is the total cooking time?'

Child A: Two hours 50 mins

Child B: Six lots of 25 minutes

Child C: 2.5 hours

Child D: You can't work it out from this information

The errors

The children respond with a range of different answers.

Why this happens

- Child A used a calculator and gained the answer 2.5. He interpreted the 0.5 incorrectly as 50 minutes.

- Child B has not completed the task. Perhaps she does not know how to find 6 × 25 minutes or she has run out of time.

- Child C has also used a calculator and used the calculator's display (2.5) as the number of hours. She has not used a conventional way to give the time because half an hour is not referred to as 0.5 of an hour.

- Child D may have found the problem too difficult, or is looking for some unnecessary information before he can complete the task.

Curriculum links

Year 4	Convert between different units of measure [for example, kilometre to metre; hour to minute]
Year 5	Convert between different units of metric measure (for example, kilometre and metre; centimetre and metre; centimetre and millimetre; gram and kilogram; litre and millilitre)
Year 6	Solve problems involving the calculation and conversion of units of measure, using decimal notation up to three decimal places where appropriate
Year 6	Use, read, write and convert between standard units, converting measurements of length, mass, volume and time from a smaller unit of measure to a larger unit, and vice versa, using decimal notation to up to three decimal places

8.30 Converting between different metric and imperial units of measure

The children are asked to work out approximately how many centimetres are in 10 inches.

Child A: 250 cm

Child B: None, they are different

Child C: Two and a half

The errors

The children respond with a range of different answers.

Why this happens

- Child A has demonstrated that she know there are approximately 2.5 cm in one inch, but has found how many centimetres in 100 inches. This is a calculation (place value) error.

- Child B does not understand that it is possible to convert between inches and centimetres. They may have been previously corrected when using centimetres and inches interchangeably.

- Child C is stating the number of centimetres in one inch. He may have misunderstood the question, or is unsure how to do the calculation.

Curriculum links

Year 5	Understand and use approximate equivalences between metric units and common imperial units such as inches, pounds and pints
Year 6	Solve problems involving the calculation and conversion of units of measure, using decimal notation up to three decimal places where appropriate
Year 6	Use, read, write and convert between standard units, converting measurements of length, mass, volume and time from a smaller unit of measure to a larger unit, and vice versa, using decimal notation to up to three decimal places
Year 6	Convert between miles and kilometres

9 Geometry

The first aspect of mathematics that young children explore is geometry. As soon as they begin to interact with the three-dimensional world they live in, babies begin to learn about their position in space and how this is related to other objects. In time children learn to become aware of a two-dimensional representation of their world, and this continues to develop into spatial reasoning.

In the Early Years Foundation Stage (DfE, 2012, page 6) practitioners are expected to provide children with opportunities to develop and improve their skills in counting, understanding and using numbers, calculating simple addition and subtraction problems; and to describe shapes, spaces and measures. In Key Stage 1 (Years 1 and 2) children develop their ability to recognise, describe, draw, compare and sort different shapes and use the related vocabulary. During lower Key Stage 2 (Years 3 and 4) children draw with increasing accuracy and develop mathematical reasoning so they can analyse shapes and their properties, and confidently describe the relationships between them. In upper Key Stage 2 (Years 5 and 6) teaching ensures that children classify shapes with increasingly complex geometric properties and that they learn the vocabulary they need to describe them.

Three- and two-dimensional shapes

Although the topic of shape and space is the first aspect of mathematics that children begin to interact with, it is a complex subject. Teachers need to be aware of its complexity in order to help them to identify the difficulties that are likely to arise for children. From a young age, children begin to draw, making sense of the three-dimensional world around them by representing it in two dimensions (Ring, 2001). This is a form of language (visual) that should be considered as important as other more conventional types of language such as written or spoken (Hall, 2007).

It is the representation of shapes in our environment that can make early understanding of properties and definitions of 3D and 2D shape difficult. This is because children are continually surrounded by prototypical shapes (Walcott et al., 2009). These have an overwhelming impact on the visual images that they develop. Much research illustrates that children tend to limit their understanding of shapes to the examples they are shown (see, for example, Yin, 2003). Even when children learn the definition of a 2D or 3D shape, the prototypical visual image they have often remains (Hershkowitz et al., 1990). As teachers, it is our responsibility to ensure that children are exposed to shapes of varying size, orientation and type, to broaden their limited understanding of shape.

Another aspect that compounds the nature of shape and space is the inclusivity and exclusivity of definitions. Children find it difficult to consider that a square is a rectangle (demonstrating the inclusive nature of the definition of rectangles), particularly when they are faced with images in and out of school where what they call a rectangle is a prototypical oblong (illustrating the exclusive nature of the definition of oblong: a rectangle that is not a square. See, for example, Hansen, 2008b; Jones, 2000; Monaghan, 2000). Orton and Frobisher (2005, page 150) highlight that *there can be confusion when one is talking to children about squares and rectangles, because children tend to classify these shapes as different, whereas mathematicians prefer to think of squares as special rectangles. To avoid this difficulty, some books use the word oblong for a non-square rectangle.*

Finally, the large variety of ways that shapes can be defined also adds to the issues of complexity. For example, we can consider the length of the individual, parallel or adjacent sides, the size of the interior angles, the order of rotation and the lines of symmetry. Lehrer *et al.* (1998) found, worryingly, that over time, children were less likely to notice attributes (such as sides or vertices) because of the conventional way geometry is being taught.

Geometry's roots lie in young children being able to manipulate objects. Physical manipulation of objects in geometry teaching has been used for over a century (e.g. Hill, 1908), and more recently the affordances that manipulation within virtual learning environments give learners have been greatly documented also (Bouck and Flanagan, 2009; Hansen, 2008b). Manipulation supports visualisation, a vital skill that children need in order to develop their geometrical understanding (Mulligan *et al.*, 2004). It also helps children to build essential mental representations (Kelly, 2006).

Resources also offer a platform for children's discussion. High-quality talk in all areas of mathematics is essential (DfE, 2010; DfES, 2008). However, there are, in fact, few findings related to young children talking about shape (Garrick, 2002). Coltman *et al.* (2002) identified the role of a supporting adult in supporting young children's understanding of aspects of 3D shape. Scaffolding and talk through structured adult intervention were shown to increase the effectiveness of learning, which in turn lead to children's secure and transferable knowledge. In an earlier, related study, Anghileri and Baron (1999) found that when sorting, children did not undertake any discussion that may have led to clarifying tasks. This was also found in Saads and Davis's (1997) study on the importance of language in the development of children's geometrical understanding. They state, *discussion involving the names and characteristics of the 3D shapes is necessary for children to clarify mathematical understanding, for example in the relationships between cubes and squares* (page 17). Likewise, Hasegawa (1997) identified that if a child does not understand concepts such as edges, sides, corners and faces, the definitions of shapes are meaningless.

Position and direction

In addition to beginning to understand the properties of shapes, at primary level children explore space through positioning themselves, objects and shapes in space.

Garrick *et al.* (2004) report that pattern-making is an activity that young children can carry out in order to naturally explore position. Appropriate use of positional language is essential to help children to make sense of position in space and to solve geometrical problems (Greeno, 1980).

Because of the dynamic environments that ICT offers, concepts of position and direction are made more accessible to all children (Jones, 2003). The collaborative nature of the environments also allow for more problem-solving strategies to be used by the children. The following difficulties relate to position and direction.

Transformation

This section is concerned with children's difficulties in the transformation of shape in space. Transformation includes enlargement and aspects of symmetry such as reflection, rotation and translation.

Garrick (2002) considered young children's perceptions of symmetrical patterns. In her research she found that 8 per cent of the 3-year-olds she worked with were able to construct their own pegboard symmetrical patterns. By four years of age, this had significantly increased to 25 per cent. Rawson (1993) looked at the pattern perception of 4–6-year-old children and identified that in several cases the children searched for a visual balance in the manipulatives and were implicitly placing importance on symmetry as a feature of pattern. Clements (2003, page 42) also reports that symmetry is an area of strength for young children.

At times it can be useful to consider symmetry as closely linked to fractions. Often teachers consider lines of symmetry as reflecting one-half of a pattern. This can, however, cause difficulties. Huckstep et al. (2002) share an example where a teacher inadvertently muddies the symmetrical properties of an oblong to her class when she is looking at halves and quarters of squares and then moves on to oblongs. The children want to halve the oblong diagonally, which then leads the teacher to use rotation to demonstrate how the oblong is cut in half. Another aspect of symmetry is reflecting shapes in one, two or more lines of symmetry.

Orton (1997) carried out a study with older children, from 9 to 16 years of age. These children identified pattern as including 'ideas of shape recognition, congruence and symmetry' (page 304). She found that although the children had a clearly established understanding of pattern recognition, they lacked the vocabulary needed to describe it. Orton identified a three-stage process that children undertake in their understanding of pattern:

Stage 1: copying shapes, detecting embedded shapes in pictures, completing simple patterns, matching shapes, recognising reflection in a vertical line, simple rotation and reflection and completing tasks with a frame of reference;

Stage 2: matching embedded shapes, matching simple shapes in different orientations, undertaking more complex reflection and rotation tasks with a frame of reference;

Stage 3: matching more complex shapes in different orientations, completing more complex tasks involving rotation, recognising most reflection and rotation (Orton, 1997, page 310).

Children first reflect in one horizontal or vertical line, with the shapes touching the line. The shapes then move a distance from the line and finally the line is set on the diagonal. The order of teaching these reflects the level of difficulty that children experience (Orton, 2004). The importance of mathematical terminology in geometrical understanding has already been highlighted in this chapter. However, once again, the issue of mathematical terminology must be raised. It appears that the importance of vocabulary and the observed lack of use of correct terminology is not limited to children. Goulding (2002) found that trainee teachers were lacking the terminology of transformations and she suggested that this may have caused trainees difficulty with their mathematical tasks. It is, of course, vital that teachers model good mathematical terminology to their children.

Angles

Angles can be defined three ways: as an amount of turning about a point between two lines; a pair of rays with a common end-point; and the region formed by the intersection of two half-planes (Mitchelmore and White, 2000). These definitions show us that we can broadly consider the concept of angle in two ways. There is the static experience, which focuses on the difference in direction of two lines. This enables us to compare, order and measure the sizes of different angles by placing one on the other or by using a protractor. The second way we can view angles is the dynamic experience, which focuses on the rotation involved when one point turns to another. This allows us to appreciate a sense of direction, movement, to look at angles of any size and to distinguish between clockwise and anti-clockwise motion. Providing experiences for children to understand both ways of viewing angles is important for the development of their concept of angles (Clements and Burns, 2005).

Mitchelmore and White (2000) undertook some research which attempted to address children's difficulties in co-ordinating different aspects of the angle concept. They aimed to relate children's angle concepts to their physical experiences. Their research identified three stages of development in children's understanding of angle:

- physical angle situations that young children experience, such as scissors, roundabouts, slides (slope is a way to consider angle), pencil points, flexible drinking straws, etc.;

- contextual angle concepts: children by the age of nine tend to have formed clear and distinct contextual angle concepts (slope, turn, intersection, corner);

- abstract angle concepts: children have generalised the contextual angle concepts and identified abstract angle concepts that may not be similar in context (intersection, corner, bend, slope, limited rotation, unlimited rotation).

9.1 Construction using three-dimensional objects

The child finds it difficult to build a stable tower and it continually topples over.

The error

The child is placing unstable blocks at the bottom of the tower.

Why this happens

From an early age, children begin to manipulate three-dimensional objects, including building tall constructions. They need to learn which shapes are the best for various parts of the tower. This is essential for children to develop their spatial understanding and reasoning. Children who continue to build unstable constructions may have been limited in the shapes or materials they have used.

Curriculum links

| EYFS | They explore characteristics of everyday objects and shapes and use mathematical language to describe them |
| Year 2 | identify and describe the properties of 3-D shapes, including the number of edges, vertices and faces |

9.2 Mathematical terminology in three-dimensional shape and space: faces

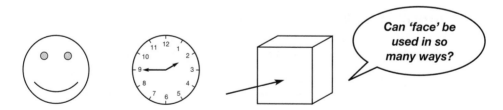

Figure 9.1   The child finds it difficult to use the term the 'face' on a 3D shape

Why this happens

From an early age, children have conversations at home and in school about the sides of an object. When they are introduced to the term face, it can be confusing and difficult as they may have been used to using this term in different ways, some non-mathematically. Without understanding the meaning of the term face, it is meaningless for children to begin to define three-dimensional objects.

Curriculum links

Year 1	Recognise and name common 2-D and 3-D shapes, including: 3-D shapes [for example, cuboids (including cubes), pyramids and spheres]
Year 2	Identify and describe the properties of 3-D shapes, including the number of edges, vertices and faces

9.3 Mathematical terminology in three-dimensional shape and space: vertices

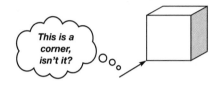

Figure 9.2

The error

The child finds it difficult to identify the vertex of a 3D shape and wants to call it a corner.

Why this happens

Children have conversations at home and in Key Stage 1 at school about the corners of an object. When they are introduced to the terms *vertex* and *vertices*, it can be confusing and difficult because they may not have used these terms before.

Curriculum links

Year 1	Recognise and name common 2-D and 3-D shapes, including: 3-D shapes [for example, cuboids (including cubes), pyramids and spheres]
Year 2	Identify and describe the properties of 3-D shapes, including the number of edges, vertices and faces

9.4 Nets

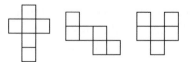

Figure 9.3

The error

The child finds it difficult to visualise which nets will form a cube.

Why this happens

Children who haven't had a lot of experience in visualising 3D shapes being opened up and folded again, often find it difficult to imagine the net of a shape or 'see' a net being folded to make a 3D shape. They may have learnt that the common cross shape (Figure 9.3, left) is a net for a cube, but may not be so sure about the others. There is some evidence to suggest that boys are able to visualise shapes more effectively than girls.

Curriculum links

Year 2	Identify 2-D shapes on the surface of 3-D shapes [for example, a circle on a cylinder and a triangle on a pyramid]
Year 3	Draw 2-D shapes and make 3-D shapes using modelling materials; recognise 3-D shapes in different orientations and describe them
Year 5	Identify 3-D shapes, including cubes and other cuboids, from 2-D representations
Year 6	Recognise, describe and build simple 3-D shapes, including making nets

9.5 2D representations of 3D objects

Figure 9.4

The error

The child finds it difficult to represent a 3D object as a 2D drawing. They may also find it difficult to recreate a model of blocks from a sketch.

Why this happens

Although the ability to transfer learning from a 2D representation to a 3D representation develops rapidly during childhood (Barr, 2010), young children (and some older people, too) find it very difficult to translate what they see in 3D space to a representation of it on paper, or 2D space. It is sometimes equally difficult to visualise a 3D shape from a 2D drawing. Young children also tend to draw what they think they see, rather than what is presented to them (Picard and Durand, 2004).

Curriculum links

Year 2	Identify 2-D shapes on the surface of 3-D shapes [for example, a circle on a cylinder and a triangle on a pyramid]
Year 5	Identify 3-D shapes, including cubes and other cuboids, from 2-D representations

9.6 Orientation of two-dimensional shapes (1)

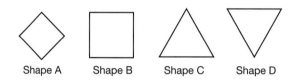

Shape A   Shape B   Shape C   Shape D

Figure 9.5

The error

The child identifies Shapes A and B as a diamond and a square respectively but does not acknowledge that they are the same shape. Likewise, the child identifies shape C as a triangle, but cannot name shape D.

Why this happens

Children who have been exposed only or mainly to prototypical images of squares or triangles (i.e. shapes with a horizontal baseline), and have not explored them in different rotations, will focus on the visual image they have of the shape. This leads to difficulties in identifying the same shape presented in different ways.

Curriculum links

Year 1	Recognise and name common 2-D and 3-D shapes, including: 2-D shapes [for example, rectangles (including squares), circles and triangles]
Year 2	Identify 2-D shapes on the surface of 3-D shapes [for example, a circle on a cylinder and a triangle on a pyramid]
Year 3	Draw 2-D shapes and make 3-D shapes using modelling materials; recognise 3-D shapes in different orientations and describe them
Year 4	Compare and classify geometric shapes, including quadrilaterals and triangles, based on their properties and sizes
Year 6	Compare and classify geometric shapes based on their properties and sizes and find unknown angles in any triangles, quadrilaterals and regular polygons

9.7 Orientation of two-dimensional shapes (2)

The teacher asks the children to identify which of the pairs of triangles are congruent.

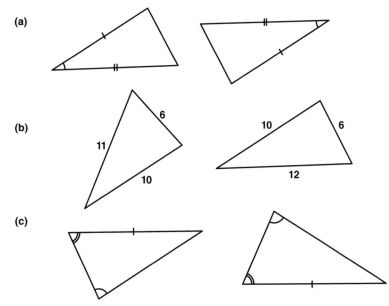

Figure 9.6

The error

The child selects only pair (a) as congruent, and does not see that pair (c) are also congruent.

Why this happens

The child has received more experience rotating shapes than flipping them. Therefore it was understandable that she did not flip the triangle in (c) to see that they are congruent.

Curriculum links

Year 6	Compare and classify geometric shapes based on their properties and sizes and find unknown angles in any triangles, quadrilaterals and regular polygons

9.8 Properties of polygons

Example 1: triangles and hexagons

See Figure 9.7.

The error

The child identifies the shapes in Set A as triangles, but cannot name the shapes in Set B as triangles. The child identifies the shapes in Set C as hexagons but does not identify the shapes in Set D as hexagons.

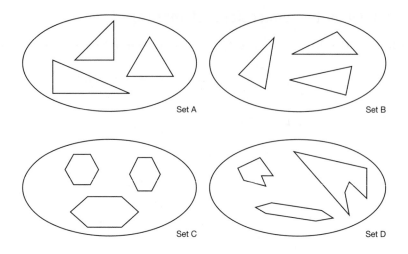

Figure 9.7

Why this happens

Children who have been exposed only or mainly to prototypical images of figures (e.g. triangles with a horizontal baseline, specific examples of right-angled triangles or only equilateral triangles; regular hexagons, hexagons with a horizontal base line or some symmetry) and have not explored them in different rotations will focus on the visual image they have of the shape. This leads to children concluding:

- all triangles have a horizontal baseline;

- only regular (equilateral) triangles are triangles;

- all hexagons have a horizontal baseline;

- only regular six-sided figures are called hexagons.

Example 2: circles

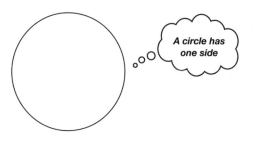

Figure 9.8

The error

The child states that a circle has only one side.

Why this happens

The child can see one side; they draw one (curved) line when they draw a circle and they follow one line when they cut out a circle. Sides create the boundary for a polygon and a side as a length. Mathematicians argue about the definition of circle, and it also depends on the context. For example, if a circle has an infinite number of sides of length of 0, the sides are no longer technically sides but rather points. In reality, of course, defining a circle as having one side is unhelpful because the use of sides should be reserved for polygons (shapes with many [straight] sides).

Example 3: polygons

Figure 9.9

The error

The child identifies all of these shapes as polygons.

Why this happens

Some children create their own logic from the images they have explored. In this example, the child has been told previously that square, triangle and rectangle are all polygons. She has extrapolated that other shapes she knows the name of, such as the heart and the crescent, are polygons. She also extrapolates that as quadrilaterals have four lines, the third shape is also a polygon. She has not yet realised that a polygon must be a closed, plane shape made up of straight lines.

Curriculum links

Year 1	Recognise and name common 2-D and 3-D shapes, including: 2-D shapes [for example, rectangles (including squares), circles and triangles]
Year 2	Identify and describe the properties of 2-D shapes, including the number of sides and line symmetry in a vertical line
Year 4	Compare and classify geometric shapes, including quadrilaterals and triangles, based on their properties and sizes
Year 5	Distinguish between regular and irregular polygons based on reasoning about equal sides and angles
Year 6	Compare and classify geometric shapes based on their properties and sizes and find unknown angles in any triangles, quadrilaterals and regular polygons

9.9 Parallel and perpendicular lines

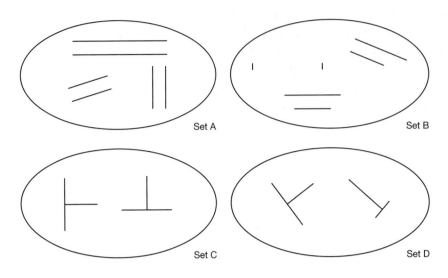

Set A Set B Set C Set D

Figure 9.10

The error

The child identifies the shapes in Set A as parallel lines, but does not acknowledge the parallel lines in Set B as parallel lines. Likewise, the child identifies the shapes in Set C as perpendicular lines, but does not acknowledge the lines in Set D as perpendicular lines.

Why this happens

Children who have been exposed only or mainly to prototypical images of parallel or perpendicular lines and have not explored them in different rotations or with lines of varying length will focus on the visual image they have. (Prototypical examples of parallel lines may include lines that are the same length, often running horizontal or vertical with lines longer than the distance between them. Prototypical examples of perpendicular lines usually include lines that are the same length and are horizontal and vertical in orientation.)

Curriculum links

Year 3	Identify horizontal and vertical lines and pairs of perpendicular and parallel lines
Year 4	Compare and classify geometric shapes, including quadrilaterals and triangles, based on their properties and sizes

9.10 Definitions of quadrilaterals

Figure 9.11   Parallelograms

The error

The child sees each of the shapes in Figure 9.11 as discrete identities and does not understand that a square is a particular example of a rectangle and that a square and rectangle are particular examples of parallelogram.

Why this happens

Children who have always been shown prototypical shapes of squares, rectangles and parallelograms (such as those above) have not explored the properties of these shapes. They may not have encountered a square as a type of rectangle, for example, as they have always related images of oblongs with the label *rectangle*.

This also occurs with other quadrilaterals such as a square being an example of a rhombus and diamonds being examples of kites (see further discussion about kites in Chapter 1).

Curriculum links

Year 4	Compare and classify geometric shapes, including quadrilaterals and triangles, based on their properties and sizes
Year 5	Use the properties of rectangles to deduce related facts and find missing lengths and angles
Year 6	Compare and classify geometric shapes based on their properties and sizes and find unknown angles in any triangles, quadrilaterals and regular polygons

9.11 Naming 2D and 3D shapes

A child refers to a ball as a 'Sophia' and a four-sided shape as a 'fourdrilateral'.

The error

The child has incorrectly named a sphere and a quadrilateral.

Why this happens

Children struggle to pronounce correctly some words and 'sphere' is commonly mispronounced. The child probably doesn't have difficulty pronouncing quadrilateral, but he may have forgotten the technical term and knows that the beginning relates to the number of sides so has made a sensible suggestion.

Curriculum links

EYFS	Explore characteristics of everyday objects and shapes and use mathematical language to describe them
Year 1	Recognise and name common 2-D and 3-D shapes, including: 2-D shapes [for example, rectangles (including squares), circles and triangles]
Year 1	Recognise and name common 2-D and 3-D shapes, including: 3-D shapes [for example, cuboids (including cubes), pyramids and spheres]

9.12 Naming parts of the circle

A child confuses the terms radius, diameter and circumference and says, 'The radius is twice the length of the diameter'.

The error

The child has confused the terms radius and diameter.

Why this happens

Primary-aged children do not tend to have the prior experience to make connections between geometric terms. Instead, this comes with repetition and experience. Therefore, a child who states 'the radius is twice the length of the diameter' should be given the opportunity to explain what they mean and this will offer the teacher the opportunity to see if the child is simply confused by the terms or if there is a deeper lack of understanding.

Curriculum links

Year 6	Illustrate and name parts of circles, including radius, diameter and circumference and know that the diameter is twice the radius

9.13 Mathematical patterns

The teacher starts a pattern (see grey shapes in Figure 9.12) and asks the child to continue it (see white shapes in Figure 9.12).

Figure 9.12

The error

The child has not continued the pattern.

Why this happens

Continuing a pattern can be difficult for young children, particularly when there are a number of variables such as shape and colour. Here, the child has used the correct shapes, but has not been able to reproduce the correct order. It may also be that because the teacher did not complete two full repeats of the pattern, the *child became confused.*

Curriculum links

EYFS	Recognise, create and describe patterns
Year 2	Order and arrange combinations of mathematical objects in patterns and sequences

9.14 Positional language

Figure 9.13

The error

The child uses the incorrect positional vocabulary to explain the position of the teddy.

Why this happens

Children come to school with a wide variation in their spoken language. This is usually dependent on how much talking about position they did prior to attending school, either at home or at nursery. A lack of specific vocabulary may not necessarily mean that a child does not understand an object's position. For example, a child with English as an additional language may already know positional words in their home language(s) but not yet fully understand the English equivalents. A child's inability to solve a geometrical problem can often be traced back to a lack of positional understanding.

Curriculum links

Year 2	Use mathematical vocabulary to describe position, direction and movement, including movement in a straight line and distinguishing between rotation as a turn and in terms of right angles for quarter, half and three-quarter turns (clockwise and anti-clockwise)

9.15 Plotting, reading and writing co-ordinates

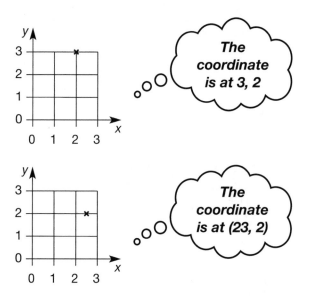

Figure 9.14

The error

The child states that the co-ordinate is at (y, x) rather than at (x, y) or the child finds it difficult to label a co-ordinate that is not at an intersection of two points.

Why this happens

The child does not understand the convention of labelling of co-ordinates according to (x-axis, y-axis). First children are expected to use co-ordinates to label spaces, for example in games like 'Battleships'. Often in this case they will use mixed notation, for example: D2. As the mathematics becomes more sophisticated, there is a need for children to move on to labelling points on lines for accuracy. This parallels children's development from a number track to a number line. A point that does not appear on an intersection requires the use and application of decimal and/or measurement (length) knowledge.

Curriculum links

Year 4	Describe positions on a 2-D grid as coordinates in the first quadrant
Year 4	Plot specified points and draw sides to complete a given polygon
Year 6	Describe positions on the full coordinate grid (all four quadrants)

9.16 Following directions: left and right, compass directions

The error

The child turns left instead of right.

Why this happens

'Left' and 'right' are only labels used to distinguish between two different directions and it is no wonder that children often confuse the two. It takes practice and reinforcement at home and school to perfect the difference. Sometimes, however, the confusion is more than just forgetting which is which. If two children are facing each other, then they will find their left and right hands are on the same side. This is the same when a child is looking in a mirror. It is challenging for children to give instructions to another child, a programmable robot, or Logo turtle, as the child has to put themselves in the other's shoes to ensure the correct command. Similar difficulties are faced by children when they begin to use compass directions: north, south, west, east, northeast, west northwest, and so on.

Curriculum links

| Year 1 | Describe position, direction and movement, including whole, half, quarter and three-quarter turns |
| Year 4 | Describe movements between positions as translations of a given unit to the left/right and up/down |

9.17 Lines of symmetry

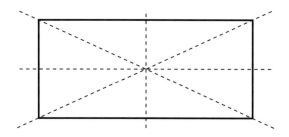

Figure 9.15

The error

The child identifies four lines of symmetry in an oblong.

Why this happens

Often when we discuss reflection with children, we use terms that include referring to 'half', such as *reflect this pattern into the other half or find the other half*. This leads children to assume that half of an object is the reflection of it, as in this case where the child has halved the oblong as many times as possible. In addition to this, the two right-angled triangles look similar visually and will in fact rotate around the centre of the oblong to fit onto each other. Identifying the diagonals as lines of symmetry also indicates a lack of understanding of the distance of the perpendicular from the line of symmetry to any point on the shape.

Curriculum links

Year 2	Identify and describe the properties of 2-D shapes, including the number of sides and line symmetry in a vertical line
Year 4	Identify lines of symmetry in 2-D shapes presented in different orientations
Year 4	Complete a simple symmetric figure with respect to a specific line of symmetry

9.18 Reflection

The following examples are illustrations of misconceptions in reflection.

Example 1: Reflection in a vertical or horizontal line

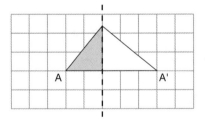

Figure 9.16

The error

The child inaccurately reflects point A.

Why this happens

The child may have simply made an error by miscalculating the distance from the line of symmetry to point A. Alternatively, this may demonstrate a misunderstanding of the need to maintain the length of the sides in the reflection or the need for the perpendicular distance between points and the line of symmetry to be equal.

Example 2: Reflection in a vertical or horizontal line at a distance

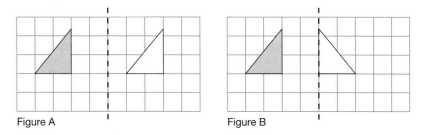

Figure A   Figure B

Figure 9.17

The error

The child inaccurately reflects the shape.

Why this happens

In Figure A, the child may have simply made an error by confusing reflection with translation or, alternatively, this may show a misunderstanding of how the shape changes orientation through reflection. Both figures may show a misunderstanding of how the perpendicular distance between points and the line of symmetry remains the same in a reflection.

Example 3: Reflection in a diagonal line of symmetry

The error

The child inaccurately reflects the shape in the line of symmetry (Figure 9.18).

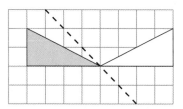

Figure 9.18

Why this happens

Children find reflecting in lines that are not horizontal or vertical a lot more difficult because of the dominant visual pictures they develop through the horizontal and vertical experience they have. These experiences allow children to count the number of squares across and up or down to identify the reflected points. In this example it is likely that the child has found it difficult to reflect in the diagonal, thus treating it as a vertical line of symmetry. It may also demonstrate that the child does not understand that each point in the reflected shape must have the same perpendicular distance from the line of symmetry.

Curriculum links

Year 4	Describe movements between positions as translations of a given unit to the left/right and up/down
Year 5	Identify, describe and represent the position of a shape following a reflection or translation, using the appropriate language, and know that the shape has not changed
Year 6	Draw and translate simple shapes on the co-ordinate plane, and reflect them in the axes

9.19 Order of rotation

The following examples illustrate misconceptions related to rotation.

Example 1: order of rotation of regular pentagons

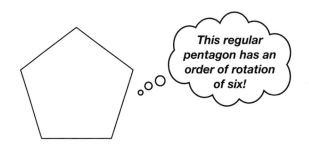

This regular pentagon has an order of rotation of six!

Figure 9.19

See Figure 9.19.

The error

The child believes they have identified the correct order of rotation because they have counted six rotations.

Why this happens

This is usually due to an incorrect counting technique. The child may have begun counting the first order of rotation before rotating it about the centre the first time, or they may have counted an extra rotation at the end as they forgot where they began the rotations. This is more common with regular shapes.

Example 2: rotation around a point

The error

See Figure 9.20. The child translates (Figure 9.20A) or reflects (Figure 9.20B) the tile rather than rotating it around the centre of rotation.

Why this happens

Children may apply the techniques they learned when studying translation or reflection earlier. They may also be confused between reflective and rotational symmetry. This could be due to the poor examples that they are asked to complete in class, as some patterns look the same after the initial tile has been reflected or rotated. (See, for example the tiles in example 3 below. These could have been produced by rotation or reflection.) If a child completes a task in this way, they are not demonstrating their knowledge of the need for all points on the tile to be the same distance from the centre of rotation and that the orientation of the tile changes.

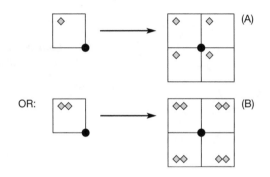

Figure 9.20

Example 3: rotation around a point at a distance

The error

The child does not leave the correct distance from the shape being rotated to the centre of rotation (Figure 9.21).

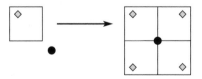

Figure 9.21

Why this happens

Along with reflecting a shape that is a distance from the line of symmetry, rotating around a centre of rotation that is not in contact with the shape is equally difficult for children. Errors often occur if children have not had a lot of experience with rotating shapes some distance from the centre of rotation.

Curriculum links

Year 4	Describe movements between positions as translations of a given unit to the left/right and up/down
Year 5	Identify, describe and represent the position of a shape following a reflection or translation, using the appropriate language, and know that the shape has not changed

9.20 Tessellation

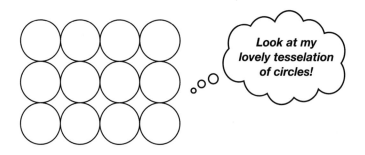

Figure 9.22

The error

The child believes they have tessellated the circles because they have created a repeating pattern.

Why this happens

Tessellation, mathematically speaking, only occurs when the vertices of the shape(s) fit together to meet at 360°. Children often focus on the repeating pattern rather than the properties of the angles where the shapes meet while tessellating shapes.

Curriculum links

Year 6	Draw and translate simple shapes on the co-ordinate plane, and reflect them in the axes

9.21 Right angles

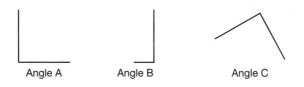

Angle A   Angle B   Angle C

Figure 9.23

The error

The child has identified that angle A is a right angle, but does not recognise angles B or C as right angles.

Why this happens

Children are often presented with prototypical examples of right angles. As a result, they do not recognise other orientations of the angle.

Curriculum links

Year 3	Recognise angles as a property of shape or a description of a turn
Year 3	Identify right angles, recognise that two right angles make a half-turn, three make three-quarters of a turn and four a complete turn; identify whether angles are greater than or less than a right angle
Year 4	Identify acute and obtuse angles and compare and order angles up to two right angles by size

9.22 Angle size dependent on bounding lines

The teacher asks the children which angle is bigger (Figure 9.24).

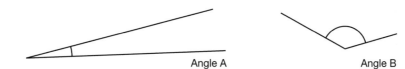

Angle A   Angle B

Figure 9.24

The error

The child states that angle A is larger than angle B.

Why this happens

Some children confuse the length of the lines bounding the angle of rotation with the size of the angle. This occurs if a child does not actually understand what the angle is measuring (i.e. the rotation of the lines). Often children are only presented with a static image of angles rather than a balance between those and the dynamic motion that angles can also portray.

Curriculum links

Year 4	Identify acute and obtuse angles and compare and order angles up to two right angles by size
Year 5	Know angles are measured in degrees: estimate and compare acute, obtuse and reflex angles
Year 5	Draw given angles, and measure them in degrees (°)
Year 6	Draw 2-D shapes using given dimensions and angles

9.23 Angle size dependent on distance of arc

The teacher asks the child which angle is bigger (Figure 9.25).

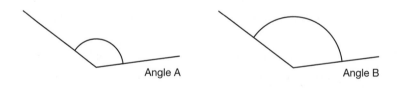

Angle A   Angle B

Figure 9.25

The error

The child states that angle A is smaller than angle B.

Why this happens

Some children confuse the length of the arc which identifies the angle with the size of the angle. This occurs if a child does not actually understand what the angle is measuring (i.e. the rotation of the lines). Often children are only presented with a static image of angles rather than a balance between those and the dynamic motion that angles can also portray. In this particular example, the angles are the same size; however, the visual impact of the arc has an impact on the child's perspective.

Curriculum links

Year 4	Identify acute and obtuse angles and compare and order angles up to two right angles by size
Year 5	Know angles are measured in degrees: estimate and compare acute, obtuse and reflex angles
Year 5	Draw given angles, and measure them in degrees (°)
Year 6	Draw 2-D shapes using given dimensions and angles

9.24 Reflex angles

The error

The child states that it is impossible to have an angle greater than 360° because 360° is the largest angle possible.

Why this happens

Children learn that there are 360 degrees in a circle and they are shown many examples of this in their shape and space work. They are also given many opportunities to measure and create angles that are smaller than 360°, so it is understandable that they make the assumption that it is not possible to find an angle larger than that. Given opportunities such as considering how many degrees the big hand of the clock has moved to rotate from one to one and then on to seven helps overcome this. There is also a need for children to see angles as dynamic measurements, rather than just static representations of a measurement.

Curriculum links

Year 5	Know angles are measured in degrees: estimate and compare acute, obtuse and reflex angles

9.25 Recognising angles

The child cannot state the size of angle abc (<abc) (Figure 9.26). He says there is not enough information to be sure.

The error

The child states she cannot find the size of <abc.

Why this happens

Sometimes teachers jump to these types of abstract questions too early without giving children enough practical experience to develop these geometric rules themselves. If so,

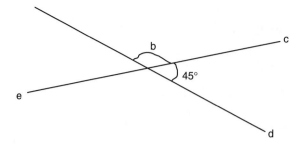

Figure 9.26

it can be difficult for some children to learn abstract rules (such as *angles on a line add up to 180°*). Alternatively, the child may have had sufficient experience finding angles on a line and now that there are angles around a point this has confused them.

Curriculum links

Year 5	Identify:
	• angles at a point and one whole turn (total 360°)
	• angles at a point on a straight line and $^1/_2$ a turn (total 180°)
	• other multiples of 90°
Year 6	Recognise angles where they meet at a point, are on a straight line, or are vertically opposite, and find missing angles

9.26 Errors when using a protractor

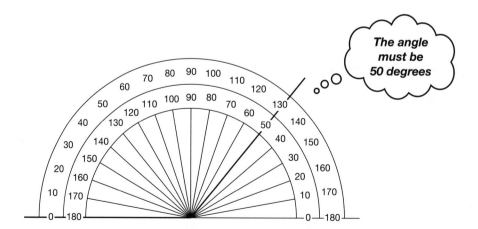

Figure 9.27

The error

The children provide many different answers.

Why this happens

1 When setting the protractor the children fail to line up the correct lines that make up the angle and so do not start from 0 degrees.

2 The children read the protractor scale but get confused with there being two different scales. They read the one going in the opposite direction to the one they need.

3 The children make errors when they identify the degrees between two known values.

Curriculum links

Year 5	Know angles are measured in degrees: estimate and compare acute, obtuse and reflex angles
Year 5	Draw given angles, and measure them in degrees (°)
Year 6	Draw 2-D shapes using given dimensions and angles

10 Statistics

Handling data presents the ideal opportunity to link mathematics to other areas of the curriculum and the real world. Children need to be introduced to the data-handling cycle – pose questions, collect data, represent data, interpret data – and wherever possible begin the cycle by raising questions that relate to a meaningful enquiry. As Nickson (2000, page 87) states, *It is this desire to use real data that motivates the students and makes the study of statistics important to the subject area.* This is supported by Williams and Easingwood (2004, page 117), who add that *Handling data is not simply making lists. It involves analysing the information and often extrapolating the results to reach definite and defined conclusions. This can only be done with real and relevant information however simple it might be.*

For example, in the upper Key Stage 2 science curriculum, children are expected to record *data and results of increasing complexity using scientific diagrams and labels, classification keys, tables, scatter graphs, bar and line graphs* (DfE, 2013, page 166).

In the Early Years Foundation Stage (DfE, 2012, page 6) practitioners are expected to provide children with opportunities to develop and improve their skills in counting, understanding and using numbers and calculating simple addition and subtraction problems, as well as describing shapes, spaces and measures. Early statistical foundations are taught through sorting, asking questions and finding answers. In Key Stage 1, children will interpret and construct simple pictograms, tally charts, block diagrams and simple tables and ask and answer simple questions by counting the number of objects in each category as well as sorting the categories by quantity. Children will also be expected to ask and answer questions about totalling and comparing categorical data.

During Key Stage 2 children continue to interpret data presented in many contexts, including discrete and continuous data. They will begin to decide which representations of data are most appropriate and why. Children will solve comparison, sum and difference problems using information presented in bar charts, pictograms, tables and other graphs. They will connect their work on co-ordinates and scales to their interpretation of time graphs, and calculate and interpret the mean as an average.

Posing questions

Few misconceptions explicitly related to posing questions have been identified by research. However, this section highlights that:

- posing questions is crucial to the data-handling process;
- it is difficult for children to pose appropriate questions;

- selecting inappropriate questions leads to errors and misconceptions within the data handling cycle.

Pepperel *et al.* (2009, page 114) stress that the cycle has various points which mark stages in the process. The first of these is a starting question. This needs to be of relevance and interest to the children. It may need to be framed so that it is clear what data it is appropriate to collect, although this is not always obvious. Many data-handling activities begin with either the teacher posing a question or the children being given data as part of an exercise from a book or worksheet. Ideally every data-handling exercise should begin with questions developed from children's interest and involvement.

> *The teacher's role so far has been to identify possible starting points and incorporate them into planning. She will need to consider the sort of questions which will provide rich starting points for children's learning. Such questions will not always be neat and focussed.*

> (Pepperel *et al.*, 2009, page 116)

However, as Back and Pumfrey (n.d.) warn:

> *{I}n schools we often undertake tasks in which we encourage children to collect data about themselves and their friends but the emphasis tends to be on presenting data in a variety of forms such as bar charts or pictograms. Analysis is often confined to identifying the most popular or least popular item. These limitations tend to restrict the interest and variety of the contexts that are explored, and fail to engage children in any significant mathematical thinking.*

These questions may well be related to work they are covering in other curriculum areas and the teacher might suggest an area or topic as a starting point. School councils can also generate interesting lines of enquiry linked with current school issues such as range of break-time activities. (Avoid sensitive issues such as pocket money that could lead to personal problems for some children.) Discussion will then be needed to make the question (or questions) suitably challenging and also practical within the school context. The type of question will determine how the data are collected, represented and analysed. According to Suggate *et al.* (2001, page 232):

> *There should be an established progression of the types of questions tackled throughout the school. In Key Stage 1 they will be fairly simple factual questions, such as the number of brothers and sisters.*

They go on to suggest that:

> *Later some relation between two measurements might be considered, such as the length of a person's hand-span and his height. More complicated questions about opinions and values might be suitable in Year 6.*

Collecting data

Once a question has been decided upon, the children will need to discuss how they are going to collect the data.

> *Using real data in examples for children to work with always used to be problematic.*
> *If numbers have to be manipulated without recourse to technology, then it is sensible to,*
> *first, keep the numbers simple, preferably whole and, secondly, to keep the number of*
> *examples to a minimum. ICT eliminates this problem.*

(Briggs and Pritchard, 2002, page 5)

The level of input from the teacher will depend on the age and ability of the children and also the intended learning outcomes. Children may learn a great deal from choosing a method that does not result in them being able to answer the question. They should be encouraged to think about why their method didn't work and about alternative methods they might have chosen. Mooney *et al.* (2000, page 105) assert that: *It may be necessary to ask questions about how data were collected in order to ascertain possible sources of error and the limitations of the data collection.* Other children may well become demotivated when they realise that they have spent a long time collecting data that they cannot organise in such a way that will allow for interpretation and hence give an answer to their question. Timely teacher intervention, through questioning, should resolve this.

> *The data which they will collect might be obvious in some cases, as in an*
> *enquiry centred on the question 'What is your favourite toy?', but less so*
> *in others. For example, if children want to investigate ways to improve the*
> *lost-property system in school, what will they need to find out? What kinds*
> *of information will help? In each case discussion will be necessary, to help*
> *children come up with ideas for themselves in the first instance.*

(Pepperel *et al.*, 2009, page 117)

Examples of appropriate questions that can help children's thinking can be found in the National Numeracy Strategy's *Mathematical Vocabulary* booklet (DfEE, 1994, pages 4–6).

Carpenter *et al.* (1993) found that young children use tally marks intuitively when solving problems. However, all too often in the excitement of recording, the accepted recording of tally marks is forgotten and leads to disorganised data that are more likely to cause errors in counting. Children will also need guidance on how to design an appropriate record sheet and record the most appropriate data in the most effective way.

With older children, questionnaires can be used to gather information, where a number of questions are asked relating to the main question. A lot of discussion and guidance will be needed here, together with a small pilot exercise, so that the children produce questions that are unambiguous and result in responses that can be interpreted productively. Thought needs to be given as to who will respond to questionnaires – if they only ask their friends then the sample will be biased. This may not raise any misconceptions related to the outcomes of the research, but needs to be recognised.

As far as possible, children should avoid 'copying out' raw data as this can lead to errors. Thought will also need to be given to what the children will record. Emergent readers and writers will need boxes to tick and labels may be drawn by the teacher rather than written. Older children may well benefit from working in mixed-ability groups.

Finally, thought needs to be given as to whether a 'free choice' is allowed and whether data need to be grouped. Restricting choice and grouping data lead to information being lost but does allow simpler, and in some cases, possible, interpretation. For example, considering the previous question, if children name the place they most enjoyed visiting, it would be possible to have as many different places as children. Grouping places, for example home town, home county, home country, Europe and other parts of the world, will lead to more manageable data.

Representing data

Graphs, pictures, tables and diagrams can be used to represent data in a mathematical way.

> *They can also present their findings to the other members of the class, perhaps using digital images in a Microsoft Powerpoint {display}along with the graphs. This is usually very striking and represents a powerful means for children to present the results of their mathematical investigations.*

> (Williams and Easingwood, 2004, page 5)

Graphs can be used to communicate information/data to a wide audience. This is a skill that needs to be used increasingly in our society which has broadening public accessibility to statistics (Ainley and Pratt, 2001). Care has to be taken to use an appropriate form of representation if its intended purpose is not to mislead or confuse. A similar view was expressed by Orton and Frobisher (2005, page 149), who stated that:

> *Often, data represented graphically are often easier to comprehend than if they were described in words or even tabulated. Sometimes, a graph might even enable us to perceive connections and relationships which are obscured by the quantity of numbers in the original data. In other words, graphs are an important means of communication, and we should obviously be aiming to enable children to communicate clearly, accurately and attractively through graphs.*

Mokros and Tinker's (2006) research reported a number of graph-related misconceptions. One of these was children looking at a graph as a picture, rather than as a source of information. It is important to keep in the children's sights the reason for the representation and for the interpretation of the data they collect. This will address some of the potential errors and misconceptions that arise through lack of purposeful understanding of their mathematics tasks.

Interpreting data/making deductions

In many classrooms the representation of data falls at the end of the data handling investigation with the initial question being left unanswered. Teachers need to remind children that they are only part way through the data-handling cycle.

The interpretation of data is critical, as stated earlier. For children to be motivated, data handling needs a purpose. Assuming the topic chosen for investigation has a purpose then it is necessary to answer any questions posed. Teachers need to allow time for this to happen and to scaffold their thinking. An extended plenary session might provide the ideal opportunity. The process is shown in Figure 10.1.

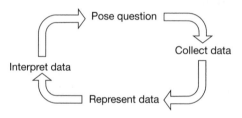

Figure 10.1

> *It may be even more meaningful for pupils, however, if the interpretive aspect is developed more, so that through discussion and collaboration, the subjective nature of pupils' interpretations will become more obvious. Misconceptions need to be identified before they can be put right and discussion can play a role in this.*

(Nickson, 2000, page 107)

With younger children a series of closed questions might be asked, for example, *Which type of rubbish did we collect most of?* With older children this may well lead to open questions such as, *Why do you think Year 5 threw away less paper than Year 4?* All children should be prompted to ask their own questions, both of their own data and of others. Not only will this support their mathematical understanding, it will also provide an opportunity for children to reveal (and for you to support/address) further misconceptions about handling data. Although the children may be able to answer the question they posed, it is likely that through discussion more questions will be raised. As Whitin and Whitin say, *by voicing her puzzlement aloud, the teacher demonstrated the importance of checking for reasonableness* (2003, page 147). In some cases, the question or data collection may have been inappropriate, or the graphs drawn misleading.

> *...teachers should give their students opportunities to revise graphs. Revising statistical information enables children to read beyond the data by posing new questions for the class to consider.*

(Couco, 2001, page 147)

In such cases discussion will arise as to what went wrong and how things could be done differently next time. Before they leave primary school, children need to begin to look critically at the data they have collected and consideration needs to be given as to the 'fairness' of their sample. They need to be asked whether the deductions they have made are reliable – a questionnaire full of biased questions is unlikely to lead to this. There is a need to apply intelligence and common sense to all interpretation of data; it is easy to 'jump to conclusions'. As Nickson (2000, page 93) says, *pupils may confuse conditionality and causality. There is a difference between the probability of having measles when a rash appears and the probability of having a rash because one has measles. Having a rash does not depend upon having measles. On the other hand, measles does cause having a rash.*

10.1 Children asking questions

After a class discussion on different types of toys, the teacher invites the children to suggest questions they might want to investigate. One child asks, *How many toys do I have?*

The error

The child poses a question that is inappropriate because once the toys have been counted the cycle will end, there is nothing to be interpreted.

Why this happens

Young children are *egocentrical thinkers* (Piaget, 1970). They find it difficult to consider situations beyond themselves and, as a result, may not understand how questions need to be considered from a perspective other than their own.

Curriculum links

Year 2	Ask and answer simple questions by counting the number of objects in each category and sorting the categories by quantity
Year 2	Ask and answer questions about totalling and comparing categorical data

10.2 Tally chart

Birds observed in the school grounds on 5 December.

Type of bird	Tally	Frequency (child)	Frequency (correct)
Blackbird	II	2	2
Robin	I	1	1
Sparrow	ЦНІ	5	6
Starling	ЦНІ ЦНІ	10	12

Figure 10.2

The error

The children make five vertical marks before making a diagonal mark on the sixth count. Children then count each group as a 'five'.

Why this happens

The children are familiar with the tally mark notation, but they do not realise that they should only make four vertical marks before making a diagonal mark on the fifth count.

Curriculum links

Year 2	Interpret and construct simple pictograms, tally charts, block diagrams and simple tables
Year 3	Solve one-step and two-step questions [for example, 'How many more?' and 'How many fewer?'] using information presented in scaled bar charts and pictograms and tables
Year 6	Complete, read and interpret information in tables, including timetables

10.3 A simple way of organising data

How children travel to school

The error

The children have used inconsistent unit sizes when representing the data in the block graph.

How children travel to school

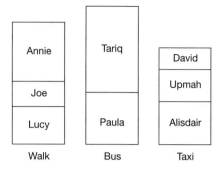

Figure 10.3

Why this happens

In handling data, we work to many conventions. In this example, the children lack awareness of the need to have units of consistent size. The issue of appropriate scales can be seen in other examples in measures in Chapter 6.

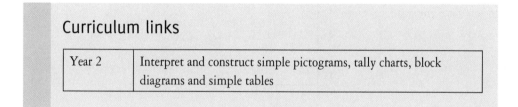

Curriculum links

Year 2	Interpret and construct simple pictograms, tally charts, block diagrams and simple tables

10.4 Block graphs

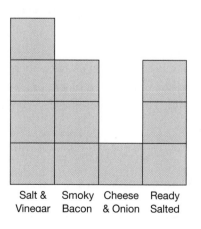

Figure 10.4 Favourite crisps

The error

The blocks do not have a gap between columns.

Why this happens

Children do not understand that for discrete data there is no 'connection' between data groups. This is also a common error seen when children draw bar charts. These are often shown incorrectly in textbooks and schemes, i.e. without gaps between the bars.

Curriculum links

Year 2	Interpret and construct simple pictograms, tally charts, block diagrams and simple tables

10.5 Bar charts: number track used on vertical axis

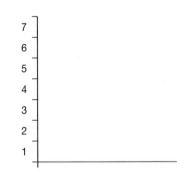

Figure 10.5

The error

The children have numbered the spaces on the vertical axis of a bar chart.

Why this happens

Children are familiar with number tracks and do not understand that a number line is required. Earlier representation of data used blocks or pictures where each item represented an individual child. This error becomes less common as they become more confident using number lines.

Curriculum links

Year 3	Interpret and present data using bar charts, pictograms and tables
Year 3	Solve one-step and two-step questions [for example, 'How many more?' and 'How many fewer?'] using information presented in scaled bar charts and pictograms and tables

Year 4	Interpret and present discrete and continuous data using appropriate graphical methods, including bar charts and time graphs
Year 5	Solve comparison, sum and difference problems using information presented in bar charts, pictograms, tables and other graphs

10.6 Bar charts: inconsistent scale used on vertical axis

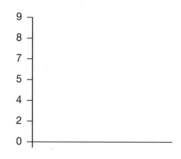

Figure 10.6

The error

The children have labelled the vertical axis using an inconsistent scale.

Why this happens

Children do not understand that once a scale has been decided upon, e.g. 1cm = 2, all of the axis must be labelled this way. They have chosen only to label the vertical axis with the values they have, 1cm representing different numbers of children.

Curriculum links

Year 3	Interpret and present data using bar charts, pictograms and tables
Year 3	Solve one-step and two-step questions [for example, 'How many more?' and 'How many fewer?'] using information presented in scaled bar charts and pictograms and tables
Year 4	Interpret and present discrete and continuous data using appropriate graphical methods, including bar charts and time graphs
Year 5	Solve comparison, sum and difference problems using information presented in bar charts, pictograms, tables and other graphs

10.7 Bar charts: inconsistent scale used on horizontal axis

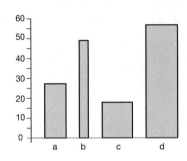

Figure 10.7

The error

The children have used different widths for their bars.

Why this happens

Children do not understand that by convention, we represent data in bar graphs using the same width.

Curriculum links

Year 3	Interpret and present data using bar charts, pictograms and tables
Year 3	Solve one-step and two-step questions {for example, 'How many more?' and 'How many fewer?'} using information presented in scaled bar charts and pictograms and tables
Year 4	Interpret and present discrete and continuous data using appropriate graphical methods, including bar charts and time graphs
Year 5	Solve comparison, sum and difference problems using information presented in bar charts, pictograms, tables and other graphs

10.8 Bar charts: incorrect labelling of axis

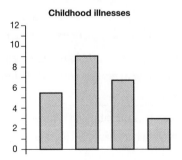

Figure 10.8

The error

The children have not labelled the items represented on the horizontal axis.

Why this happens

Children fail to understand the importance of labelling axes/graphs and in this case the graph cannot be interpreted by others. This shows a lack of awareness of an intended audience.

This error is not restricted to just the horizontal axis.

Curriculum links

Year 3	Interpret and present data using bar charts, pictograms and tables
Year 3	Solve one-step and two-step questions [for example, 'How many more?' and 'How many fewer?'] using information presented in scaled bar charts and pictograms and tables
Year 4	Interpret and present discrete and continuous data using appropriate graphical methods, including bar charts and time graphs
Year 5	Solve comparison, sum and difference problems using information presented in bar charts, pictograms, tables and other graphs

10.9 Bar charts: scale used on vertical axis does not begin at zero

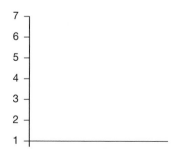

Figure 10.9

The error

Children have labelled the vertical axis starting at 'one'.

Why this happens

Children do not understand that the vertical scale should start at zero, not one. Because children start counting at one, they are confused when labelling the vertical axis. They need to be aware that the axis is a scale of measurement.

Curriculum links

Year 3	Interpret and present data using bar charts, pictograms and tables
Year 3	Solve one-step and two-step questions [for example, 'How many more?' and 'How many fewer?'] using information presented in scaled bar charts and pictograms and tables
Year 4	Interpret and present discrete and continuous data using appropriate graphical methods, including bar charts and time graphs
Year 5	Solve comparison, sum and difference problems using information presented in bar charts, pictograms, tables and other graphs

10.10 Bar charts

Crisps	No. of children
Salt & vinegar	12
Cheese & onion	7
Ready salted	3
Smoky bacon	5

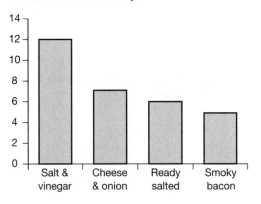

Favourite flavours of crisps

Figure 10.10

The error

Only three children chose ready salted as their favourite flavour of crisps; however, this is misrepresented in the graph as six children.

Why this happens

Children count the number of lines or squares and ignore the scale.

Curriculum links

Year 3	Interpret and present data using bar charts, pictograms and tables
Year 3	Solve one-step and two-step questions [for example, 'How many more?' and 'How many fewer?'] using information presented in scaled bar charts and pictograms and tables
Year 4	Interpret and present discrete and continuous data using appropriate graphical methods, including bar charts and time graphs
Year 5	Solve comparison, sum and difference problems using information presented in bar charts, pictograms, tables and other graphs

10.11 Scatter graph: same scale on both axes

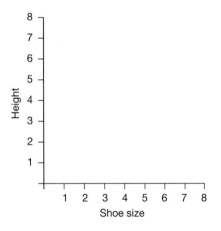

Figure 10.11

The error

An inappropriate scale is used on the vertical axis.

Why this happens

The children incorrectly believe that by convention, they must use the same scale on both axes. The children may have also decided to use a scale of 10cm, but omitted this detail when labelling the *y*-axis increments.

10.12 Misuse of line graphs for discrete data

Shoe size	Y4 frequency	Y5 frequency
2	1	0
3	4	1
4	5	3
5	7	6
6	8	10
7	4	5
8	0	2
9	0	1

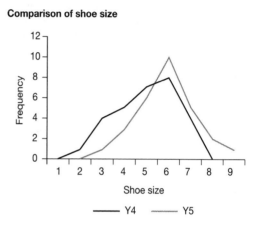

Figure 10.12

The error

The children have represented discrete data as line graphs. They have confused shoe size (3, 3½, etc.), which is a discrete variable, with the measurement of foot length, a continuous variable.

Why this happens

The chart functions associated with computer spreadsheets allow the user to draw graphs regardless of suitability. In this case discrete data have been represented in a form only appropriate for continuous data.

10.13 Inappropriate representation using pie charts

How many children play these sports?

Sport	No. of children
Football	16
Netball	12
Swimming	27
Tennis	5
Gymnastics	8
Golf	3
Rugby	4
Total:	75

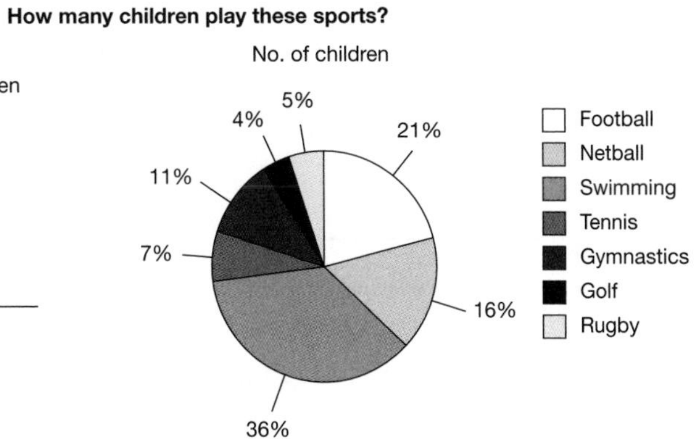

No. of children

Figure 10.13

The error

The children have inappropriately represented the data in a pie chart.

Why this happens

Children in the class are included more than once, or not at all. A *chart wizard* enables the user to create a variety of charts, some of which may not be appropriate and actually lead to misconceptions.

Curriculum links

Year 5	Solve comparison, sum and difference problems using information presented in bar charts, pictograms, tables and other graphs
Year 6	Interpret and construct pie charts and line graphs and use these to solve problems

10.14 Comparison of pie charts

The error

The children say that more people live in three-bedroom houses in Penrith than Carlisle.

Why this happens

Children can see that the sector for three-bedroom houses is larger for Penrith than Carlisle. They interpret this as meaning that there are therefore more three-bedroom houses in Penrith. They do not understand that the sector represents a percentage of the total number of houses.

Number of bedrooms, Penrith	Frequency	Number of bedrooms, Carlisle	Frequency
1	5	1	13
2	8	2	22
3	30	3	45
4	17	4	53
5	4	5	16
6	1	6	8
7	2	7	5
	—		—
	67		162

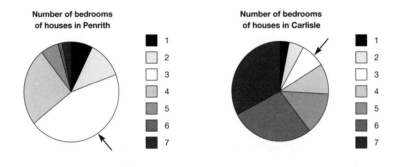

Figure 10.14

Curriculum links

Year 5	Solve comparison, sum and difference problems using information presented in bar charts, pictograms, tables and other graphs
Year 6	interpret and construct pie charts and line graphs and use these to solve problems

10.15 Venn diagrams: the intersection

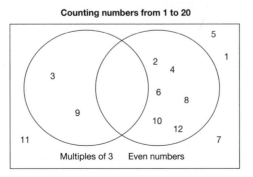

Figure 10.15

The error

The children have not placed 6 and 12 within the intersection of the Venn diagram.

Why this happens

Children do not understand that the intersection of the two sets contains those items of data that fulfil the criteria for both sets.

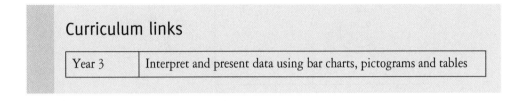

Curriculum links

Year 3	Interpret and present data using bar charts, pictograms and tables

10.16 Venn diagrams: the universal set

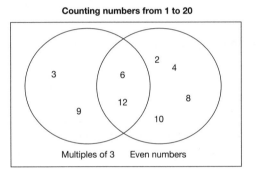

Figure 10.16

The error

The children have omitted 1, 5, 7, 11 from the Venn diagram.

Why this happens

Children do not understand that numbers that are not members of either of the two sets need to be placed within the universal set.

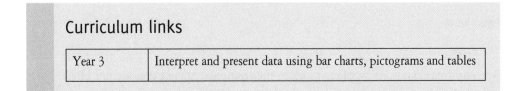

Curriculum links

Year 3	Interpret and present data using bar charts, pictograms and tables

10.17 First-stage binary sorting: Carroll diagram

Figure 10.17

The error

The children do not know where to place the shapes that are sun, moon or wheel.

Why this happens

Children do not understand *negation*, that sun/moon/wheel are 'not face'.

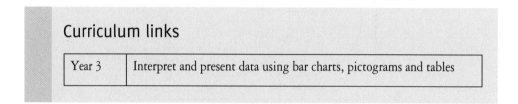

Curriculum links

Year 3	Interpret and present data using bar charts, pictograms and tables

10.18 Second-stage binary sorting: Carroll diagram

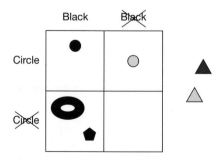

Figure 10.18

The error

The children do not know where to place the triangular shapes that are not black.

Why this happens

The children may not have understood the notion of *negation*, that the other colours are 'not black' and a triangle is 'not a circle'.

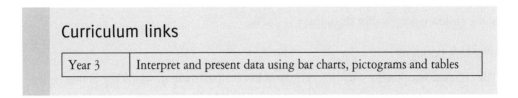

Curriculum links

Year 3	Interpret and present data using bar charts, pictograms and tables

10.19 Correlation

The children investigate scores in spelling tests within their class. A child produces the graph shown in Figure 10.19.

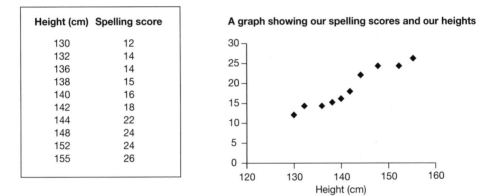

Height (cm)	Spelling score
130	12
132	14
136	14
138	15
140	16
142	18
144	22
148	24
152	24
155	26

A graph showing our spelling scores and our heights

Figure 10.19

The error

The children say that tall children do better in spelling tests.

Why this happens

The children have concluded that since the majority of high marks scored in spelling tests are gained by children who are taller, then there must be a relationship between two variables. Those children who score highly in spelling tests may be taller than average or vice versa but one variable does not necessarily cause the other.

Curriculum links

Year 4	Solve comparison, sum and difference problems using information presented in bar charts, pictograms, tables and other graphs

10.20 Measure of average: mean

Children are asked to calculate the mean of the following numbers: 5, 6, 7, 2, 7, 9.

The error

Some children accept that the answer is 28.5.

Why this happens

The children have used a scientific calculator to calculate their answer. They do not realise that a scientific calculator uses algebraic logic (BODMAS) and therefore will divide the last number, 9, by the number of items in the sample, 6, before adding the remaining numbers. They also do not understand that the mean must lie within the range of values given. They have not checked that the *solution is reasonable in the context of the problem* (DfEE, 1999b, page 73) and have merely followed the rule to calculate the mean.

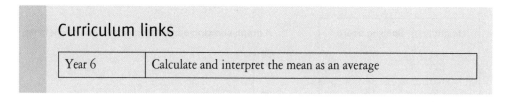

Curriculum links

Year 6	Calculate and interpret the mean as an average

10.21 Measure of average: median

Children are asked to calculate the median of the following heights: 134cm, 156cm, 133cm, 142cm, 147cm.

The error

Some children say that the answer is 133cm.

Why this happens

The children have remembered that in order to find the median of a set of data they must select the middle value. They have not understood the importance of putting the values in numerical order first. They have not considered whether or not their solution is reasonable.

Curriculum links

Year 6	Calculate and interpret the mean as an average

10.22 Measure of average: mode and mean

Children are asked to calculate the mode of the following shoe sizes: 5, 6, 7, 4, 7, 9, 7, 4, 5.

The error

Some children say that the answer is 6.

Why this happens

The children have confused mode and mean, finding the sum of all the values and dividing the answer by nine rather than looking for the most frequently occurring value.

> ## Curriculum links
>
> | Year 6 | Calculate and interpret the mean as an average |
> | --- | --- |

10.23 Measure of average: mode

Children are asked to calculate the mode of the following shoe sizes: 5, 6, 7, 2, 7, 9, 7, 4, 5.

The error

Some children say that the answer is 3.

Why this happens

The children have realised that there are more size 7s than any other size and that there are three of them. This has formed the basis for their answer. They have not understood that the mode is always one of the values of the variable and is used to represent all the data.

> ## Curriculum links
>
> | Year 6 | Calculate and interpret the mean as an average |
> | --- | --- |

10.24 Measure of spread: range

Children are asked to find the range of the following numbers: 5, 6, 7, 2, 7, 9.

The error

Some children say that the answer is 2 to 9.

Why this happens

The children have used their own understanding of the word 'range' (and applied it correctly) rather than applying the mathematical term, i.e. $9 - 2 = 7$.

> ## Curriculum links
>
> | Year 6 | Calculate and interpret the mean as an average |
> | --- | --- |

Appendix: curriculum objectives

This Appendix provides a list of objectives that are related to the errors found in Chapters 3–10. You will find objectives from the Statutory Framework for the Early Years Foundation Stage and National Curriculum in England objectives (pages 204–15). The objectives from the 2006 Revised Primary Framework for Mathematics that existed in the 2nd edition have been removed from this edition due to significant changes in the curriculum. The referencing uses a numerical code, x.y, where x is the chapter, and y is the number of the error in the chapter.

STATUTORY FRAMEWORK FOR THE EARLY YEARS FOUNDATION STAGE (March 2012)	POSSIBLE ERRORS
Numbers	
Children count reliably with numbers from 1 to 20, place them in order and say which number is one more or one less than a given number.	3.1; 3.2; 3.3; 3.4
They solve problems, including doubling, halving and sharing.	6.1; 6.2
Using quantities and objects, they add and subtract two single-digit numbers and count on or back to find the answer.	4.1; 4.5
Shape, space and measures	
Children use everyday language to talk about size, weight, capacity, position, distance, time and money to compare quantities and objects and to solve problems.	8.1; 8.3; 8.4; 8.5; 8.6; 8.7; 8.23; 8.24
They recognise, create and describe patterns.	9.13
They explore characteristics of everyday objects and shapes and use mathematical language to describe them.	9.1; 9.11

NATIONAL CURRICULUM OBJECTIVES	POSSIBLE ERRORS
KEY STAGE 1	
YEAR 1	
Number: number and place value	
Count to and across 100, forwards and backwards, beginning with 0 or 1, or from any given number	3.1; 3.2; 3.5; 3.6; 3.10
Count, read and write numbers to 100 in numerals; count in multiples of twos, fives and tens	3.1; 3.2; 3.4; 3.7; 3.8; 3.9; 3.10; 3.11; 3.12; 3.13; 3.16
Given a number, identify one more and one less	3.15
Identify and represent numbers using objects and pictorial representations including the number line, and use the language of: equal to, more than, less than (fewer), most, least	3.1; 3.2; 3.3; 3.15; 3.18; 3.19
Read and write numbers from 1 to 20 in numerals and words	3.4; 3.7; 3.9; 3.10; 3.11
Number: addition and subtraction	
Read, write and interpret mathematical statements involving addition (+), subtraction (−) and equals (=) signs	4.2
Represent and use number bonds and related subtraction facts within 20	4.3
Add and subtract one-digit and two-digit numbers to 20, including zero	4.5; 4.8
Solve one-step problems that involve addition and subtraction, using concrete objects and pictorial representations, and missing number problems such as $7 = \square - 9$	4.1; 4.7
Number: multiplication and division	
Solve one-step problems involving multiplication and division, by calculating the answer using concrete objects, pictorial representations and arrays with the support of the teacher	5.1; 5.2
Number: fractions	
Recognise, find and name a half as one of two equal parts of an object, shape or quantity	6.1; 6.2; 6.8
Recognise, find and name a quarter as one of four equal parts of an object, shape or quantity	6.1; 6.2; 6.8
Measurement	
Compare, describe and solve practical problems for: lengths and heights [for example, long/short, longer/shorter, tall/short, double/half]	8.1; 8.6; 8.7
Compare, describe and solve practical problems for: mass/weight [for example, heavy/light, heavier than, lighter than]	8.3; 8.5; 8.6; 8.7
Compare, describe and solve practical problems for: capacity and volume [for example, full/empty, more than, less than, half, half full, quarter]	8.4; 8.6; 8.7
Compare, describe and solve practical problems for: time [for example, quicker, slower, earlier, later]	8.20
Measure and begin to record the following: lengths and heights	8.8; 8.9
Measure and begin to record the following: mass/weight	8.14
Measure and begin to record the following: capacity and volume	8.15
Measure and begin to record the following: time (hours, minutes, seconds)	8.20
Recognise and know the value of different denominations of coins and notes	8.23; 8.24

NATIONAL CURRICULUM OBJECTIVES	POSSIBLE ERRORS
Sequence events in chronological order using language [for example, before and after, next, first, today, yesterday, tomorrow, morning, afternoon and evening]	8.16
Recognise and use language relating to dates, including days of the week, weeks, months and years	8.17
Tell the time to the hour and half past the hour and draw the hands on a clock face to show these times.	8.18
Geometry: properties of shapes	
Recognise and name common 2-D and 3-D shapes, including: 2-D shapes [for example, rectangles (including squares), circles and triangles]	9.6; 9.8; 9.11
Recognise and name common 2-D and 3-D shapes, including: 3-D shapes [for example, cuboids (including cubes), pyramids and spheres]	9.2; 9.3; 9.11
Geometry: position and direction	
Describe position, direction and movement, including whole, half, quarter and three-quarter turns.	9.16
YEAR 2	
Number: number and the place-value system	
Count in steps of 2, 3 and 5 from 0, and in tens from any number, forward and backward	3.5; 3.12; 3.13; 3.16
Recognise the place value of each digit in a two-digit number (tens, ones)	3.4; 3.7; 3.8
Identify, represent and estimate numbers using different representations, including the number line	3.6; 3.18; 3.19
Compare and order numbers from 0 up to 100; use <, > and = signs	3.6
Read and write numbers to at least 100 in numerals and in words	3.7; 3.9; 3.10; 3.11
Use place value and number facts to solve problems.	3.8
Number: addition and subtraction	
Solve problems with addition and subtraction: • using concrete objects and pictorial representations, including those involving numbers, quantities and measures • applying their increasing knowledge of mental and written methods	4.8
Recall and use addition and subtraction facts to 20 fluently, and derive and use related facts up to 100	4.2; 4.3; 4.5
Add and subtract numbers using concrete objects, pictorial representations, and mentally, including: • a two-digit number and ones • a two-digit number and tens • two two-digit numbers • adding three one-digit numbers	4.1; 4.6; 4.8
Show that addition of two numbers can be done in any order (commutative) and subtraction of one number from another cannot	4.7
Recognise and use the inverse relationship between addition and subtraction and use this to check calculations and solve missing number problems	4.3; 4.4
Number: multiplication and division	
Recall and use multiplication and division facts for the 2, 5 and 10 multiplication tables, including recognising odd and even numbers	5.4; 5.6

NATIONAL CURRICULUM OBJECTIVES	POSSIBLE ERRORS
Calculate mathematical statements for multiplication and division within the multiplication tables and write them using the multiplication (×), division (÷) and equals (=) signs	5.4
Show that multiplication of two numbers can be done in any order (commutative) and division of one number by another cannot	5.4
Solve problems involving multiplication and division, using materials, arrays, repeated addition, mental methods, and multiplication and division facts, including problems in contexts	5.1; 5.2
Number: fractions	
Recognise, find, name and write fractions $^1/_3$, $^1/_4$, $^2/_4$ and $^3/_4$ of a length, shape, set of objects or quantity	6.1; 6.2; 6.8; 6.9
Write simple fractions for example, $^1/_2$ of 6 = 3 and recognise the equivalence of $^2/_4$ and $^1/_2$	6.5; 6.6; 6.7; 6.13; 6.14; 6.15
Measurement	
Choose and use appropriate standard units to estimate and measure length/height in any direction (m/cm); mass (kg/g); temperature (°C); capacity (litres/ml) to the nearest appropriate unit, using rulers, scales, thermometers and measuring vessels	8.8; 8.9; 8.14; 8.15
Compare and order lengths, mass, volume/capacity and record the results using >, < and =	8.6
Recognise and use symbols for pounds (£) and pence (p); combine amounts to make a particular value	8.25
Find different combinations of coins that equal the same amounts of money	8.25
Solve simple problems in a practical context involving addition and subtraction of money of the same unit, including giving change	8.26
Compare and sequence intervals of time	8.20
Tell and write the time to five minutes, including quarter past/to the hour and draw the hands on a clock face to show these times	8.18
Know the number of minutes in an hour and the number of hours in a day	8.21
Geometry: properties of shapes	
Identify and describe the properties of 2-D shapes, including the number of sides and line symmetry in a vertical line	9.8; 9.16
Identify and describe the properties of 3-D shapes, including the number of edges, vertices and faces	9.1; 9.2; 9.3
Identify 2-D shapes on the surface of 3-D shapes [for example, a circle on a cylinder and a triangle on a pyramid]	9.4; 9.5
Compare and sort common 2-D and 3-D shapes and everyday objects	9.6
Geometry: position and direction	
Order and arrange combinations of mathematical objects in patterns and sequences	9.13
Use mathematical vocabulary to describe position, direction and movement, including movement in a straight line and distinguishing between rotation as a turn and in terms of right angles for quarter, half and three-quarter turns (clockwise and anti-clockwise)	9.14
Statistics	
Interpret and construct simple pictograms, tally charts, block diagrams and simple tables	10.2; 10.3; 10.4

NATIONAL CURRICULUM OBJECTIVES	POSSIBLE ERRORS
Ask and answer simple questions by counting the number of objects in each category and sorting the categories by quantity	10.1
Ask and answer questions about totalling and comparing categorical data	10.1

LOWER KEY STAGE 2	
YEAR 3	
Number: number and place value	
Count from o in multiples of 4, 8, 50 and 100; find 10 or 100 more or less than a given number	3.12; 3.13
Recognise the place value of each digit in a three-digit number (hundreds, tens, ones)	3.4; 3.7; 3.8
Compare and order numbers up to 1000	3.7
Identify, represent and estimate numbers using different representations	3.5; 3.6; 3.18; 3.19
Read and write numbers up to 1000 in numerals and in words	3.7; 3.9; 3.10; 3.11; 3.12
Solve number problems and practical problems involving these ideas	All of the above
Number: addition and subtraction	
Add and subtract numbers mentally, including: • a three-digit number and ones • a three-digit number and tens • a three-digit number and hundreds	4.6; 4.8; 4.11
Add and subtract numbers with up to three digits, using formal written methods of columnar addition and subtraction	4.9; 4.10; 4.12;
Estimate the answer to a calculation and use inverse operations to check answers	4.13
Solve problems, including missing number problems, using number facts, place value, and more complex addition and subtraction.	4.4; 4.7; 4.9; 4.10; 4.11; 4.13; 4.14
Number: multiplication and division	
Recall and use multiplication and division facts for the 3, 4 and 8 multiplication tables	5.4
Write and calculate mathematical statements for multiplication and division using the multiplication tables that they know, including for two-digit numbers times one-digit numbers, using mental and progressing to formal written methods	5.3; 5.11
Solve problems, including missing number problems, involving multiplication and division, including positive integer scaling problems and correspondence problems in which n objects are connected to m objects.	5.5; 5.17
Number: fractions	
Count up and down in tenths; recognise that tenths arise from dividing an object into 10 equal parts and in dividing one-digit numbers or quantities by 10	6.18; 6.19
Recognise, find and write fractions of a discrete set of objects: unit fractions and non-unit fractions with small denominators	6.2
Recognise and use fractions as numbers: unit fractions and non-unit fractions with small denominators	6.3
Recognise and show, using diagrams, equivalent fractions with small denominators	6.13; 6.14; 6.15

LOWER KEY STAGE 2	
Add and subtract fractions with the same denominator within one whole [for example, $5/_7 + 1/_7 = 6/_7$]	6.20
Compare and order unit fractions, and fractions with the same denominators	6.10; 6.11
Solve problems that involve all of the above	All of the above
Measurement	
Measure, compare, add and subtract: lengths (m/cm/mm); mass (kg/g); volume/ capacity (l/ml)	8.8; 8.9; 8.14; 8.15
Measure the perimeter of simple 2-D shapes	8.9; 8.11
Add and subtract amounts of money to give change, using both £ and p in practical contexts	8.25
Tell and write the time from an analogue clock, including using Roman numerals from I to XII, and 12-hour and 24-hour clocks	8.18; 8.19
Estimate and read time with increasing accuracy to the nearest minute; record and compare time in terms of seconds, minutes and hours; use vocabulary such as o'clock, a.m./p.m., morning, afternoon, noon and midnight	8.18; 8.19; 8.21
Know the number of seconds in a minute and the number of days in each month, year and leap year	8.22
Compare durations of events [for example to calculate the time taken by particular events or tasks]	8.20
Geometry: properties of shapes	
Draw 2-D shapes and make 3-D shapes using modelling materials; recognise 3-D shapes in different orientations and describe them	9.4; 9.6
Recognise angles as a property of shape or a description of a turn	9.21
Identify right angles, recognise that two right angles make a half-turn, three make three-quarters of a turn and four a complete turn; identify whether angles are greater than or less than a right angle	9.21
Identify horizontal and vertical lines and pairs of perpendicular and parallel lines	9.9
Statistics	
Interpret and present data using bar charts, pictograms and tables	10.5; 10.6; 10.7; 10.8; 10.9; 10.10; 10.15; 10.16; 10.17; 10.18
Solve one-step and two-step questions [for example, 'How many more?' and 'How many fewer?'] using information presented in scaled bar charts and pictograms and tables	10.2; 10.5; 10.6; 10.7; 10.8; 10.9; 10.10
YEAR 4	
Number: number and place value	
Count in multiples of 6, 7, 9, 25 and 1000	3.12; 3.13
Find 1000 more or less than a given number	3.14
Count backwards through zero to include negative numbers	3.5; 3.6; 3.17
Recognise the place value of each digit in a four-digit number (thousands, hundreds, tens and ones)	3.4; 3.8
Order and compare numbers beyond 1000	3.9
Identify, represent and estimate numbers using different representations	3.5; 3.18; 3.19
Round any number to the nearest 10, 100 or 1000	3.20

LOWER KEY STAGE 2	
Solve number and practical problems that involve all of the above and with increasingly large positive numbers	All of the above
Read Roman numerals to 100 (I to C) and know that, over time, the numeral system changed to include the concept of zero and place value	3.8; 3.21
Number: addition and subtraction	
Add and subtract numbers with up to 4 digits using the formal written methods of columnar addition and subtraction where appropriate	4.9; 4.10; 4.11; 4.12
Estimate and use inverse operations to check answers to a calculation	4.3; 4.7; 4.13
Solve addition and subtraction two-step problems in contexts, deciding which operations and methods to use and why.	4.14
Number: multiplication and division	
Recall multiplication and division facts for multiplication tables up to 12	5.4
Use place value, known and derived facts to multiply and divide mentally, including: multiplying by 0 and 1; dividing by 1; multiplying together three numbers	5.6; 5.9
Recognise and use factor pairs and commutativity in mental calculations	5.10
Multiply two-digit and three-digit numbers by a one-digit number using formal written layout	5.11; 5.12; 5.13
Solve problems involving multiplying and adding, including using the distributive law to multiply two digit numbers by one digit, integer scaling problems and harder correspondence problems such as n objects are connected to m objects	5.5; 5.14; 5.17
Number: fractions (including decimals)	
Recognise and show, using diagrams, families of common equivalent fractions	6.13; 6.15
Count up and down in hundredths; recognise that hundredths arise when dividing an object by one hundred and dividing tenths by ten	6.18; 6.19
Solve problems involving increasingly harder fractions to calculate quantities, and fractions to divide quantities, including non-unit fractions where the answer is a whole number	6.17
Add and subtract fractions with the same denominator	6.20
Recognise and write decimal equivalents of any number of tenths or hundredths	6.18; 6.19
Recognise and write decimal equivalents to $\frac{1}{4}, \frac{1}{2}, \frac{3}{4}$	6.16
Find the effect of dividing a one- or two-digit number by 10 and 100, identifying the value of the digits in the answer as ones, tenths and hundredths	6.18; 6.19
Round decimals with one decimal place to the nearest whole number	6.27
Compare numbers with the same number of decimal places up to two decimal places	6.26
Solve simple measure and money problems involving fractions and decimals to two decimal places.	6.28
Measurement	
Convert between different units of measure [for example, kilometre to metre; hour to minute]	8.28; 8.29
Measure and calculate the perimeter of a rectilinear figure (including squares) in centimetres and metres	8.9; 8.11
Find the area of rectilinear shapes by counting squares	8.2; 8.10; 8.11

LOWER KEY STAGE 2	
Estimate, compare and calculate different measures, including money in pounds and pence	8.1; 8.3; 8.4; 8.5; 8.6; 8.7; 8.8; 8.9; 8.14; 8.15; 8.23; 8.24; 8.25; 8.26; 8.27
Geometry: properties of shape	
Compare and classify geometric shapes, including quadrilaterals and triangles, based on their properties and sizes	9.6; 9.8; 9.9; 9.10
Identify acute and obtuse angles and compare and order angles up to two right angles by size	9.21; 9.22; 9.22
Identify lines of symmetry in 2-D shapes presented in different orientations	9.17
Complete a simple symmetric figure with respect to a specific line of symmetry	9.17
Geometry: position and direction	
Describe positions on a 2-D grid as co-ordinates in the first quadrant	9.15
Describe movements between positions as translations of a given unit to the left/right and up/down	9.16; 9.18; 9.19
Plot specified points and draw sides to complete a given polygon	9.15
Statistics	
Interpret and present discrete and continuous data using appropriate graphical methods, including bar charts and time graphs	10.5; 10.6; 10.7; 10.8; 10.9; 10.10; 10.12
Solve comparison, sum and difference problems using information presented in bar charts, pictograms, tables and other graphs	10.5; 10.6; 10.7; 10.8; 10.9; 10.10; 10.11; 10.13; 10.14; 10.19

UPPER KEY STAGE 2	
Year 5	
Number: number and place value	
Read, write, order and compare numbers to at least 1 000 000 and determine the value of each digit	3.4; 3.7; 3.8
Count forwards or backwards in steps of powers of 10 for any given number up to 1 000 000	3.14
Interpret negative numbers in context, count forwards and backwards with positive and negative whole numbers, including through zero	3.5; 3.6; 3.17
Round any number up to 1 000 000 to the nearest 10, 100, 1000, 10 000 and 100 000	3.20
Solve number problems and practical problems that involve all of the above	All of the above
Read Roman numerals to 1000 (M) and recognise years written in Roman numerals	3.21
Number: addition and subtraction	
Add and subtract whole numbers with more than 4 digits, including using formal written methods (columnar addition and subtraction)	4.9; 4.10; 4.11; 4.12
Add and subtract numbers mentally with increasingly large numbers	4.9
Use rounding to check answers to calculations and determine, in the context of a problem, levels of accuracy	4.13
Solve addition and subtraction multi-step problems in contexts, deciding which operations and methods to use and why	4.14

UPPER KEY STAGE 2	
Number: multiplication and division	
Identify multiples and factors, including finding all factor pairs of a number, and common factors of two numbers	5.10
Know and use the vocabulary of prime numbers, prime factors and composite (non-prime) numbers	5.10
Establish whether a number up to 100 is prime and recall prime numbers up to 19	5.10
Multiply numbers up to 4 digits by a one- or two-digit number using a formal written method, including long multiplication for two-digit numbers	5.11; 5.12; 5.13
Multiply and divide numbers mentally drawing upon known facts	5.6; 5.7; 5.8
Divide numbers up to 4 digits by a one-digit number using the formal written method of short division and interpret remainders appropriately for the context	5.15
Multiply and divide whole numbers and those involving decimals by 10, 100 and 1000 and use square numbers and cube numbers, and the notation for squared (^{2}) and cubed (^{3})	5.6; 5.7; 5.8
Number: multiplication and division	
Identify multiples and factors, including finding all factor pairs of a number, and common factors of two numbers	5.10
Know and use the vocabulary of prime numbers, prime factors and composite (non-prime) numbers	5.10
Establish whether a number up to 100 is prime and recall prime numbers up to 19	5.10
Multiply numbers up to 4 digits by a one- or two-digit number using a formal written method, including long multiplication for two-digit numbers	5.11; 5.12; 5.13
Multiply and divide numbers mentally drawing upon known facts	5.4; 5.9
Divide numbers up to 4 digits by a one-digit number using the formal written method of short division and interpret remainders appropriately for the context	5.13
Multiply and divide whole numbers and those involving decimals by 10, 100 and 1000; recognise and use square numbers and cube numbers, and the notation for squared (^{2}) and cubed (^{3})	5.6; 5.7; 5.8
Solve problems involving multiplication and division including using their knowledge of factors and multiples, squares and cubes	5.10
Solve problems involving addition, subtraction, multiplication and division and a combination of these, including understanding the meaning of the equals sign	5.14; 5.15; 5.18
Solve problems involving multiplication and division, including scaling by simple fractions and problems involving simple rates	5.19
Number: fractions (including decimals and percentages)	
Compare and order fractions whose denominators are all multiples of the same number	6.10; 6.11
Identify, name and write equivalent fractions of a given fraction, represented visually, including tenths and hundredths	6.13; 6.14; 6.15
Recognise mixed numbers and improper fractions and convert from one form to the other and write mathematical statements > 1 as a mixed number [for example, $^2/_5 + ^4/_5 = ^6/_5 = 1\,^1/_5$]	6.12
Add and subtract fractions with the same denominator and denominators that are multiples of the same number	6.20; 6.21
Multiply proper fractions and mixed numbers by whole numbers, supported by materials and diagrams	6.22; 6.23

UPPER KEY STAGE 2	
Read and write decimal numbers as fractions [for example, 0.71 = $^{71}/_{100}$]	6.16; 6.17; 6.18; 6.19
Recognise and use thousandths and relate them to tenths, hundredths and decimal equivalents	6.19
Round decimals with two decimal places to the nearest whole number and to one decimal place	6.27
Read, write, order and compare numbers with up to three decimal places	6.25; 6.26
Solve problems involving number up to three decimal places	6.25; 6.28; 6.29
Recognise the per cent symbol (%) and understand that per cent relates to 'number of parts per hundred', and write percentages as a fraction with denominator 100, and as a decimal	6.32; 6.33
Solve problems which require knowing percentage and decimal equivalents of $^1/_2$, $^1/_4$, $^1/_5$, $^2/_5$, $^4/_5$ and those fractions with a denominator of a multiple of 10 or 25	6.32; 6.33
Measurement	
Convert between different units of metric measure (for example, kilometre and metre; centimetre and metre; centimetre and millimetre; gram and kilogram; litre and millilitre)	8.28; 8.29
Understand and use approximate equivalences between metric units and common imperial units such as inches, pounds and pints	8.30
Measure and calculate the perimeter of composite rectilinear shapes in centimetres and metres	8.9; 8.11
Calculate and compare the area of rectangles (including squares), including using standard units, square centimetres (cm²) and square metres (m²), and estimate the area of irregular shapes	8.2
Estimate volume [for example, using 1 cm³ blocks to build cuboids (including cubes)] and capacity [for example, using water]	8.5
Solve problems involving converting between units of time	8.21
Use all four operations to solve problems involving measure [for example, length, mass, volume, money] using decimal notation, including scaling	All of the above
Geometry: properties of shapes	
Identify 3-D shapes, including cubes and other cuboids, from 2-D representations	9.4; 9.5
Know angles are measured in degrees: estimate and compare acute, obtuse and reflex angles	9.21; 9.22; 9.23; 9.24; 9.26
Draw given angles, and measure them in degrees (°)	9.21; 9.22; 9.23; 9.25; 9.26
Identify: <ul><li>angles at a point and one whole turn (total 360°)</li><li>angles at a point on a straight line and half a turn (total 180°)</li><li>other multiples of 90°</li></ul>	9.25
Use the properties of rectangles to deduce related facts and find missing lengths and angles	9.10
Distinguish between regular and irregular polygons based on reasoning about equal sides and angles.	9.8
Geometry: position and direction	
Identify, describe and represent the position of a shape following a reflection or translation, using the appropriate language, and know that the shape has not changed	9.18; 9.19

UPPER KEY STAGE 2	
Statistics	
Solve comparison, sum and difference problems using information presented in a line graph	10.12
Complete, read and interpret information in tables, including timetables	10.2
YEAR 6	
Number: number and place value	
Read, write, order and compare numbers up to 10 000 000 and determine the value of each digit	3.5; 3.7; 3.8
Round any whole number to a required degree of accuracy	3.20
Use negative numbers in context, and calculate intervals across zero	3.5; 3.6; 3.17
Solve number and practical problems that involve all of the above	All of the above
Number: addition, subtraction, multiplication and division	
Multiply multi-digit numbers up to 4 digits by a two-digit whole number using the formal written method of long multiplication	5.11; 5.12
Divide numbers up to 4 digits by a two-digit whole number using the formal written method of long division, and interpret remainders as whole number remainders, fractions, or by rounding, as appropriate for the context	5.11; 5.15
Divide numbers up to 4 digits by a two-digit number using the formal written method of short division where appropriate, interpreting remainders according to the context	5.11; 5.16
Perform mental calculations, including with mixed operations and large numbers	5.8; 5.20
Identify common factors, common multiples and prime numbers	5.10
Use their knowledge of the order of operations to carry out calculations involving the four operations	5.14; 5.18
Solve addition and subtraction multi-step problems in contexts, deciding which operations and methods to use and why	4.14; all of the above
Number: fractions (including decimals and percentages)	
Use common factors to simplify fractions; use common multiples to express fractions in the same denomination	6.13; 6.15
Compare and order fractions, including fractions › 1	6.26
Add and subtract fractions with different denominators and mixed numbers, using the concept of equivalent fractions	6.12; 6.21
Multiply simple pairs of proper fractions, writing the answer in its simplest form [for example, $\frac{1}{4} \times \frac{1}{2} = \frac{1}{8}$]	6.23
Divide proper fractions by whole numbers [for example, $\frac{1}{3} \div 2 = \frac{1}{6}$]	6.22
Associate a fraction with division and calculate decimal fraction equivalents [for example, 0.375] for a simple fraction [for example, $\frac{3}{8}$]	6.16; 6.17; 6.18
Identify the value of each digit in numbers given to three decimal places and multiply and divide numbers by 10, 100 and 1000 giving answers up to three decimal places	6.19; 6.24
Ratio and proportion	
Solve problems involving the relative sizes of two quantities where missing values can be found by using integer multiplication and division facts	6.36; 6.37
Solve problems involving the calculation of percentages [for example, of measures, and such as 15% of 360] and the use of percentages for comparison	6.30; 6.31; 6.32; 6.34; 6.35
Solve problems involving similar shapes where the scale factor is known or can be found	6.38

UPPER KEY STAGE 2	
Solve problems involving unequal sharing and grouping using knowledge of fractions and multiples	6.4
Algebra	
Use simple formulae	7.2; 7.5
Generate and describe linear number sequences	7.1; 7.4; 7.5
Express missing number problems algebraically	7.2; 7.8
Find pairs of numbers that satisfy an equation with two unknowns	7.3; 7.6; 7.7
Enumerate possibilities of combinations of two variables	7.3; 7.7
Measurement	
Solve problems involving the calculation and conversion of units of measure, using decimal notation up to three decimal places where appropriate	8.28; 8.29; 8.30
Use, read, write and convert between standard units, converting measurements of length, mass, volume and time from a smaller unit of measure to a larger unit, and vice versa, using decimal notation to up to three decimal places	8.8; 8.13; 8.14; 8.15; 8.21; 8.26; 8.27; 8.28; 8.29; 8.30
Convert between miles and kilometres	8.30
Recognise that shapes with the same areas can have different perimeters and vice versa	8.2
Recognise when it is possible to use formulae for area and volume of shapes	8.2; 8.12; 8.13
Calculate the area of parallelograms and triangles	8.12
Calculate, estimate and compare volume of cubes and cuboids using standard units, including cubic centimetres (cm^3) and cubic metres (m^3), and extending to other units [for example, mm^3 and km^3]	8.5
Geometry: properties of shapes	
Draw 2-D shapes using given dimensions and angles	9.22; 9.23; 9.26
Recognise, describe and build simple 3-D shapes, including making nets	9.4
Compare and classify geometric shapes based on their properties and sizes and find unknown angles in any triangles, quadrilaterals, and regular polygons	9.6; 9.7; 9.8; 9.10
Illustrate and name parts of circles, including radius, diameter and circumference and know that the diameter is twice the radius	9.12
Recognise angles where they meet at a point, are on a straight line, or are vertically opposite, and find missing angles	9.26
Geometry: position and direction	
Describe positions on the full coordinate grid (all four quadrants)	9.15
Draw and translate simple shapes on the coordinate plane, and reflect them in the axes	9.18; 9.20
Statistics	
Interpret and construct pie charts and line graphs and use these to solve problems	10.12; 10.13; 10.14
Calculate and interpret the mean as an average	10.20; 10.21; 10.22; 10.23; 10.24

Bibliography

Ackermann, E. (1991) From decontextualized to situated knowledge: revisiting Piaget's water-level experiment. In: I. Harel and S. Papert (eds) *Constructionism*. Norwood, NJ: Ablex Publishing Corporation.

Ainley, J., Bagnib, G.T., Hefendehl-Hebekerc, L. and Lagranged, J.B. (2009) Algebraic thinking and mathematics education. In: *Proceedings of CERME 6*, January 28, February 1 2009, Lyon, France, pp. 415–419.

Ainley, J. and Pratt, D. (2001) Introducing a special issue on constructing meanings from data, *Educational Studies in Mathematics*, 45(1/3): 1–8.

Ainley, J., Bills, L. and Wilson, K.E. (2005) Designing spreadsheet-based tasks for purposeful algebra, *International Journal of Computers for Mathematical Learning*, 10(3): 191–215.

Ainley, J., Nardi, E. and Pratt, D. (2000) Towards the construction of meanings for trend in active graphing, *International Journal of Computers for Mathematical Learning* 5(2): 85–114.

Ainley, J., Pratt, D. and Hansen, A. (2006) Connecting engagement and focus in pedagogic task design. *British Educational Research Journal*, 32(1): 23–38.

Anghileri, J. (ed.) (1995) *Children's Mathematical Thinking in the Primary Years: Perspectives on Children's Learning*. London: Cassell.

Anghileri, J. (2000) *Teaching Number Sense*. London: Continuum.

Anghilieri, J. and Baron, S. (1999) Playing with the materials of study: poleidoblocs, *Education 3–13*, 27(2): 57–64.

Alloway, T.P. (2006) How does working memory work in the classroom? *Educational Research and Reviews*, 1(4): 134–139.

Askew, M. and Wiliam, D. (1995) Recent Research in Mathematics Education 5–16. London: HMSO.

Askew, M., Brown, M., Rhodes, V., Johnson, D. and Wiliam, D. (1997) *Effective Teachers of Numeracy: Final Report*. London: King's College.

Atiyah, M. (2001) Mathematics in the 20th century: geometry versus algebra, *Mathematics Today*, 37(2): 47–49.

Back, J. and Pumfrey, L. (n.d.) Enriching data handling. Available at: http://nrich.maths.org/public/viewer.php?obj_id=5449 (last accessed 25/8/09).

Bailey, D.H. and Borwein, J.M. (2010) The greatest mathematical discovery? Available at: http://www.fas.org/sgp/eprint/discovery.pdf (last accessed 7/9/10).

Barmby, P., Bilesborough, L., Harries, T. and Higgins, S. (2009) *Primary Mathematics: Teaching for Understanding*. Berkshire: Open University Press.

Barmby, P., Harries, T., Higgins, S. and Suggate, J. (2009) The array representation and primary children's understanding and reasoning in multiplication, *Educational Studies in Mathematics*, 70: 217–241.

Baroody, A.J., Lai, M. and Mix, K.S. (2006) The development of young children's early number and operation sense and its implications for early childhood education. In: B. Spodek and O.N. Saracho (eds) *Handbook of Research on the Education of the Young*, 2nd edn. Mahwah, NJ: Lawrence Erlbaum Associates, pp. 187–222.

Barr, R. (2010) Transfer of learning between 2D and 3D sources during infancy: informing theory and practice, *Developmental Review*, 30(2): 128–154.

Barrett, J.E. and Clements, D.H. (2003) Quantifying path length: fourth-grade children's developing abstractions for linear measurement, *Cognition and Instruction*, 21(4): 475–520.

Battista, M.T. (1990) Spatial visualisation and gender differences in high school geometry, *Journal for Research in Mathematics Education*, 21: 47–60.

Becta (1998) *Using IT to Support English, Maths and Science at KS2*. Becta.

Bell, A., Swan, M., Onslow, B., Pratt, K. and Purdy, D. (1985) *Diagnostic Teaching for Long Term Learning: Report of ESRC Project HR8491/1*. Nottingham: Shell Centre for Mathematical Education, University of Nottingham.

Bell, A.W. (1993) Some experiments in diagnostic teaching, *Education Studies in Mathematics*, 24(1): 115–137.

Boaler, J. (2009) *The Elephant in the Classroom: Helping Children Learn and Love Mathematics*. London: Souvenir Press Ltd.

Booth, D. (1981) Aspects of logico-mathematical intuition in the development of young children's spontaneous pattern painting. Unpublished PhD thesis, La Trobe University.

Bouck, E.C. and Flanagan, S.M. (2009) Virtual manipulatives: what they are and how teachers can use them, *Intervention in School and Clinic*. Sage Publications. Available at: http://isc.sagepub.com/content/early/2009/11/04/1053451209349530.full.pdf (last accessed 9/9/10).

Brannon, E.M., Lutz, D. and Cordes S. (2006) The development of area discrimination and its implications for number representation in infancy, *Development Science*, 9(6): F59–F64.

Briggs, M. and Davis, S. (2008) *Creative Teaching: Mathematics in the Early Years and Primary Classrooms*. London: Routledge.

Briggs, M. and Pritchard, A. (2002). *Using ICT in Primary Mathematics Teaching*. Exeter: Learning Matters.

Brown, M. (1981) Number operations. In: K.M. Hart (ed.) *Children's Understanding of Mathematics 11–16*. London: John Murray.

Brueckner, L.J. (1928) Analysis of errors in fractions, *The Elementary School Journal*, 28(10): 760–770.

Bruner, J. (1960) *The Process of Education*, 1st edn. Cambridge, MA: Harvard University Press.

Bruner, J. (1977) *The Process of Education*, 2nd edn. Cambridge, MA: Harvard University Press.

Bryant, P. (1982) The role of conflict and agreement between intellectual strategies in children's ideas about measurement, *British Journal of Psychology*, 73: 243–252.

Burger, M. and Shaugnessy, J.M. (1986) Characterizing the van Hiele levels of development in geometry, *Journal for Research in Mathematics Education*, 17: 31–34.

Burton, L. (1990) *Gender and Mathematics: An International Perspective*. London: Cassell.

Carpenter, T., Fennema, E. and Romberg, T. (1993) *Rational Numbers: An Integration of Research*. Hillsdale, NJ: Lawrence Erlbaum Associates.

Carpenter, T.P. and Moser, J.M. (1979) The development of addition and subtraction concepts in young children. In: *Proceedings of the Third International Conference for the Psychology of Mathematics Education*. University of Warwick, Mathematics Education Research Centre.

Carpenter, T.P. and Moser, J.M. (1982) The development of addition and subtraction problem solving skill. In T.P. Carpenter, J.M. Moser and T.A. Romberg (eds) *Addition and Subtraction: A Cognitive Perspective*. Hillsdale, NJ: Lawrence Erlbaum.

Carruthers, E. and Worthington, M. (2006) *Children's Mathematics: Making Marks, Making Meaning*, 2nd edn. London: SAGE Publications.

Casey, R. (2002) A framework for teaching mathematically promising pupils. In: V. Koshy and J. Murray (eds) *Unlocking Numeracy*. London: David Fulton, pp. 122–145.

Castle, K. and Needham, J. (2007) First graders' understanding of measurement, *Early Childhood Education Journal*, 35(3): 215–221.

Charalambous, C.Y. and Pitta-Pantazi, D. (2005) Revisiting a theoretical model on fractions: implications for teaching and research. In: H.L. Chick and J.L. Vincent (eds) *Proceedings of the 29th Conference of the International Group for the Psychology of Mathematics Education*, Vol. 2. Melbourne: PME, pp. 233–240. Available at: http://www.emis.de/proceedings/PME29/PME29RRPapers/PME29Vol2CharalambousEtAl.pdf (last accessed 7/9/10).

Circa (1997) Pictures from data, *Circa: The Mathematical Magazine*, Volume 6.

Clements, D.D. and Burns, B.A. (2005) Students' development of strategies for turn and angle measure, *Educational Studies in Mathematics*, 41(1): 31–45.

Clements, D.D., Battista, M.T., Sarama, J. and Swaminathan, S. (1996) Development of turn and turn measurement concepts in a computer-based instructional unit, *Educational Studies in Mathematics*, 18: 109–124.

Clements, D.D., Sarama, J. and Swaminathan, S. (1997) Young children's concepts of shape, *Proceedings for International Group for Mathematics Education*, 21: 356–371.

Clements, D.H. (2003) Major themes and recommendations. In: D.H. Clements, J. Sarama and A.M. DiBiase (eds) *Engaging Young Children in Mathematics: Standards for Early Childhood Mathematics Education*. London: Routledge, pp. 7–72.

Clements, D.H. and Battista, M.T. (1990a) Constructivist learning and teaching, *Arithmetic Teacher*, 38(1): 34–35.

Clements, D.H. and Battista, M.T. (1990b) The effects of Logo on children's conceptualisations of angle and polygons, *Journal for Research in Mathematics Education*, 21: 356–371.

Clements, D.H. and Battista, M.T. (1992) Geometry and spatial reasoning. In D.A. Grouws (ed.) *Handbook of Research in Mathematics Teaching and Learning*. New York: Macmillan Publishing Company, pp. 420–464.

Clements, D.H. and Sarama, J. (2009) *Learning and Teaching Early Math*. New York: Routledge.

Clements, M.A. (1980) Analyzing children's errors on written mathematical tasks, *Educational Studies in Mathematics*, 11(1): 1–21.

Cobb, P. (1987) Information-processing psychology and mathematics education – a constructivist perspective, *Journal of Mathematical Behaviour*, 6: 3–40.

Cobb, P., Confrey, I., diSessa, A., Lehrer, R. and Schauble, L. (2003) Design experiments in educational research, *Educational Researcher*, 32(4): 9–13.

Cobb, P., Yackel, E. and Wood, T. (1989) Young children's emotional acts while doing mathematical problem solving. In: D.B. McLeod and V.M. Adams (eds) *Affect and Mathematical Problem Solving: A New Perspective*, New York: Springer-Verlag, pp. 117–148.

Cockburn, A. (1999) *Teaching Mathematics with Insight*. London: Falmer Press.

Cockcroft, W.H. (1982) *Mathematics Counts*. London: HMSO.

Cole, R. (2009) Why today's children don't understand money: a cashless society has left today's children with no understanding of the value of real money – let alone where it actually comes from, *The Times*, 1 August.

Collins, A., Brown, J.S. and Newton, S.E. (1990) Cognitive apprenticeship: teaching the crafts of reading, writing and mathematics. In: L.B. Resnick (ed.) *Knowing, Learning and Instruction: Essays in Honor of Robert Glaser*. Hillsdale, NJ: Lawrence Erlbaum.

Coltman, P., Anghileri, J. and Petyaeva D. (2002) Scaffolding learning through meaningful tasks and adult interaction, Early Years, 22(1): 39–49.

Couco, A. (2001) *The Roles of Representation in School Mathematics*. NCTM Yearbook for 2001.

Cross, C.T., Woods, T.A and Schweingruber, H. (2009) Mathematics Learning in Early *Childhood: Paths Toward Excellence and Equity*. Washington, DC: The National Academies Press.

Critchley, P. (2002) Chocolate fractions, *Times Educational Supplement*, 19 January.

Dauben, J.W. and Scriba, C. J. (eds) (2002) *Writing the History of Mathematics: Its Historical Development*. Berlin: Birkhäuser Verlag.

Davis, R.B. (1986) Conceptual and procedural knowledge in mathematics: a summary analysis, in J. Heibert (ed.) *Conceptual and Procedural Knowledge: The Case of Mathematics*. Hillsdale, NJ: Lawrence Erlbaum Associates, pp. 265–300.

Deboys, M. and Pitt, E. (1988) *Lines of Development in Primary Mathematics*, 3rd edn. Belfast: The Blackstaff Press.

de Court, E., Greer, B. and Verschaffel, L. (2000) *Making Sense of Word Problems*. London: Taylor & Francis.

Department for Education (DfE) (2010) *Developing Mathematics in Initial Teacher Training*. London: DfE.

Department for Education (DfE) (2012) *Statutory Framework for the Early Years Foundation Stage: Setting the Standards for Learning, Development and Care for Children from Birth to Five*. London: DfE.

Department for Education (DfE) (2013) *The National Curriculum in England: Key Stages 1 and 2 Framework Document.* London: DfE.

Department for Education and Employment (DfEE) (1999a) *Professional Development Materials 3 and 4: Guide for your Professional Development, Book 2: Raising Standards in Mathematics at Key Stage 2.* London: DfEE.

Department for Education and Employment (DfEE) (1999b) *Professional Development Materials 3 and 4: Guide for your Professional Development, Book 3: Raising Standards in Mathematics at Key Stage 2.* London: DfEE.

Department for Education and Employment (DfEE) (1994) *Mathematical Vocabulary.* London: DfEE.

Department for Education and Employment (DfEE) (2002a) *Qualifying to Teach Professional Standards for Qualified Teacher Status and Requirements for Initial Teacher Training.* London: Teacher Training Agency.

Department for Education and Employment (DfEE) (2002b) Mathematics unit plans. www.standards.dfes.gov.uk/numeracy/unit_plans/ (accessed 21/3/05).

Department for Education and Employment/Qualifications and Curriculum Authority (DfEE/QCA) (1998) *Science: A Scheme of Work for Key Stages 1 and 2.* London: DfEE.

Department for Education and Skills (DfES) (2003) *Models and Images: Y1–Y3.* London: DfES Publications. Ref. 0508–2003 GCDI.

Department for Education and Skills (DfES) (2004) *Primary National Strategy. Excellence and Enjoyment: Learning and Teaching in the Primary Years. Creating a Learning Culture: Conditions for Learning.* London: DfES Publications. Ref. 0523–2004.

Department for Education and Skills (DfES) (2005a) *Wave 3: Supporting Children with Gaps in their Mathematical Understanding.* London: DfES Publications. Ref. DFES 1165–2005G.

Department for Education and Skills (DfES) (2005b) *Primary National Strategy. Targeting Support: Implementing Interventions for Children with Significant Difficulties in Mathematics.* London: DfES Publications. Ref. 1083–2005.

Department for Education and Skills (2007) *The Primary National Strategies. Primary Framework CPD Day 2 'Developing Language and Reasoning Through Guided Group Work in Mathematics'.* London: DfES Publications. In: *CPD Day 2 Professional Development Meeting Notes*, Ref : 0087–2007-DWO-EN.

Department for Education and Skills (DfES) (2008) *Independent Review of Mathematics Teaching in Early Years Settings and Primary Schools: Final report.* Ref. 00433–2008BKT-EN. Available at: http://publications.education.gov.uk/eOrderingDownload/WMR%20Final%20Report.pdf (last accessed 1/12/10).

Dewey, J. (1926) *Democracy and Education: An Introduction to the Philosophy of Education.* New York: The Macmillan Company.

Dickson, L., Brown, M. and Gibson, O. (1984) *Children Learning Mathematics: A Teacher's Guide to Recent Research.* London: Cassell Education.

DiSessa, A. and Sherin, B. (1998) What changes in conceptual change? *International Science Education*, 20(10): 1155–1191.

DiSessa, A.A. and Cobb, P. (2004) Ontological innovation and the role of theory in design experiments, *Journal of the Learning Sciences*, 13(1): 77–103

Donaldson, M. (1978) *Children's Minds*. London: Fontana Press.

Donlan, C. (2003) Numeracy development in children with specific language impairments: the interaction of conceptual and procedural knowledge. In: A.J. Baroody and A. Dowker (eds) *The Development of Arithmetic Concepts and Skills: Constructing Adaptive Expertise*. Mahwah, NJ: Erlbaum, pp. 337–358.

Dowker, A. (2009) *What Works for Children with Mathematical Difficulties? The Effectiveness of Intervention Schemes*. Nottingham: DCSF Publications, Ref: 00086–2009BKT-EN.

Driscoll, M.P. (1994) *Psychology of Learning for Instruction*. Needham, MA: Allyn and Bacon.

Dubinsky, E., Weller, K., McDonald, M. and Brown, A. (2005). Some historical issues and paradoxes regarding the concept of infinity: an APOS-based analysis: Part 1, *Educational Studies in Mathematics*, 58: 335–359.

Duncan, A. (1996) *What Primary Teachers Should Know about Maths*. London: Hodder and Stoughton.

Elwood, J. and Gipps, C. (1998) *Review of Recent Research on the Achievement of Girls in Single Sex Schools*. London: Institute of Education, University of London.

English, L. (2002) Development of 10-year-olds' mathematical modelling. In A.D. Cockburn and E. Nardi (eds) *Proceedings of the Twenty-sixth Annual Conference of the International Group for the Psychology of Mathematics Education Conference*, 3: 329–335.

English, L.D. (2007) Cognitive psychology and mathematics education: reflections on the past and the future, *The Montana Mathematics Enthusiast*, Monograph 2, pp. 119–126. The Montana Council of Teachers of Mathematics.

Ericsson, K.A. and Kintsch, W. (1995) Long-term memory, *Psychological Review*, 102: 211–245.

Fischbein, E. (1993) The theory of figural concepts, *Educational Studies in Mathematics*, 24: 139–162.

Fischbein, E. (1994) The interaction between the formal, the algorithmic and the intuitive components in a mathematical activity. In: R. Biehler *et al.* (eds) *Didactics of Mathematics as a Scientific Discipline*. Dordrecht: Reidel.

Fisher, I. (2001) Maths resource introducing probability, *Mathematics in School*, 30(3).

Flegg, G. (ed.) (1989) *Number Through the Ages*. London and Milton Keynes: Macmillan Education in association with the Open University.

Foster, R. (1994) Counting on success in simple addition tasks. In: *Proceedings of the 18th Conference of the International Group for the Psychology of Mathematics Education*, 2: 360–367.

Foster, R. (1996) Practice makes imperfect, *Mathematics Teaching*, 143 (June): 34–36.

Freudenthal, H. (1971) Geometry between the devil and the deep sea, *Educational Studies in Mathematics*, 3: 413–435.

Freudenthal, H. (1973) *Mathematics as an Educational Task*. Dordrecht: Reidel.

Freudenthal, H. (1981) Major problems of mathematical education, *Educational Studies in Mathematics*, 12: 133–150.

Freudenthal, H. (1991) *Revisiting Mathematics Education.* Dordrecht: Kluwer Academic Publishers.

Frobisher, L., Monaghan, J., Orton, A., Roper, T. and Threlfall, J. (1999) *Learning to Teach Number.* Cheltenham: Stanley Thornes.

Fujita, T. and Jones, K. (2002) The design of geometry teaching: learning from the geometry textbooks of Godfrey and Siddons. In: O. McNamara (ed.) *Proceedings of the Twenty-third Day Conference of the British Society for Research into Learning Mathematics.* London: British Society of Research into Learning Mathematics.

Furani, H.A. (2003) Misconceiving or misnaming? Some implications of toddlers' symbolizing for mathematics education, *Philosophy of Mathematics Education Journal*, 17(May). Available at: http://www.people.ex.ac.uk/PErnest/pome17/miscon.htm (accessed 23/8/10).

Fuson, K.C. (1992) Research on whole number addition and subtraction. In: D.A. Grows (ed.) Handbook of Research on Mathematics Teaching and Learning. New York: Macmillan.

Fuys, D., Geddes, D. and Tischler, R. (1988) The van Hiele model of thinking in geometry among adolescents, *Journal for Research in Mathematics Education Monograph*, 3.

Garrick, R. (2002) Pattern-making and pattern play in the nursery: special organisation. Paper presented at the *Annual Conference of the British Educational Research Association*, University of Exeter, England, 12–14 September.

Garrick, R., Threlfall, J. and Orton, A. (2004) Pattern in the nursery. In: A. Orton, *Pattern in Teaching and Learning of Maths.* London: Continuum, pp. 1–17.

Geary, D.C. (1996) Sexual selection and sex differences in mathematical abilities, *Behavioural and Brain Sciences*, 19: 224–247.

Gelman, R. and Gallistel, C.R. (1986) *The Child's Understanding of Number.* London: Harvard University Press.

Gelman, R. and Gallistel, C.R. (2004) Language and the origin of numerical concepts. *Science*, 306(5695): 441–443.

Gibson, O.E. (1981) A study of the ability of children with spina bifida to handle money. PhD thesis, University of London.

Ginsburg, H.P. (1977) *Children's Arithmetic: How They Learn It and How You Teach It.* Austin, TX: PRO-ED.

Goulding, M. (2002) Primary teacher trainees' self-assessment of their mathematical subject knowledge. Paper presented at the Annual Conference of the British Educational Research Association, University of Exeter, England, 12–14 September.

Graham, A. (1990) *Supporting Primary Mathematics: Probability.* Milton Keynes: Centre for Mathematics Education, Open University.

Gravemeijer, K. and Doorman, M. (1999) Context problems in realistic mathematics education: a calculus course as an example, *Educational Studies in Mathematics*, 39: 111–129.

Gray, E. (2008) Compressing the counting process: strength from the flexible interpretation of symbols. In: I. Thompson (ed.) (2008) *Teaching and Learning Early Number*, 2nd edn. Buckingham: Open University Press, pp. 82–94.

Gray, E.M. and Tall, D. (1994) Duality, ambiguity and flexibility: a proceptual view of simple arithmetic, Journal for Research in Mathematics Education, 26: 115–141.

Gray, E.M. and Tall, D.O. (2007) Abstraction as a natural process of mental compression, *Mathematics Education Research Journal*, 19(2): 23–40

Greeno, J.G. (1980) Some examples of cognitive task analysis with instructional implications. In: R.E. Snow, P. Frederico and W.E. Montague (eds) *Aptitude, Learning and Instruction, Vol. 2: Cognitive Process Analysis of Learning and Problem-Solving*. Hillsdale, NJ: Lawrence Erlbaum Associates, pp. 1–21.

Guitierréz, A., Jaime, A. and Fortuny, J.M. (1991) An alternative paradigm to evaluate the van Hiele levels, *Journal for Research into Mathematics Education*, 3: 17–24.

Hall, E. (2007) Mixed messages: The role and value of drawing in early education. Paper presented at the British Educational Research Association Annual Conference, Institute of Education, University of London. 5–8 September, 2007. Available at: http://www.leeds.ac.uk/educol/documents/165704.htm (last accessed 10/9/10).

Hall, J.S. (2000) Psychology and schooling: the impact of Susan Isaacs and Jean Piaget on 1960s science education reform. *History of Education*, 29(2): 153–170.

Hansen, A. (2008a) *Primary Mathematics: Extending Knowledge in Practice*. London: Learning Matters/SAGE.

Hansen, A. (2008b) Children's geometric defining and a principled approach to task design. Unpublished doctoral thesis, Warwick University.

Hansen, A. and Pratt, D. (2005) How do we design tasks to help children understand the definitions of quadrilaterals? Paper presented to the Mathematics Education Research Group of Australia Annual Conference.

Harel, I. and Papert, S. (1991) *Constructionism*. Norwood, NJ: Ablex Publishing Corporation.

Hasegawa, J. (1997) Concept formation of triangles and quadrilaterals in second grade, *Educational Studies in Mathematics*, 32: 157–179.

Hatch, G. (1998) Replace your mental arithmetic test with a game, *Mathematics in School*, 27(1): 32–35.

Haylock, D. (2001) *Mathematics Explained for Primary Teachers*, 2nd edn. London: Paul Chapman Publishing.

Haylock, D. and Cockburn, A. (1997) *Understanding Mathematics in the Lower Primary Years*. London: Paul Chapman Publishing.

Hausfather, S.J. (1996) Vygotsky and schooling: creating a social context for learning, *Action in Education*, 18: 1–10.

Hershkowitz, R. (1990) Psychological aspects of learning geometry. In P. Nesher and J. Kilpatrick (eds) *Mathematics and Cognition*. Cambridge: Cambridge University Press, pp. 70–95.

Hershkowitz, R., Ben-Chaim, D., Hoyles, C., Lappan, G., Mitchelmore, M. and Vinner, S. (1990) Psychological aspects of learning geometry. In: P. Nesher and J. Kilpatrick (eds) *Mathematics and Cognition: A Research Synthesis by the International Group for the Psychology of Mathematics Education.* Cambridge: Cambridge University Press, pp. 70–95.

Hilbert, D. and Cohn-Vossen, S. (1932) *Geometry and the Imagination.* New York: Chelsea.

Hill, P.S. (1908) The Value and Limitations of Froebel's Gifts as Educative Materials Parts I, II *The Elementary School Teacher*, Vol. 9, No. 3. pp. 129–137.

Hopkins, C., Gifford, S. and Pepperell, S. (1999) *Mathematics in the Primary School: A Sense of Progression.* 2nd edn. London: David Fulton Publishers.

Hopkins, C., Pope, S. and Pepperell, S. (2004) *Understanding Primary Mathematics.* London: David Fulton Publishers.

Howat, H. (2006) Participation in elementary mathematics: an analysis of engagement, attainment and intervention. Unpublished PhD thesis, University of Warwick.

Hoyles, C. (1985) What is the point of group discussion in mathematics? *Educational Studies in Mathematics*, 16: 205–214.

Hoyles, C. and Sutherland, R. (1986) *When 45 Equals 60.* London: University of London Institute of Education, Microworlds Project.

Huckstep, P., Rowland, T. and Thwaites, A. (2002) Primary teachers' mathematics content knowledge: what does it look like in the classroom? Paper presented at the Annual Conference of the British Educational Research Association, University of Exeter, England, 12–14 September.

Hughes, M. (1986) *Children and Number: Difficulties in Learning Mathematics.* Oxford: Blackwell.

Hughes, M. and Vass, A. (2001) *Strategies for Closing the Learning Gap.* Stafford: Network Educational Press.

John-Steiner, V. and Mahn, H. (2003) Sociocultural contexts for teaching and learning. In: W.M. Reynolds and G.E. Miller (eds) *Handbook of Psychology.* Hoboken, NJ: Wiley, pp. 125–151.

Johnson, S. (1996) The contribution of large scale assessment programmes to research on gender differences, *Educational Research and Evaluation*, 2(1): 25–49.

Jones, K. (2000) Providing a foundation for deductive reasoning: students' interpretations when using dynamic geometry software and their evolving mathematical explanations, *Educational Studies in Mathematics*, 44: 55–85.

Jones, K. (2003) Classroom implications of research on dynamic geometry software. Paper presented to the Thematic Working Group: tools and technologies in mathematical didactics, CERME 3: Third Conference of the European Society for Research in Mathematics Education 28 February–3 March 2003 in Bellaria, Italy.

Kafai, Y. and Harel, I. (1991a) Learning through design and teaching: exploring social and collaborative aspects of constructionism. In: I. Harel and S. Papert (eds) *Constructionism.* Norwood, NJ: Ablex.

Kafai, Y. and Harel, I. (1991b) Learning through consulting: when mathematical ideas, knowledge of programming and design, and playful discourse are intertwined. In: I. Harel and S. Papert (eds) *Constructionism*. Norwood, NJ: Ablex.

Karmarkar, U.R. and Buonomano, D.V. (2007) Telling time in the absence of clocks, *Neuron*, 53(3): 427–438.

Kazemi, E. (1998) Discourse that promotes conceptual understanding, *Teaching Children Mathematics Journal*, March: 410–414.

Keat, J.B. and Wilburne, J.M. (2009) The impact of storybooks on kindergarten children's mathematical achievement and approaches to learning, *US-China Education Review*, 6(7): 61–67.

Kelly, C.A. (2006) Using manipulatives in mathematical problem solving: a performance-based analysis. *The Montana Mathematics Enthusiast (TMME)*, 3(2): 184–193. Available at: http://www.math.umt.edu/tmme/vol3no2/tmmevol3no2_colorado_pp184_193.pdf (last accessed 10/9/10).

Koedinger, K.R. and Nathan, M.J. (2004) The real story behind story problems: effects of representations on quantitative reasoning, *Journal of the Learning Sciences*, 13(2): 129–164.

Koshy, V. (2000) Children's mistakes and misconceptions. In V. Koshy, P. Ernest and R. Casey (eds) *Mathematics for Primary Teachers*. London: Routledge.

Lamberg, T. and Middleton, J. (2002) The role of inscriptional practices in the development of mathematical ideas in a fifth grade classroom. In A.D. Cockburn and E. Nardi (eds) *Proceedings of the Twenty-sixth Annual Conference of the International Group for the Psychology of Mathematics Education Conference*. Norwich: University of East Anglia.

Lamon, S. (1999) *Teaching Fractions and Ratios for Understanding*. London: Erlbaum.

Lamon, S.L. (2001) Presenting and representing: from fractions to rational numbers. In: A. Cuoco and F. Curcio (eds) *The Roles of Representation in School Mathematics –2001 Yearbook*. Reston: NCTM, pp. 146–165.

Lamon, S.L. (2008) *Teaching Fractions and Ratios for Understanding: Essential Content Knowledge and Instructional Strategies for Teachers*, 2nd edn. Mahwah, NJ: Lawrence Erlbaum Associates.

Lave, J. (1988) *Cognition in Practice: Mind, Mathematics and Culture in Everyday Life*. Cambridge: Cambridge University Press.

Lave, J. and Wenger, E. (1991) *Situated Learning: Legitimate Peripheral Participation*. Cambridge: Cambridge University Press.

Lee, C. (2006) *Language for Learning Mathematics: Assessment for Learning in Practice*. Berkshire: Open University Press.

Lehrer, R., Jenkins, M. and Osana, H. (1998) Longitudinal study of children's reasoning about space and geometry. In: R. Lehrer and D. Chazan (eds) *Designing Learning Environments for Developing Understanding of Geometry and Space*. Mahwah: NJ: Lawrence Erlbaum Associates, pp. 137–168.

Liebeck, P. (1984) *How Children Learn Mathematics*. London: Penguin Books.

Masingila, J.O. (1993) Connecting the ethnomath of carpet layers with school learning, *International Study Group on Ethnomathematics (ISGEm) Newsletter*, 8: 2.

Mathematics Association (1987) *Maths Talk*. Cheltenham: Stanley Thornes.

Matthews, J. (1999) *The Art of Childhood and Adolescence: The Construction of Meaning*. London: Falmer Press.

Miller, G.A. (1956) The magical number seven, plus or minus two: some limits on our capacity for processing information, *Psychological Review*, 63: 81–97.

Misailidou, C. and Williams, J. (2002) Ratio: raising teachers' awareness of children's thinking. *Proceedings of the 2nd International Conference on the Teaching of Mathematics at the Undergraduate Level* (ICTM2). Available at: http://www.math.uoc.gr/~ictm2/Proceedings/pap143.pdf (last accessed 9/9/10).

Mitchelmore, M.C. and White, P. (2000) Development of angle concepts by progressive abstraction and generalisation, *Educational Studies in Mathematics*, 41: 209–238.

Mokros, J.R. and Tinker, R.F. (2006) The impact of microcomputer-based labs on children's ability to interpret graphs, *Journal of Research in Science Teaching*, 24(4): 369–383.

Moloney, K. and Stacey, K. (1997) Changes with age in students' conceptions of decimal notation, *Mathematics Education Research Journal*, 9(1): 25–38.

Monaghan, F. (2000) What difference does it make? Children's views of the difference between some quadrilaterals, *Educational Studies in Mathematics*, 42: 179–196.

Monroe, E. and Clark, H. (1998) Rote or reason, *Mathematics in School*, 27(3): 26–27.

Mooney, C., Ferrie, L., Fox, S., Hansen, A. and Wrathmell, R. (2000) *Achieving QTS. Primary Mathematics: Knowledge and Understanding*. Exeter: Learning Matters.

Mooney, C., Ferrie, L., Fox, S., Hansen, A. and Wrathmell, R. (2002) *Achieving QTS. Primary Mathematics: Knowledge and Understanding*, 2nd edn. Exeter: Learning Matters.

Mooney, C., Ferrie, L., Fox, S., Hansen, A. and Wrathmell, R. (2014) *Achieving QTS. Primary Mathematics: Knowledge and Understanding*, 7th edn. Exeter: Learning Matters.

Morton, R.L. (1924) An analysis of pupils' errors in fractions, *The Journal of Educational Research*, 9(2): 117–125.

Mulligan, J., Prescott, A. and Mitchelmore, M. (2004) Children's development of structure in early mathematics. In: J. Watson and K. Beswick (eds) *Proceedings of the 30th Annual Conference of the Mathematics Education Research Group of Australasia (MERGA)*.

Munn, P. (2008) Children's beliefs about counting. In: I. Thompson (ed.) *Teaching and Learning Early Number*, 2nd edn. Buckingham: Open University Press, pp. 19–33.

National Institute for Budget Advice (2009) *Learning to Manage Money: NIBUD Learning Goals and Competences for Children and Young People*. Utrecht: NIBUD.

NCTM (2000) *Data Analysis and Probability Standard for Grades 6–8*. Reston, VA: NCTM.

Newman, M.A. (1977) An analysis of sixth-grade pupils' errors in written mathematical tasks. In: M. Clements and J. Foyster (eds) *Research in Mathematics Education in Australia*, 2: 269–287.

Nickson, M. (2000) *Teaching and Learning Mathematics: A Teacher's Guide to Recent Research and its Application.* London: Cassell.

Noss, R. and Hoyles, C. (1996) *Windows on Mathematical Meanings: Learning Cultures and Computers.* Dordrecht: Kluwer Academic Publishers.

Nunes, T. and Bryant, P. (1996) *Children Doing Mathematics.* Oxford: Blackwell Publishers.

Nunes, T., Bryant, P., Evans, D., Bell, D., Gardner, S., Gardner, A. and Carraher, J. (2007) The contribution of logical reasoning to the learning of mathematics in primary school, *British Journal of Developmental Psychology*, 25(1): 147–166.

Nunes, T., Schliemann, A.D. and Carraher, D.W. (1993) *Street Mathematics and School Mathematics.* Cambridge: Cambridge University Press.

Nyabanyaba, T. (1999) Wither relevance? Mathematics teachers' discussion of the use of 'real-life' contexts in school mathematics, *For the Learning of Mathematics*, 19(3): 10–14.

Ofsted (2003) *The National Literacy and Numeracy Strategies and the Primary Curriculum.* London: HMI.

Ofsted (2009) *Mathematics: Understanding the Score. Improving Practice in Mathematics Teaching at Primary Level.* London: Ofsted. Ref 080283.

Ollerton, M. (2000) Learning mathematics through 'real-life' problems: texts, contexts and con-tricks, *Mathematics Teaching*, 166: 12.

Orton, A. (1992) *Learning Mathematics: Issues, Theory and Classroom Practice*, 2nd edn. London: Cassell.

Orton, A. and Frobisher, L. (2005) *Insights into Teaching Mathematics*, 2nd edn. London: Continuum.

Orton, J. (1997) Pupils' perception of pattern in relation to shape. *Proceedings of the 21st Conference of the International Group for the Psychology of Mathematics Education*, 3: 304–311.

Orton, J. (2004) Children's perception of pattern in relation to shape. In: A. Orton *Pattern in the Teaching and Learning of Mathematics.* London: Continuum, pp.149–167.

Pagni, D. (2004) Fractions and decimals, *Australian Mathematics Teacher*, 60(4): 28–30.

Pegg, J. and Tall, D. (2002) Fundamental cycles of cognitive growth. In: A.D. Cockburn and E. Nardi (eds) *Proceedings of the Twenty-sixth Annual Conference of the International Group for the Psychology of Mathematics Education Conference*, 4: 41–48.

Pepperel, S., Hopkins, C., Gifford, S. and Tallant, P. (2009) *Mathematics in the Primary School: A Sense of Progression.* London: David Fulton

Personal Finance Education Group (2010) Financial capability in England. Available at http://www.pfeg.org/curriculum_and_policy/england/index.html (last accessed 7/9/10).

Peters, M. (2010) Parsing Mathematical constructs: results from a preliminary eye tracking study. In: M. Joubert (ed.) *Proceedings of the British Society for Research into Learning Mathematics*, 30(2).

Peterson, L. and Peterson, M. (1959) Short-term retention of individual verbal items. Journal of *Experimental Psychology*, 58: 193–198.

Piaget, J. (1953) *How Children Form Mathematical Concepts*. San Francisco: W.H. Freeman and Co. (reprinted from *Scientific American*, November 1953).

Piaget, J. (1970) *The Science of Education and the Psychology of the Child*. New York: Crossman.

Piaget, J. (1971) *The Psychology of Intelligence*. London: Routledge and Kegan Paul.

Piaget, J. and Inhelder, B. (1969) *The Psychology of the Child*. London: Routledge and Kegan Paul.

Piaget, J., Inhelder, B. and Szeminska, A. (1970) *The Child's Conception of Geometry*. London: Routledge.

Picard, D. and Durand, K. (2004) Are young children's drawings canonically based? *Journal of Experimental Child Psychology*, 90(1): 48–64.

Pound, L. (1999) *Supporting Mathematical Development in the Early Years*. Buckingham: Open University Press.

Pound, L. (2008) *Thinking and Learning about Mathematics in the Early* Years. Oxford: Routledge.

Poynter, A. and Tall, D.O. (2005) Relating theories to practice in the teaching of mathematics. Fourth Congress of the European Society for Research in Mathematics Education.

Pratt, D. and Noss, R. (2002) The micro-evolution of mathematical knowledge: the case of randomness, *Journal of Learning Sciences*, 11(4): 453–488.

Qualifications and Curriculum Authority (QCA) (1999) *The National Numeracy Strategy: Teaching Written Calculations, Guidance for Teachers at Key Stages 1 and 2*. London: QCA.

Qualifications and Curriculum Authority (QCA) (2001) *Using Assessment to Raise Achievement in Mathematics. Key Stages 1, 2 and 3*. Research report, November. London: QCA.

Rawson, B. (1993) Searching for pattern, *Education 3–13*, 21(3): 26–33.

Rees, R. and Barr, G. (1984) *Diagnostics and Prescription in the Classroom: Some Common Maths Problems*. London: Harper and Row.

Ring, K. (2001) Young children drawing: the significance of the context. Paper presented at The British Educational Research Association Annual Conference. University of Leeds, 13–15 September.

Rocke, J. (1995) A common-cents approach to fractions, *Teaching Children Mathematics*, 2(4): 234–236.

Ryan, J. and Williams, J. (2007) *Children's Mathematics 4–15: Learning from Errors and Misconceptions*. Berkshire: Open University Press.

Saads, S. and Davis, G. (1997) Spacial abilities, van Hiele levels and language used in three dimensional geometry. In: *Proceedings of the 22nd Conference of the International Group for the Psychology of Mathematics Education*, 4: 104–111.

Sadi, A. (2007) Misconceptions in numbers, *UGRU Journal*, 5. Available at: http://www.ugru.uaeu.ac.ae/UGRUJournal/UGRUJournal_files/SR5/MIN.pdf (last accessed 9/9/10).

Sáiz, M. (2003) Primary teachers' conceptions about the concept of volume: the case of volume-measurable objects. In: N.A. Pateman, B.J. Dougherty and J.T. Zilliox (eds) *Proceedings of the 27th Psychology of Mathematics Education International Conference*, 4: 95–102.

Sáiz, M. and Figueras, O. (2009) A research-based workshop design for volume tasks. In: B. Clarke, B. Grevholm and R. Millman (eds) *Tasks in Primary Mathematics Teacher Education: Purpose, Use and Exemplars*. New York: Springer, pp. 147–160.

Sfard, A. (1991) On the dual nature of mathematical conceptions: reflections on processes and objects as different sides of the same coin, *Educational Studies in Mathematics*, 22: 1–36.

Shuard, H. and Rothery, A. (eds) (1984) *Children Reading Mathematics*. London: John Murray.

Simpson, A.R. (2009) The micro-evolution and transfer of conceptual knowledge about negative numbers. A thesis submitted in partial fulfilment of the requirements for the degree of Doctor of Philosophy in Education, University of Warwick.

Skemp, R. (1977) Relational understanding and instrumental understanding, *Arithmetic Teacher*, 77: 20–26.

Skemp, R.R. (1986) *The Psychology of Learning Mathematics*, 2nd edn. London: Penguin Books.

Smedslund, J. (1961) The acquisition of conservation of substance and weight in children, *Scandinavian Journal of Psychology*, 2: 11–20.

Smeets, E. and T. Mooij (2001) Pupil-centred learning, ICT, and teacher behaviour: observations in educational practice, *British Journal of Educational Technology*, 32: 403–417.

Smith, C. (1999) Pencil and paper numeracy, *Mathematics in School*, 8(5): 10–13.

Sotto, E. (1994) *When Teaching Becomes Learning: A Theory and Practice of Teaching*. London: Continuum.

Spooner, M. (2002) *Errors and Misconceptions in Maths at Key Stage 2: Working Towards Successful SATS*. London: David Fulton Publishers.

Star, S.L. (1989) The structure of ill-structured solutions: boundary objects and heterogeneous distributed problem solving. In: L. Glasser and M.N. Huhns (eds) *Distributed Intelligence*, 2: 37–54.

Steffe, L.P., Thompson, P.W. and Richards, J. (1982) Children counting in arithmetic problem solving, In: T.P. Carpenter, J.M. Moser and T.A. Romberg (eds) *Addition and Subtraction: A Cognitive Perspective*. Hillsdale NJ: Lawrence Erlbaum.

Suggate, J., David, A. and Goulding, M. (2001) *Mathematical Knowledge for Primary Teachers*, 2nd edn. London: David Fulton Publishers.

Swan, M. (2001) Dealing with misconceptions in mathematics. In: P. Gates (ed.) Issues in *Mathematics Teaching*. London: RoutledgeFalmer, pp. 147–165.

Swan, M. (2003) Making sense of mathematics. In: I. Thompson (ed.) *Enhancing Primary Mathematics Teaching*. Berkshire: Open University Press, pp. 112–124.

Sweller, J. (1988) Cognitive load during problem solving: effects on learning, *Cognitive Science*, 12: 257–285.

Tabbers, H.K. (2002) The modality of text in multimedia instructions: refining the design guidelines. Unpublished doctoral thesis, Open University of the Netherlands, Heerlen.

Tall, D.O. (2007) Developing a theory of mathematical growth, *ZDM*, 39: 145–154.

Tanner, H. and Jones, S. (2000) *Becoming a Successful Teacher of Mathematics*. London: RoutledgeFalmer, pp. 86–107.

Tartre, L.A. (1990) Spatial orientation skill and mathematical problem solving. *Journal for Research in Mathematics Education*, 21: 216–229.

Teacher Training Agency (2003) *Qualifying to Teach: Handbook of Guidance*. London: Teacher Training Agency.

Tennyson, R.D. (1996) Concept learning. In: T. Plomp and D.P. Ely (eds) *International Encyclopedia of Educational Technology*, 2nd edn. Oxford, UK: Elsevier Science Ltd, pp. 52–55.

Thompson, I. (ed.) (1997) *Teaching and Learning Early Number*. Buckingham: Open University Press.

Thompson, I. (ed.) (2008) *Teaching and Learning Early Number*, 2nd edn. Buckingham: Open University Press.

Treffers, A. (1987) *Three Dimensions: A Model of Goal and Theory Description in Mathematics Instruction: The Wiskobas Project*. Dordrecht: Reidel Publishing Company.

Twidle, J. (2006) Is the concept of conservation of volume in solids really more difficult than for liquids, or is the way we test giving us an unfair comparison? *Educational Research*, 48(1): 93–109.

van den Heuvel-Panhuizen (2003) The didactical use of models in realistic mathematics education: an example from a longitudinal trajectory on percentage. *Educational Studies in Mathematics*, 54(1): 9–35.

Van Hiele, P.M. (1986) *Structure and Insight: A Theory of Mathematics Education*. London: Academic Press.

Vergnaud, G. and Durand, C. (1976) Structures additives et complexité psychogénétique, *La Revue Francaise de Pedagogie*, 36: 28–43.

von Glasersfled, E. (1995) *Radical Constructivism: A Way of Knowing and Learning*. London: RoutledgeFalmer.

Vygotsky, L.S. (1978) *Mind in Society: The Development of Higher Psychological Processes*. Cambridge, MA: Harvard University Press.

Walcott, C., Mohr, D. and Kastberg, S.E. (2009) Making sense of shape: an analysis of children's written responses, *The Journal of Mathematical Behavior*, 28(1): 30–40.

Warren, E. (2005) Young children's ability to generalise the pattern rule for growing patterns. In: H.L. Chick and J.L. Vincent (eds) *Proceedings of the 29th Conference of the International Group for the Psychology of Mathematics Education*, Vol. 4, pp. 305–312. Melbourne: PME.

Watson, A. and Mason, J. (1998) *Questions and Prompts for Mathematical Thinking*. Derby: Association of Teachers of Mathematics.

Watson, D. (ed.) (1993) *The Impact Report: An Evaluation of the Impact of Information Technology on Children's Achievements in Primary and Secondary Schools*. London: Kings College University Press.

Weber, K. (2005) Students' understanding of trigonometric functions, *Mathematics Education Research Journal*, 17, 91–112.

Wells, G. (1999) *Dialogic Inquiry: Toward a Sociocultural Practice and Theory of Education*. New York: Cambridge University Press.

White, P., Wilson, S., Faragher, R. and Mitchelmore, M. (2007) Percentages as part whole relationships. In: J. Watson and K. Beswick (eds) *Proceedings of the 30th Annual Conference of the Mathematics Education Research Group of Australasia (MERGA)*, pp. 805–814. Available at: http://www.merga.net.au/documents/RP762007.pdf (last accessed 9/9/10).

Whitin, D.J. and Whitin, P. (2003) Task counts: discussing graphs with young children, *Teaching Mathematics*, 10(13): 142–149.

Wilensky, U. (1991) Abstract meditation on the concrete and concrete implications for mathematics education. In: I. Harel and S. Papert (eds) *Constructionism*. Norwood, NJ: Ablex.

Williams, E.M. and Shuard, H. (1970) *Primary Mathematics Today*. London: Longman.

Williams, J. and Easingwood, N. (2004) *ICT and Primary Mathematics: A Teacher's Guide*. Abingdon: RoutledgeFalmer.

Wood, D. (1998) *How Children Think and Learn*. Oxford: Blackwell Publishers.

Wood, D., Bruner, J.S. and Ross, G. (1979) The role of tutoring in problem solving, *Journal of Child Psychology and Psychiatry*, 17: 89–100.

Yackel, E. and Cobb, P. (1996) Sociomathematical norms, argumentation, and autonomy in mathematics, *Journal for Research in Mathematics Education*, 27(4): 458–477.

Yackel, E., Cobb, P. and Wood, T. (1991) Small-group interactions as a source of learning opportunities in second-grade mathematics, *Journal for Research in Mathematics Education*, 22: 390–408.

Yeo, K.K.J. (2008) Teaching area and perimeter: Mathematics-Pedagogical-Content Knowledge-in-Action. In: M. Goos, R. Brown and K. Makar (eds) *Proceedings of the 31st Annual Conference of the Mathematics Education Research Group of Australasia*.

Yin, H.S. (2003) Young children's concept of shape: van Hiele Visualization Level of geometric thinking, *The Mathematics Educator*, 7(2): 71–85. Available at: http://repository.nie.edu.sg/jspui/bitstream/10497/65/1/ME-7-2-71.pdf (last accessed 10/9/10).

Index